# Scott Foresman - Addison Wesley

## Problem Solving Masters

### Grade 4

Scott Foresman - Addison Wesley

Editorial Offices: Menlo Park, California • Glenview, Illinois
Sales Offices: Reading, Massachusetts • Atlanta, Georgia • Glenview, Illinois
Carrollton, Texas • Menlo Park, California

http://www.sf.aw.com

ISBN 0-201-31271-9

Printed in the United States of America

1 2 3 4 5 6 7 8 9 10 – BW – 01 00 99 98 97

# Contents

## Overview

*Problem Solving Masters* provide a variety of problem solving opportunities designed to complement the lessons in the student edition.

For Learn lessons, these masters provide a wealth of additional problems, employing the skills acquired up to that point in the course. Some masters provide interdisciplinary connections and others include problems that require students to first choose a strategy from the following list:

*Use Objects/Act It Out, Draw a Picture, Work Backward, Look for a Pattern, Guess and Check, Solve a Simpler Problem, Use Logical Reasoning, Make an Organized List, and Make a Table.*

For the Analyze Strategies and Analyze Word Problems lessons, the masters are in the form of a **Guided Problem Solving** worksheet. These worksheets lead students through the four-step Problem Solving Guide: *Understand, Plan, Solve,* and *Look Back.* The problem used on the worksheet is one of the problems from the "Practice and Apply" or "Problem Solving and Reasoning" sections of the student edition. To encourage students to map out the problem solving steps and solve a problem on their own, the Guided Problem Solving Masters include an additional problem similar to the one being analyzed (under the section *Solve Another Problem*).

The four steps of the Problem Solving Guide are described below.

The **Understand** step asks questions about the *question* in the problem and the data provided.

The **Plan** step maps out a problem solving strategy or approach. At times the worksheet suggests a particular strategy or approach. Other times the worksheet offers students choices of strategies, methods, or operations.

The **Solve** step prompts students to do the computation and then answer the question.

The **Look Back** step allows students to reflect on their answers and the strategy they used to solve the problem. It also encourages the students to consider the reasonableness of their answers.

The Guided Problem Solving master on the next page can be used to assist students in solving any problem as they complete the four steps of the Problem Solving Guide.

Name _____

 **PROBLEM** _____

**— Understand —**

**— Plan —**

**— Solve —**

**— Look Back —**

Name _____

# Pictographs and Bar Graphs

**Science** The deepest places on earth are trenches beneath the ocean. The deepest trench is the Mariana Trench. It is close to 7 miles deep!

Below is a bar graph that shows the depths of some trenches:

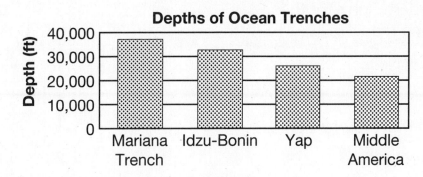

**Depths of Ocean Trenches**

1. Which trench in the graph is the shallowest? _____

2. About how deep is the deepest trench? _____

3. Which trenches shown in the graph are deeper than the Yap trench? _____

Use the pictograph to answer **4–5**.

4. List the number of pets from the pictograph in order from most to least.

_____

5. Students at Cleveland Elementary have 40 pet birds. How many pictures would you draw to show the number of birds?

_____

| Number of Pets Cleveland Elementary School Students Have | |
|---|---|
| Cats | 🐱 🐱 🐱 🐱 🐱 🐱 🐱 |
| Dogs | 🐱 🐱 🐱 🐱 🐱 🐱 |
| Rodents | 🐱 |

🐱 = 10
🐱 = 5

# Ordered Pairs

**Geography** Knowing how to use ordered pairs to locate points on a coordinate grid is helpful for reading a map. Below is a coordinate grid map of a town.

Give the ordered pair for these points on the map:

**1.** The Library _____

**2.** The Post Office _____

**3.** The Hardware Store _____

**4.** The Town Hall _____

**5.** The Bank _____

**6.** The School _____

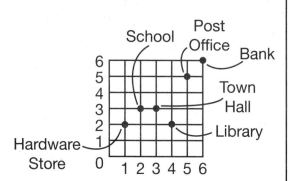

Use the grid to locate the points to answer the questions.

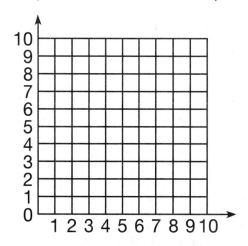

**7.** Use the grid to locate the points (1,2), (1,4), (5,4), (5,2), and (1,2). Connect them in this order: (1,2), (1,4), (5,4), (5,2), and back to (1,2). What shape do they make? _____

**8.** Use the grid to locate the points (3,6), (6,9), (6,6), and (3,7). Connect them in order: (3,7), (6,9), (6,6), and back to (3,7). What shape do they make? _____

# Reading Line Graphs

**Geography** The temperature in Portland, Maine remains relatively cool throughout the year because it is so far north. This graph shows the average temperature in Portland, Maine.

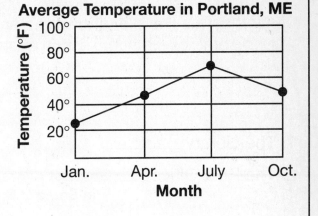

**Average Temperature in Portland, ME**

1. Estimate the average temperature in Portland in

   January. _____

2. In which month is the average temperature about 70 degrees? _____

3. About how many degrees warmer is it in Portland in April than in January? _____

**Number of Hits Scored by Top National League Baseball Players**

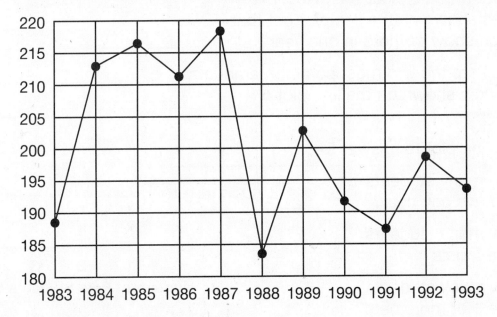

Use the line graph to answer **4–5**.

4. About how many hits were made in 1990? _____

5. About how many more hits were made in 1987 than in 1988? _____

Name _____

# Reading Line Plots

**Geography** Most of the snowiest cities in the U.S. are in the North. This line plot shows the amount of snowfall that falls on some of the snowiest cities in the country.

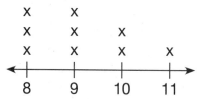

**Greatest Average Snowfall in Some U.S. Cities (ft)**

Use the line plot to answer **1–4**.

1. How many cities get about 11 feet of snow in one year? _____

2. How many cities get about 9 feet of snow in one year? _____

3. Syracuse, New York gets about 10 feet of snow in a typical year. How many cities shown on the line plot get that much snow or more in one year? _____

4. What are the two most common amounts of snow shown on the line plot? _____

Use the line plot to answer **5–8**.

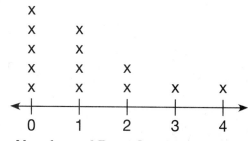

**Number of Pets Students Have**

5. How many students do not have any pets? _____

6. How many students have 4 pets? _____

7. How many students have 1 or more pets? _____

8. Do most of the students have pets? Explain.

_____

# Reading Stem-and-Leaf Plots

**Science** The largest animals known were dinosaurs. From their skeletons, scientists can estimate how long they were.

**Lengths of the Largest Dinosaurs (meters)**

| Stem | Leaf |
|------|------|
| 1 | 5 2 2 |
| 2 | 7 5 5 1 |
| 3 | 6 0 0 |

Use the stem-and-leaf plot to answer **1–4**.

1. The Seismosaurus is the longest known dinosaur. About how many meters long was a Seismosaurus?  _____

2. The Tyrannosaurus and Spinosaurus were the same length. How many meters long could they have been?

   _____

3. How many types of dinosaurs were longer than 15 meters?  _____

4. Suppose a new dinosaur was discovered tomorrow. If its length is 10 meters, would it be one of the 9 largest dinosaurs? Explain.

   _____

   _____

Use the stem-and-leaf plot to answer **5–7**.

**Lengths of the Longest Snakes (ft)**

| Stem | Leaf |
|------|------|
| 1 | 1 2 4 6 |
| 2 | 4 |
| 3 | 3 |

5. The python is the longest snake. What is its length? _____

6. How many snakes are longer than 16 feet? _____

7. How many snakes are between 11 and 24 feet long? _____

**GPS** **PROBLEM 6, STUDENT PAGE 21**

What is the difference in length between the San Francisco garter snake and the Texas blind snake?

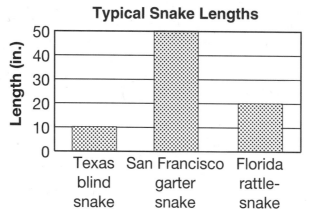

**Typical Snake Lengths**

## ━ Understand ━

**1.** What facts do you know? _____

_____

**2.** What do you need to find out?

_____

## ━ Plan ━

**3.** What operation do you use to find a difference? _____

## ━ Solve ━

**4.** Find the difference. _____

**5.** Write your answer. _____

_____

## ━ Look Back ━

**6.** How can you check to see if your answer makes sense?

_____

**SOLVE ANOTHER PROBLEM**

Find the difference in length between the
Florida rattlesnake and the Texas blind snake. _____

Fennecs, the smallest kind of foxes, are about 16 inches long. A red fox is about 25 inches long. What is the difference in length between a fennec and a red fox?

## — Understand —

**1.** What do you know?

_____

**2.** What is the length of a fennec? _____

**3.** What is the length of a red fox? _____

**4.** What are you asked to find?

_____

## — Plan —

**5.** Which operation is used to find the *difference* between two numbers?

_____

**6.** Looking at the two numbers, can you estimate their difference?

_____

## — Solve —

**7.** Write the number sentence. _____

**8.** What is the difference in length between a fennec and a red fox?

_____

## — Look Back —

**9.** How can you check your answer?

_____

SOLVE ANOTHER PROBLEM

On Monday morning, there were 12 dogs at the city animal shelter. During the day, 9 more dogs were brought in. How many dogs are at the shelter now? _____

# Exploring Making Bar Graphs

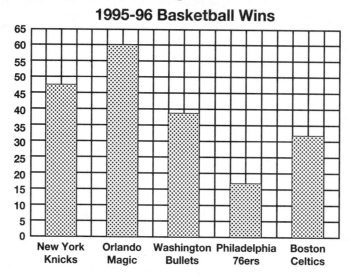

**1.** What does this bar graph compare?

_____

**2.** What scale does the graph use? _____

**3.** Which team won between 45 and 50 games? _____

**4.** If you wanted to add the Chicago Bulls (72 wins) to the bar graph, how would you change the graph?

_____

**5.** Describe how the graph would look using a scale of 10.

_____

_____

**6.** Use this grid to make the graph with a scale of 10.

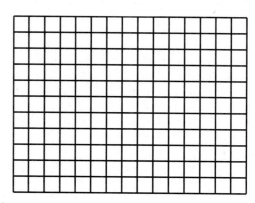

# Exploring Making Line Plots

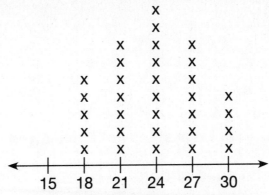

| | | | x | | |
| | | | x | | |
| | | x | x | x | |
| | | x | x | x | |
| | x | x | x | x | |
| | x | x | x | x | x |
| | x | x | x | x | x |
| | x | x | x | x | x |
| | x | x | x | x | x |

15  18  21  24  27  30

**Hamsters' Lifespans (Months)**

**1.** What does this line plot compare?

_____

**2.** Based on the line plot, would you say most hamsters live to 30 months? Explain.

_____

_____

**3. a.** If two more hamsters that lived 21 months each were included in the data, how would you change the line plot?

_____

**b.** How would your answer in Part **a** change your answer to **2**?

_____

**4.** Why are there no Xs at 15?

_____

**5.** Write a question that can be answered by the line plot.

_____

**6.** Answer your question.

_____

# Exploring Range, Median, and Mode

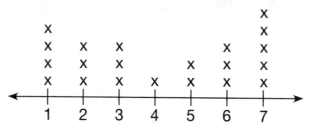

**Ages of Dogs at the Pet Shelter (yrs)**

**1.** Find the range of the ages of dogs. _____

**2.** Find the median age of dogs. _____

**3.** Find the mode of the ages of dogs. _____

**4.** How does the line plot help you find the range?

_____

**5.** How does the line plot help you find the mode?

_____

**6.** What if another 6-year-old dog arrived at the pet shelter.

   **a.** Would the range change? Explain.

   _____

   **b.** Would the mode change? Explain.

   _____

   **c.** Would the median change? Explain.

   _____

**7.** What if an additional 9-year-old dog arrived at the pet
shelter. Would the range, mode, or median change?
Explain.

   _____

   _____

# Exploring Algebra: What's the Rule?

A rule can use addition or subtraction. It can also use multiplication or division.

| In | 4 | 1 | 6 | 7 | 2 |
|-----|----|----|----|----|----|
| Out | 12 | 3 | 18 | | |

**1. a.** Write the table's rule in words. _____

    **b.** Write the table's rule with a variable. _____

    **c.** Complete the table.

    **d.** Describe how you discovered the rule.

_____

_____

_____

| In | 8 | 10 | 14 | 6 | 18 | 20 |
|-----|----|----|----|----|----|----|
| Out | 4 | 5 | 7 | | | |

**2. a.** Write a rule for the first pair of numbers that doesn't work for the second pair. _____

    **b.** Write a rule with a variable that works for all pairs of numbers. _____

    **c.** Complete the table.

**3.** Make your own table. Your rule can use addition, subtraction, multiplication, or division. Leave some spaces blank. Give your table to a classmate to complete.

| In | | | | | |
|-----|---|---|---|---|---|
| Out | | | | | |

Rule: _____

Name _____

**GPS** | PROBLEM 3, STUDENT PAGE 38

Dmitri and Wayne spent a total of $12 for books. Dmitri spent $2 more than Wayne. How much did each spend?

## ━ Understand ━

1. How much did the two boys spend all together? _____

2. What else do you know about how much the two boys spent?

_____

## ━ Plan ━

3. What is your first guess? _____

4. What should the difference be between the two amounts? _____

## ━ Solve ━

5.

| Guesses | | Difference | Sum |
|---------|---------|------------|------|
| Dmitri | Wayne | $2 | $12 |
|  |  |  |  |
|  |  |  |  |
|  |  |  |  |

Continue the table with your guesses. Continue guessing until you find the answer.

6. How much did each boy spend?

_____

## ━ Look Back ━

7. How can you check your answer? _____

---

SOLVE ANOTHER PROBLEM

Amanda ran 8 miles in two days. The first day she ran 4 more miles than the second day. How many miles did she run each day?

Day 1: _____   Day 2: _____

# Place Value Through Thousands

**Careers** Here are the number of Americans who work in each career. Write the word name for each number.

1. Actors/directors/producers—129,000 people

_____

2. Aircraft pilots—85,000 people

_____

3. Auto mechanics—739,000 people

_____

4. Bank tellers—525,000 people

_____

5. All these numbers have been rounded to what place?

_____

**Patterns** What number comes next?

6. 23; 230; 2,300 _____

7. 439; 4,390; 43,900 _____

8. 124; 1,240; 12,400 _____

9. 309; 3,090; 30,900 _____

10. 31; 313; 3,131 _____

11. 472; 1,472; 10,472 _____

12. 100; 1,000; 10,000 _____

13. 700; 700,000; 700,000,000 _____

14. The letters of the word "wonderful" have each been assigned a number. Using the chart, write the number for each word below, then write its word name.

| W | O | N | D | E | R | F | U | L |
|---|---|---|---|---|---|---|---|---|
| 1 | 2 | 3 | 4 | 5 | 6 | 7 | 8 | 9 |

a. FOLDER _____

_____

b. LOWER _____

_____

# Exploring Place-Value Relationships

Complete the table. Use place-value blocks.

| | Number | Ones | Tens | Hundreds |
|---|---|---|---|---|
| **1.** | 1 | | | |
| **2.** | 10 | | | |
| **3.** | 100 | | | |
| **4.** | 1,000 | | | |

**5.** What pattern(s) do you see in the table?

_____

_____

_____

_____

**6.** How many tens are in 6,000? _____

**7.** How many hundreds are in 5,000? _____

**8.** How could you find the number of hundreds in 9,000 without using place-value blocks or paper and pencil?

_____

_____

**9.** Michael has 2,400 comics in his collection. How many stacks would he have if he stacked them in

   **a.** hundreds? _____

   **b.** tens? _____

   **c.** thousands? _____

   _____

Use with pages 54–55.

# Place Value Through Millions

**Science** The Earth is $4\frac{1}{2}$ billion years old. Scientists divide the Earth's history into time periods according to the fossils they find in rocks. Use the table of periods in Earth's history to solve the problems.

| Time Period | When It Began |
|---|---|
| Late Triassic Period | 225,000,000 years ago |
| Jurassic Period | 213,000,000 years ago |
| Cretaceous Period | 144,000,000 years ago |
| Tertiary Period | 65,000,000 years ago |

**1.** Write the word name for the number that tells when the Tertiary period began. _____

**2.** Which period began one hundred forty-four million years ago? _____

**3.** Which two periods began more than two-hundred million years ago?

_____

Solve the riddles.

**4.** I'm a seven-digit number with digits from 1 to 7. Each digit is used once. From left to right the digits go from least to greatest. What number am I? _____

**5.** I'm an odd six-digit number whose tens digit is less than the tens digit in 345,211. My ones digit is greater than the ones digit in 345,208. The rest of my digits are the same as these two numbers. What number am I? _____

**6.** I'm a number that ends in 0 or 5. I have exactly three 1s and three 0s for digits. What number could I be?

_____

**GPS** | PROBLEM 3, STUDENT PAGE 60

Suppose you have 5 neon markers: green, purple, blue, yellow, and pink.
You choose 2 markers to make a drawing.

**a.** How many different choices do you have?

**b.** If one color must be green, how many choices do you have?

## ━ Understand ━

**1.** What do you know?

Part **a.** _____

Part **b.** _____

**2.** What must you find?

Part **a.** _____

Part **b.** _____

## ━ Plan ━

How can you organize your answers? _____

## ━ Solve ━

List your choices. How many are there?

Part **a.** _____

Part **b.** _____

## ━ Look Back ━

How can you check your answers? _____

| SOLVE ANOTHER PROBLEM |

What if the same set of 5 markers had 2 blue markers and
no green markers? What are your choices?

_____

## Comparing Numbers

**Literature** In a library, the Dewey Decimal System groups books by subjects. Here are the first five categories.

| Number | Category |
|--------|----------|
| 000-099 | Encyclopedias, magazines, almanacs, bibliographies |
| 100-199 | Philosophy, psychology, ethics |
| 200-299 | Religion and myths |
| 300-399 | Sociology (Civics, economics, education) |
| 400-499 | Language, dictionaries, grammar |

1. In which category does a book with the number 317 belong?

   _____

2. What is the greatest number a book could have if it were an encyclopedia?

   _____

3. Could a book with the number 452 be a dictionary? Explain.

   _____

4. What is the least number a book could have if it was about Native American myths?

   _____

Solve the riddles.

5. I am greater than 23,451 by 1,000. What number am I?

   _____

6. I am less than 34,211 by 2 hundreds. What number am I?

   _____

7. I'm the number between 9,999 and 10,001. _____

# Ordering Numbers

**Social Studies** Groups of years are sometimes given names. Some of these are:

Decade: 10 years        Century: 100 years        Millennium: 1,000 years

Place the groups of years in order from shortest to longest.

**1.** 3 centuries, 1 millennium, 9 decades

_____

**2.** 18 decades, 1 century, 5 millenniums

_____

**3.** 47 centuries, 2 millenniums, 89 decades

_____

**4.** In Abraham Lincoln's Gettysburg Address he said "four score and seven years ago." He could have said "eight decades and seven years ago." How many years was Lincoln referring to in this quote?

_____

Solve.

**5.** Use the digits 1, 2, and 3. Create as many 3-digit numbers as you can. Order the numbers from least to greatest.

_____

**6.** Use the digits 5, 5, 5 and 1. Create as many 4-digit numbers as you can. Order the numbers from greatest to least.

_____

**7.** Write three numbers in order from least to greatest that are greater than 21,894 but less than 42,189.

_____

# Exploring Rounding

Show the height of each of these famous mountains on a number line. On each number line, show the number that is the mountain's height rounded to the nearest thousand. Then answer the questions.

**Famous Mountains of the World**

| Mountain | Height in feet |
|---|---|
| Mt. Everest | 29,028    0  5,000  10,000  15,000  20,000  25,000  30,000 |
| Mt. McKinley | 20,320    0  5,000  10,000  15,000  20,000  25,000  30,000 |
| Mt. Ararat | 16,946    0  5,000  10,000  15,000  20,000  25,000  30,000 |
| Mt. Olympus | 9,550    0  5,000  10,000  15,000  20,000  25,000  30,000 |
| Mt. Rushmore | 5,725    0  5,000  10,000  15,000  20,000  25,000  30,000 |

1. How did you decide where to show Mt. Ararat's rounded height on the number line?

2. You are climbing Mt. Olympus, and are at 6,405 ft high. Round this number to the nearest 1,000. Show your position on the Mt. Olympus number line. About how far from the mountain top are you? How do you know?

3. Explain how to decide if Mt. Rushmore's height is closer to 5,000 feet or 10,000 feet.

# Telling Time

**Careers** A work schedule shows when certain things happen every day, such as starting times and work breaks.

Use the clocks to write the missing times.

**1.** _____ Work begins.

**2.** _____ Morning break ends.

**3.** _____ Lunch break ends.

**4.** _____ Afternoon break ends.

**5.** _____ Work ends.

**6.** Doreen's dentist appointment is at half past two in the afternoon. She arrives at 2:15 P.M. Is she early or late? Explain.

_____

**7.** Ron and Will met to go ice skating. Ron arrived at quarter to three. Will arrived at 2:55. Who arrived first? Explain.

_____

# Exploring Time: Exact or Estimate?

Read the following story. Change all the inappropriate units of time to make a sensible story. Write the correct sentences below.

Mrs. Spoon woke up at 6:20 A.M. It took her 1 minute to get ready for work. On her way out to the car, she noticed her neighbor, Emily, was having car trouble. She told Emily she would go inside in a few days and call the tow truck. The tow-truck service said they would be there in 15 years. Mrs. Spoon slipped on a patch of ice as she walked back to her car. She looked around for an hour before getting up, so she could find a less slippery place to walk. In a couple of months she was in her car. It usually took her 30 seconds to get to work, but today it took her a week. Mrs. Spoon finally arrived at the office. She had been working there since she left college 5 hours ago.

_____

_____

_____

_____

_____

_____

_____

_____

_____

_____

_____

# Elapsed Time

**Careers** Flight attendants and pilots may fly between many cities in a day. Karyn is a pilot. Her schedule for Monday is shown below. Use the schedule to answer the questions.

| Departure | Arrival |
|---|---|
| St. Louis 7:35 A.M. | Chicago - O'Hare 8:25 A.M. |
| Chicago - O'Hare 9:40 A.M. | Houston 2:55 P.M. |

**1.** How long is Karyn's flight from St. Louis to Chicago?

_____

**2.** How long is Karyn's break between flights?

_____

**3.** On Monday, how many hours will Karyn be flying the plane?

_____

**4.** Sam and his dad start to play checkers at 7:57 P.M. They play until 8:22 P.M. How long does their game last? _____

**5.** A play begins at 7:30 P.M. and lasts for 2 hours and 17 minutes. What time does the play end? _____

Use the bus schedule to answer the questions below.

| Leave Station | Arrive | | | | |
|---|---|---|---|---|---|
| | A St. | B St. | 3rd Ave. | Pier St. | Mall |
| 11:55 a.m. | 12:00 p.m. | 12:05 p.m. | 12:11 p.m. | 12:15 p.m. | 12:25 p.m. |
| 12:15 p.m. | 12:20 p.m. | 12:25p.m. | 12:31 p.m. | 12:35 p.m. | 12:45 p.m. |
| 12:35 p.m. | 12:40 p.m. | 12:45 p.m. | 12:51 p.m. | 12:55 p.m. | 1:05 p.m. |

**6.** If you take the 12:15 bus and get off 20 minutes later, where will you be? _____

**7.** How long does it take to go from the station to the mall? _____

# Exploring the Calendar

June is a busy month! It's time to fill in the calendar!

| Sunday | Monday | Tuesday | Wednesday | Thursday | Friday | Saturday |
|---|---|---|---|---|---|---|
|  |  |  |  |  |  | 1 |
| 2 | 3 | 4 | 5 | 6 | 7 | 8 |
| 9 | 10 | 11 | 12 | 13 | 14 | 15 |
| 16 | 17 | 18 | 19 | 20 | 21 | 22 |
| 23 | 24 | 25 | 26 | 27 | 28 | 29 |
| 30 |  |  |  |  |  |  |

Find the correct date for each Special Day listed below and follow the *What to do* directions to mark it on the calendar.

| Special Day | When | What to do |
|---|---|---|
| Swimming pool opens | the first Wednesday | Write an "S." |
| Craft Fair | the second Saturday | Write a "C." |
| Puppet Show | every other Sunday, starting June 2 | Write a "P." |
| Bike Race | the third Tuesday | Write a "B." |
| Camera Day at Park | 9 days after bike race | Write a "K." |
| Flag Day | 1 day before new moon | Draw a flag. |
| The full moon | 4 weeks after the first puppet show | Draw a circle. |
| The new moon | 1 week after craft fair | Draw a dark circle. |
| Summer begins! | 1 week before camera day | Draw a sun. |
| Father's Day | the third Sunday | Write "FD." |

If Flag Day falls on a weekend, workers are given Friday and Monday off. Otherwise, workers just get Flag Day off. Write "off" on the calendar on each day workers will have off.

Name _____

# Decision Making

Your class is making a fifteen-minute video about
your school for new students. The video will include an
introduction, information about the teachers, students,
after-school activities, and a tour of the building.

You need to plan your video so that you cover all your
information in the time allowed.

**1.** What do you need to decide?

_____

_____

**2.** How many different kinds of information will you have in
your video?

_____

**3.** Do you think you should have a separate part for each
kind of information, or combine some of them together?
Why?

_____

_____

**4.** Do you think all the parts should be the same length, or
should some parts be longer than other? Why?

_____

**5.** Make a schedule for your video and write it in the space below.

_____

_____

_____

_____

_____

# Exploring Addition and Subtraction Patterns

**1.** Oakdale School is collecting cans for a recycling center.
Fourth grade students collected 800 cans. Third grade
students collected 500 cans. Josh wants to know the
total number of cans collected by the third and fourth
grade students.

**a.** Explain how Josh can add 800 and 500 mentally.

_____

**b.** What basic fact could help him find the sum? _____

**c.** What is the total number of cans collected by the
third and fourth grade students? _____

**d.** How many more cans were collected by fourth
grade students than by third grade students? _____

**2.** Students at the Wilson School also collected cans for
the recycling center. The third grade students collected
700 cans. Fourth grade students collected 400 cans.

**a.** How can you use mental math to find the total number
of cans collected by students at Wilson School?

_____

**b.** What basic fact could help you find the sum? _____

**c.** What is the total number of cans collected by the
third and fourth grade students at Wilson School? _____

**d.** How many more cans were collected by third
grade students than by fourth grade
students? _____

**e.** How did you use 7 − 4 to solve 700 − 400?

_____

_____

**3.** Which school collected the most cans?
How many more cans did they collect? _____

# Exploring Adding and Subtracting on a Thousand Chart

Marty saves baseball cards. He has a total of 730 cards in his collection. He wants to give 180 cards to his friend Marie.

1. Marty wants to know how many cards he will have left in his collection after he gives Marie 180 cards.

   **a.** How could Marty use a thousand chart to find his new card total?

   _____

   **b.** How could Marty use mental math to find his new card total?

   _____

   **c.** Use mental math or a thousand chart to find Marty's new card total.  _____

2. Marie had 260 of her own cards. Then Marty gave her 180 cards from his collection.

   **a.** Describe two ways Marie could use a thousand chart to find her new card total.

   _____

   _____

   _____

   **b.** How could Marie use mental math to find her new card total?

   _____

   **c.** Use mental math or a thousand chart to find Marie's new card total.  _____

3. Who has more cards, Marty or Marie? How many more?  _____

4. Marty buys another 170 cards and Marie buys another 90. Now how many do each have?  _____

Name _____

# Estimating Sums and Differences

**Social Studies** The chart shows the number of inventions registered in the United States between 1800 and 1860. Use the chart to answer the questions below.

| Year | Number of Inventions |
|------|---------------------|
| 1800 | 41 |
| 1810 | 223 |
| 1820 | 155 |
| 1830 | 544 |
| 1840 | 458 |
| 1850 | 883 |
| 1860 | 4,357 |

**1.** About how many more inventions were created in 1850 than in 1820? _____

**2.** About how many inventions were created from 1810 through 1820? _____

**3.** About how many more inventions were created in 1860 than from 1810 through 1830? _____

**4.** In which years were there almost the same number of inventions? _____

The Zigot company makes bicycles. The chart shows how many bicycles were made over a five-day period.

| Day | Monday | Tuesday | Wednesday | Thursday | Friday |
|-----|--------|---------|-----------|----------|--------|
| Bicycles Made | 1,745 | 2,319 | 2,832 | 1,601 | 1,459 |

**5.** About how many bicycles were made during the first two days of the week? _____

**6.** What is the approximate difference between the greatest and the least number of bicycles made during the week? _____

Name _____

| GPS | PROBLEM 5, STUDENT PAGE 101 |

The table shows the number of school lunches served in a week.

| Day | Lunch | Number Served |
|-----|-------|---------------|
| Monday | Hamburgers | 285 |
| Tuesday | Baked chicken | 189 |
| Wednesday | Spaghetti | 329 |
| Thursday | Chicken nuggets | 423 |
| Friday | Pizza | 397 |

The cafeteria provides milk with each meal. It also sells milk to students who bring bag lunches. Last Wednesday, 20 students bought milk. How many cartons of milk did the cafeteria need that day?

## ━ Understand ━

**1.** What do you know?

_____

**2.** What do you need to know? _____

_____

## ━ Plan ━

**3.** Do you need an exact answer or will an estimate do? _____

## ━ Solve ━

**4.** What operation will you use? _____

**5.** How many cartons of milk did the cafeteria need on Wednesday? _____

## ━ Look Back ━

**6.** Is your answer reasonable? Explain why.

_____

| SOLVE ANOTHER PROBLEM |

Last Friday, the cafeteria sold 28 more pizza lunches than it did this Friday. How many pizza lunches were sold last Friday? _____

Name _____

# Adding

**Sports** This table shows how many games were won and lost by five NBA head coaches. Use the table to answer **1–4.**

| Coach | Won | Lost | Teams |
|---|---|---|---|
| Pat Riley | 533 | 194 | Los Angeles Lakers (1981–90) |
| K.C. Jones | 463 | 193 | Washington Bullets (1973–76) Boston Celtics (1983–88) |
| Billy Cunningham | 454 | 196 | Philadelphia 76ers (1977–85) |
| Red Auerbach | 938 | 479 | Washington Capitols (1946–49) Tri-Cities Blackhawks (1949–50) Boston Celtics (1950–66) |
| Tom Heinsohn | 427 | 263 | Boston Celtics (1969–77) |

1. Red Auerbach was the head coach of three different teams. How many games did he coach? _____

2. What is the total number of games won by Pat Riley and Billy Cunningham? _____

3. What is the total number of games lost by Tom Heinsohn and K.C. Jones? _____

4. What is the total number of games won by all five coaches? _____

5. Frieda makes beaded necklaces. She has 325 blue beads and 219 red beads. How many beads does she have in all?

_____

6. **Choose a strategy** For the high school football games on Saturday and Sunday, 257 and 394 tickets were sold. How many more tickets were sold for the Sunday game than the Saturday game?

   a. What strategy would you use to solve the problem?

   _____

   b. Answer the problem. _____

- Use Objects/Act It Out
- Draw a Picture
- Look for a Pattern
- Guess and Check
- Use Logical Reasoning
- Make an Organized List
- Make a Table
- Solve a Simpler Problem
- Work Backward

Name _____

## Column Addition

---

**History** Marco Polo is known for his 4-year journey from Italy to China in the 13th century. He returned to Italy 24 years later where he shared his knowledge of useful Chinese customs. The map below shows the approximate path of Marco Polo's trip.

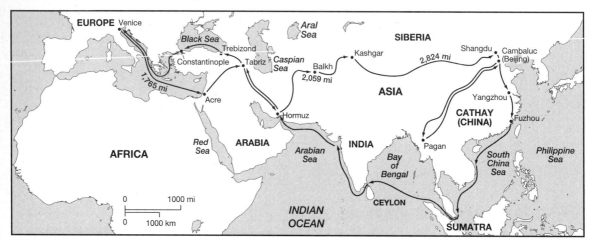

**1.** Marco Polo began his journey in Venice. How far did he travel to arrive at Hormuz? The distance from Acre to Hormuz is 3,029 miles. _____

**2.** How far did Marco Polo travel to arrive at Kashgar? _____

**3.** Was the distance from Venice to Hormuz greater or less than the distance from Hormuz to Cambaluc? Explain.

_____

_____

_____

---

**5.** Landon has a coin collection with 789 pennies, 231 nickels, 408 dimes, and 149 quarters. How many coins does he have in his collection? _____

**6.** Patti's school library has 27 encyclopedias, 14 dictionaries, 348 fiction books, and 13 atlases. How many books are in the library? _____

# Subtracting

Use the table for **1–4**.

1. Which place gets the least snowfall?

   _____

2. How much more snowfall does Juneau get than Buffalo?

   _____

| Average Snowfall | |
|---|---|
| **Place** | **Snowfall in Inches** |
| Buffalo, NY | 92 |
| Caribou, ME | 113 |
| Juneau, AK | 103 |
| Mt. Washington, NH | 247 |

3. How much more snow does the place with the most snowfall get than the place with the least snowfall? _____

4. What is the total amount of snowfall in the places listed in the table?

   _____

5. Michael had 397 stickers in his collection. He gave away 49 and lost 126. How many stickers does Michael have left?

   _____

6. **Choose a strategy** Suppose you offered juice or milk to 10 guests. Three guests said, "I would like juice, but only if you have apple juice. Otherwise, I would like milk." Two guests said, "I would like milk, but only if you have chocolate milk. Otherwise, I would like juice." Five guests said, "I would like juice, but only if you have orange juice. Otherwise, I would like milk." If you had only orange juice and regular milk, how many guests would have juice?

   - Use Objects/Act It Out
   - Draw a Picture
   - Look for a Pattern
   - Guess and Check
   - Use Logical Reasoning
   - Make an Organized List
   - Make a Table
   - Solve a Simpler Problem
   - Work Backward

   **a.** What strategy would you use to solve the problem?

   _____

   **b.** Answer the problem. _____

# Subtracting with Middle Zeros

**Science** Scientists have discovered about 500 active volcanoes on Earth. A few are listed below.

| Volcano | Height |
|---|---|
| Kilauea, USA | 4,090 feet |
| Mt. Katmai, Alaska | 6,700 feet |
| Mt. Melbourne, Antarctica | 9,000 feet |
| Mt. Saint Helens, USA | 9,677 feet |
| Mt. Tarawera, New Zealand | 3,645 feet |

**1.** Which of these volcanoes is the tallest? _____

**2.** What is the difference in height between the tallest volcano and the shortest volcano? _____

**3.** How much taller is Mt. Katmai than Mt. Tarawera? _____

**4.** How much taller is Mt. St. Helens than Mt. Melbourne? _____

**5.** One mile is 5,280 feet.

  **a.** Which volcanoes are under 1 mile in height?

  _____

  **b.** How many feet less than 2 miles is Mt. St. Helens? _____

**6.** Felicia has 2,003 animals on her farm. The only animals she has are sheep and goats. She has 1,379 sheep. How many goats does she have? _____

**7.** Arthur made 205 scones for a school bake sale. Joe bought 28 scones. How many scones were left? _____

**8.** A stationery store had 4,000 greeting cards. If they sold 2,750, how many cards are left? _____

Name _____

**Guided Problem Solving**
## 3-9

**GPS PROBLEM 3, STUDENT PAGE 119**

Kyle's first published story is 117 words long. His second story is 42 words longer. His third story is 56 words shorter than his second story. How long is his third story?

## ━ Understand ━

**1.** How long is Kyle's first story? _____

**2.** What do you need to know to answer the question?

_____

## ━ Plan ━

**3. a.** How will you find the length of the second story? Explain.

_____

_____

**b.** Write the number sentence. _____

**4. a.** How will you find the length of the third story? Explain.

_____

_____

**b.** Write the number sentence. _____

## ━ Solve ━

**5.** How long is Kyle's second story? _____

**6.** How long is Kyle's third story? _____

## ━ Look Back ━

**6.** What strategy could you use to check your answer?

_____

**SOLVE ANOTHER PROBLEM**

Keesha's first draft of a story was 223 words long. When she edited the story, she crossed out 51 words and added 74 new ones. How long was the edited story? _____

© Scott Foresman Addison Wesley 4

# Using Mental Math

**Health** Different activities burn different amounts of calories. Here is a chart showing about how many calories Alex burned doing various things on Saturday and Sunday.

| Activity | Time | Calories Burned |
|---|---|---|
| Light housework | $1\frac{1}{4}$ hours | 248 |
| Sitting at the movies | $3\frac{3}{4}$ hours | 375 |
| Riding a bike | $4\frac{3}{4}$ hours | 997 |
| Playing tennis | $1\frac{1}{4}$ hours | 552 |
| Walking | 1 hour | 298 |
| Studying | 2 hours | 230 |

Add or subtract mentally. Use any method you choose.

1. How many fewer calories did Alex burn doing housework than playing tennis? _____

2. It took Alex 1 hour to walk to the library to study. He studied for 2 hours. How many calories did this burn? _____

3. Alex spent Saturday afternoon riding his bike and played tennis on Sunday. Together, how many calories did these activities burn? _____

4. Donna bought a book for $24.95. She bought a CD for $16.99. About how much more did the book cost than the CD? _____

5. Donna read 136 pages of her 434-page book. How many pages are left? _____

6. Joanne was exercising. She did 255 push-ups and 347 sit-ups. About how many more sit-ups did she do? _____

# Choosing a Calculation Method

**Social Studies** Information about four American cities is shown in the table.

| City | Population in 1994 | Tallest Building | Height of Building |
|------|-------------------|------------------|-------------------|
| Boston | 547,725 | John Hancock Tower | 790 feet |
| Atlanta | 396,052 | Nation's Bank Tower | 1,050 feet |
| Denver | 493,559 | Republic Plaza | 714 feet |
| San Francisco | 734,676 | Transamerica Pyramid | 853 feet |

Use the data to solve. Choose any method.

1. How many more people lived in San Francisco than in Denver in 1994? _____

2. What was the total population of Boston and Atlanta in 1994? _____

3. How many more people lived in the two cities with the greatest population than the two cities with the least population? _____

4. How much taller is the Transamerica Pyramid than the John Hancock Tower? _____

5. How much taller is the tallest building listed than the shortest one? _____

6. The Toddler Toy Factory produced 57,327 toys on Monday and 62,571 toys on Tuesday.

   a. How many more toys did it produce on Tuesday than on Monday? _____

   b. How many toys did it produce all together on Monday and Tuesday? _____

7. Caroline had 236 building bricks, and her sister had 264. How many did they have in total? _____

# Counting Money

**Careers** Mr. Conte, the clerk at the music store, processed the following two orders:

piano lesson books for $30.99

sheet music for $67.95

1. Mr. Conte received only five-dollar bills for the books.

   **a.** How many bills did he receive? _____

   **b.** Should he give change? _____

   **c.** If so, how much? _____

2. Mr. Conte received 6 bills and 5 coins to pay for the sheet music. He received the exact amount. What were the bills and coins?

   _____

   _____

3. What is the least number of bills and coins you could use to make a $15.27 purchase?

   _____

4. **a.** If you have 3 ten-dollar bills, 8 dollars, 16 dimes, and 21 pennies, could you make a $47.56 purchase? Explain.

   _____

   **b.** What is the least number of bills and coins you could use to make the $47.56 purchase?

   _____

   _____

5. If you only had 10-dollar bills how many would you use to pay for an item that costs $56.15? _____

# Adding and Subtracting Money

**History** In November 1929, during the time in American History known as the Great Depression, you could buy a candy bar for as little as 3¢! But a worker earned only about $25 a week.

Here are some typical Depression Age prices for items you would buy today. Find the difference in prices.

| | Item | Price in 1929 | Price in 1997 | Difference |
|---|---|---|---|---|
| 1. | Hamburger | $0.05 | $0.69 | |
| 2. | Ice cream cone | $0.03 | $1.19 | |
| 3. | Ticket to the movies | $0.10 | $5.50 | |
| 4. | Bus fare | $0.08 | $1.00 | |

5. How much would a hamburger and an ice-cream cone combined cost in

   **a.** 1929? _____

   **b.** 1997? _____

6. If you pay $20 for a shirt that costs $12.79, how much change should you receive? _____

7. Sue went to a movie that cost $5.50. Her popcorn cost $2.50 and her soda cost $2.25.

   **a.** How much did Sue spend? _____

   **b.** If Sue brought $15 to the movies with her, did she have enough money left to buy a book that cost $3.29 on the way home? Explain.

   _____

8. Write your own subtraction problem about money. Use $30.76 and $41.80. Be sure to include the answer.

   _____

# Exploring Making Change

**1.** When you give change to a customer, you usually count on from the price of the purchase to the amount which the customer has given to you. Write what the cashier should say when counting change from a $43.27 purchase paid for with a $50 dollar bill.

_____

_____

**2.** Have you ever noticed that in some stores, next to the cash register, there is a small container of pennies? Customers are allowed to take pennies out to pay for their purchase.

**a.** Why is this helpful?

_____

_____

_____

**b.** Suppose there are 10 pennies in the container. If your purchase was $12.27 and you paid with a 20-dollar bill, how many pennies would you take from the container? Why? How would this affect your change?

_____

_____

_____

**3.** If a customer paid for a $4.89 purchase with a $20-dollar bill, what is the least number of coins and bills they could get in change?

_____

**4.** If you had no bills, what is the least number of coins you could use for the customer in change?

_____

# Exploring Algebra: Balancing
# Number Sentences

**1. a.** Write the following problem as a number sentence:

$$
\begin{array}{r}
106 \\
+\ \ n \\
\hline
178
\end{array}
$$  _____

**b.** What is the value of $n$? _____

**2. a.** Write the number sentence each workmat shows. _____

**b.** What is the value of $n$? _____

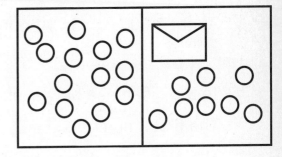

**3. a.** Draw a number sentence workmat that shows $6 + n = 13$.

**b.** What is the value of $n$? _____

**4.** Write three number sentences with the same meaning as $n + 5 = 12$.

_____

**5. a.** Draw a number sentence workmat that shows $n + n = 10$.

**b.** What is the value of $n$? _____

**GPS** PROBLEM 6, STUDENT PAGE 137

Continue the pattern. Describe the rule.

2,001; 1,901; 1,811; 1,731; 1,661; _____; _____; _____

## ━ Understand ━

**1.** What does the problem ask you to find?

_____

**2.** Would it seem reasonable to assume your answer would begin with:

**a.** About 3,000      **b.** About 1,751      **c.** About 1,600

## ━ Plan ━

**3.** Write the difference between:

**a.** The first 2 numbers _____

**b.** The second and third numbers _____

**c.** The third and fourth numbers _____

## ━ Solve ━

**4. a.** What is the pattern so far? _____

**b.** What will you do to continue the pattern? _____

**5. a.** What are the next 3 numbers? Describe the rule?

_____

## ━ Look Back ━

**6.** Describe one way you can check your answer.

_____

_____

| SOLVE ANOTHER PROBLEM |
|---|

Continue the pattern. Describe the rule.

Z, X, Y, W, X, _____, _____, _____

Name _____

# Reviewing the Meaning of Multiplication

**Science** Earth is not the only planet that has a moon. Most of the other planets in our solar system also have moons. In many cases, they have more than one moon.

1. In 1610, Galileo discovered 4 moons on Jupiter. Today, scientists believe that Jupiter has 4 times as many moons as Galileo saw. How many known moons does Jupiter have? _____

2. Mars has 2 known moons. Saturn is known to have 9 times as many moons as Mars. How many known moons does Saturn have? _____

3. Until 1989, scientists had only discovered 2 of Neptune's moons. Since then, scientists have found 4 times as many moons orbiting Neptune as they originally thought. How many known moons does Neptune have? _____

4. Uranus is known to have 5 times as many moons as Earth. How many known moons does Uranus have? _____

5. Suppose you go to soccer practice 5 days a week. How many days would you go to practice in 4 weeks? _____

6. Suppose you work on homework 2 hours a day. How many hours would you work in 5 days? _____

7. A magazine costs $3. How much would you pay for 6 magazines? _____

8. A tray of blueberry muffins contains 2 cups of blueberries. How many blueberries are in 3 trays? _____

Name ____________________

Problem Solving
4-2

# Exploring Patterns in Multiplying by 0, 1, 2, 5, and 9

| | | | | | | | | | |
|---|---|---|---|---|---|---|---|---|---|
| 51 | 52 | 53 | 54 | 55 | 56 | 57 | 58 | 59 | 60 |
| 61 | 62 | 63 | 64 | 65 | 66 | 67 | 68 | 69 | 70 |
| 71 | 72 | 73 | 74 | 75 | 76 | 77 | 78 | 79 | 80 |
| 81 | 82 | 83 | 84 | 85 | 86 | 87 | 88 | 89 | 90 |
| 91 | 92 | 93 | 94 | 95 | 96 | 97 | 98 | 99 | 100 |

Use the half of a hundred chart above to answer **1–3** below.

**1.** Do you think that 10 would have more or fewer multiples than 5 on a hundred chart? Explain.

____________________

____________________

**2.** How many multiples does 1 have on the half of a hundred chart above? Explain.

____________________

**3.** How many multiples does 0 have on the half of a hundred chart above? Explain.

____________________

**4.** How do you know that $45 \times 23 = 23 \times 45$ without finding their products?

____________________

**5.** Tell if each number is a multiple of 2, 5, both, or neither.

**a.** 714 __________ **b.** 1,850 __________

**c.** 30 __________ **d.** 765 __________

# Multiplying with 3 and 4 as Factors

**History** Presidential elections happen every 4 years. This 4-year cycle is called a term.

1. Franklin D. Roosevelt served a little more than 3 full terms as president. About how long was he president? _____

2. In 1944, Roosevelt was elected to serve a 4th term, which he never completed. How many years would Roosevelt have been in office if he had completed a 4th term? _____

3. Because Roosevelt won so many elections, Congress passed a law. It states that presidents can only serve 2 terms. How many years can a president remain in office today? _____

4. Adrienne and Derrick each bought 4 comic books.

   **a.** How many comic books did they buy in all? _____

   **b.** Each comic book they bought cost $3. How much did they spend in all? _____

5. Aaron practices the piano 7 days a week. How many days does he practice in 4 weeks? _____

6. Joel made 3 roundtrips to the next town. The roundtrip is a total of 6 miles. How many miles did he travel? _____

7. Keith went swimming 3 days a week during his summer vacation. His summer vacation was 9 weeks long. How many days did he go swimming? _____

8. It takes Alan 4 minutes to complete a puzzle. How long will it take him to complete 5 puzzles? _____

# Multiplying with 6, 7, and 8 as Factors

1. Niles multiplied two numbers. The product was 32. One factor was 8. What was the other factor?   _____

2. Dawn multiplied two numbers. The product was 63. One factor was 9. What was the other factor?   _____

3. Tickets to the movie cost $7.00 each. How much money would you need to buy 6 tickets?   _____

4. Kenneth paid $4.00 each for himself and 7 other people to see a show. How much did all the tickets cost?   _____

5. Notebooks cost $6.00 each. How much money would you need to buy 4 notebooks?   _____

6. Suppose a pool has 8 lanes for lap swimming. Each lane is 5 feet wide. How wide is the pool?   _____

7. Steve can cook only 2 eggs at a time in his saucepan. He wants to boil 6 eggs for 7 minutes each. How long will it take?   _____

8. **Choose a strategy**   Garden A has 6 rows. Each row in Garden A has 8 heads of lettuce growing in it. Garden B has 4 rows. There are the same number of heads of lettuce in Garden A as there are in Garden B. How many heads of lettuce are there in each row in Garden B?

   | |
   |---|
   | • Use Objects/Act It Out |
   | • Draw a Picture |
   | • Look for a Pattern |
   | • Guess and Check |
   | • Use Logical Reasoning |
   | • Make an Organized List |
   | • Make a Table |
   | • Solve a Simpler Problem |
   | • Work Backward |

   a. What strategy would you use to solve the problem?

   _____

   b. Answer the problem.

   _____

# Exploring Patterns in Multiples of 10, 11, and 12

Use a hundred chart to help you answer each question.

**1.** List the multiples of 10 in order.

_____

**2.** Write a rule using addition for the multiples of 10.

_____

**3.** List the multiples of 11 in order.

_____

**4.** Write a rule using addition for the multiples of 11.

_____

**5.** List the multiples of 12 in order.

_____

**6.** Write a rule using addition for the multiples of 12.

_____

**7.** Write a rule using addition to find the multiples of any number.

_____

**8.** What other patterns do you see on a hundred chart?

_____

_____

**9.** What patterns can you find in the sums of digits in a column?

_____

**10.** What patterns do you notice in the diagonal from 1 to 100?

_____

# Decision Making

The cross country ski club is planning a weekend trip to Manchester, Vermont. They are leaving for the trip in 6 weeks. They need to raise about $40 per person for the trip. There are 12 students in the club, so they need to raise $480 in 6 weeks. How should the club raise money?

### Facts and Data
6 students are not free on Tuesdays.
4 students are not free on Thursdays.

Possible jobs:

| Day | Job | Number of Hours per Student | Pay |
|---|---|---|---|
| Tuesday | Shoveling Snow | 2 hours | $5 per hour |
| Thursday | Walking Dogs | 2 hours | $4 per hour |

1. How many students are available to work on Tuesdays? _____

2. How many students are available to work on Thursdays?_____

3. How much can the club earn in a week shoveling snow? _____

4. How much can the club earn in a week walking dogs? _____

5. How many weeks will it take to earn $480 shoveling snow? walking dogs?

_____

6. a. If the club members worked at both jobs each week, how much would they earn per week? _____

   b. About how many weeks would it take to earn $480?

_____

7. What do you think the club should do to earn the money they need for the trip? Explain.

_____

_____

_____

# Reviewing the Meaning of Division

**Language Arts** Books are often divided into sections called chapters. Sometimes chapters are grouped together to form parts. *Gulliver's Travels*, by Jonathan Swift, is divided into 4 parts, and each one of those parts is divided into chapters.

1. Mark is reading Part I (A Voyage to Lilliput) of *Gulliver's Travels*. He has 63 pages to read. If he reads 7 pages each day, how long will it take him to read Part I? _____

2. Part I of *Gulliver's Travels* has 8 chapters. If your class spends 16 days studying Part I, how many days will you spend on each chapter? _____

3. Chapter 1 of Part I is 9 pages long. If you want to read the chapter in 3 days, how many pages should you read each day? _____

4. Lila, who is planning on competing in a spelling bee, needs to study the spelling of 72 frequently misspelled words. She has 9 days to get ready. How many words should she study each day? _____

5. Gary is assigned a role in a play on May 1st. He has 36 lines to memorize. He needs to know all of his lines by heart by May 6th.

   a. If he studies the same number of lines each day, how many should he memorize each day? _____

   b. Suppose Gary forgets to study his lines on May 1st and 2nd. How many lines does he need to memorize each of the remaining days? _____

6. Graham is backpacking with his family. They have 56 miles to cover in a week. How many miles should they walk in a day? _____

Name _____

# Exploring Multiplication and Division Stories

1. Suppose you wanted to write a multiplication and division story with the numbers 4, 20, and 5. Write the number sentences you could use.

   _____

2. Some fact families only have 2 number sentences.

   a. Write four fact families that have only 2 number sentences.

   _____

   _____

   b. What do the fact families with 2 number sentences have in common? Explain.

   _____

   _____

3. Suppose you want to write a multiplication or division story with the number 36. Write all of the possible basic facts (using factors under 10) you could use.

   _____

   _____

4. Describe a situation with money where you could use multiplication and division facts.

   _____

   _____

5. Write a multiplication or division story using the basic facts $4 \times 3$ and $12 \div 3$.

   _____

   _____

# Dividing with 2, 5, and 9

---

**Physical Education** Mike's gym teacher, Ms. Whitman, formed a bicycle club in the spring. Nine students joined the club. The club goes biking every day after school and sometimes on the weekends.

1. One day after school, everybody on the bike team rode the same number of miles. If the total number of miles the team rode was 36 miles, how many miles did each team member ride that day?  _____

2. Mike rode 40 miles over five days. If he traveled the same numbers of miles each day, how many miles did Mike ride each day?  _____

3. Mike rode for 2 hours each day for an entire week. How many hours did he ride during that week?  _____

---

4. Angie gets paid $5 per hour mowing lawns. If Angie makes $45 one week, how many hours did she work?  _____

5. There are 27 students in Mr. Morelli's 4th grade class. He asks the students to split into groups of 3 for a math lesson. How many groups of 3 students will there be?  _____

6. Joyce bought 18 marbles. She gave each of her 2 children an equal number of marbles. How many marbles did each child get?  _____

7. Nora bought 2 shirts. Each shirt was the same price. If she paid $24.00, how much was each shirt?  _____

8. Ben is playing a game with 5 friends. 25 counters are divided equally among them. How many counters does each one get?  _____

Name _____

# Special Quotients

**Fine Arts** The City Museum is putting on a small exhibit of paintings by famous European artists. A curator at the museum, Mrs. Hanson, had to research, select, and obtain the paintings for the exhibit.

1. Mrs. Hanson obtained 6 different paintings by the French artist, Claude Monet. How many Monet paintings were in the exhibit? Write a number sentence for this problem.  _____

2. Mrs. Hanson obtained 9 different paintings from 9 different artists. How many paintings did each artist have in the exhibit? Write a number sentence for this problem.  _____

3. Mrs. Hanson wanted to get 3 paintings by Matisse for the exhibit. The 3 Matisse paintings are being shared by 3 museums including the City Museum. How many paintings by Matisse were in the exhibit? Write a number sentence for this problem.  _____

4. If the dividend of a number sentence is 0, and the divisor is greater than 0, what do you know about the quotient?

_____

5. John gets paid $5 per hour for his job stocking shelves at the hardware store. If he makes $5 one day, how many hours did he work?  _____

6. Karen has 3 flower beds. She has planted 3 different types of flowers in each bed. How many different types of flowers did Karen plant?  _____

7. Jim is playing a game of tiddlywinks with Cathy. Cathy says she will add 3 counters to Jim's winnings, or multiply Jim's winnings by 3. If Jim is not likely to win anything, which choice do you think he should make? Explain.

_____

_____

# Dividing with 3 and 4

---

**Fine Arts** When a composer writes a piece of music, he or she divides the music into *measures*. A measure is a part of a song. Each measure has the same number of beats. Composers sometimes write music with 3, 4 or 6 beats per measure.

1. A composer writes a short children's song with 27 beats, total. If there are 3 beats per measure, how many measures does the song contain? _____

2. Another song contains 32 beats, total. If there are 4 beats per measure, how many measures does this song contain? _____

3. If a third song is 11 measures long and has 44 beats total, how many beats per measure are there? _____

---

4. Jason played 9 quarters during 3 football games.

   a. If he played the same number of quarters in each game, how many quarters did he play per game? _____

   b. If one of the games went into overtime, and continued to 5 quarters, how many quarters did Jason spend on the bench? _____

5. Complete the table. Write the rule.

| In | 16 | 21 | 24 | 27 | 32 | 33 | 36 |
|-----|----|----|----|----|----|----|----|
| Out | 4 | 7 | 6 | 9 | | | |

Rule: _____

6. Mark is having 3 guests to visit. He makes 12 sandwiches.

   a. How many sandwiches can each guest have? _____

   b. Another guest joins them. How many sandwiches will each guest have now? _____

# Dividing with 6, 7 and 8

**Science** Don't call a spider an insect! A spider is an *arachnid*. Insects have 6 legs while arachnids have 8 legs.

Some insects: flies, beetles, mosquitoes, ants

Some arachnids: spiders, scorpions, mites, aphids

1. A very careful scientist was studying photographs of her ant farm. In one picture, she counted 54 individual ant legs. How many ants were in the picture? _____

2. The same scientist came across some bug tracks in the sand. She decided the tracks were made by a scorpion. If there were 56 individual footprints in the sand, how many times did each of the scorpion's legs touch the ground? _____

3. Eight scientists on the project agreed to share the research time equally. If 40 hours are needed, how many hours is each scientist responsible for? _____

4. It takes 14 days for a canary egg to incubate (get ready to hatch). How many weeks is this?

_____

5. Find the incubation period for each bird:

   **a.** Chickens: 21 days or _____ weeks

   **b.** Turkeys: _____ days or 4 weeks

6. It takes 28 days for a squirrel to gestate (get ready to be born). How many weeks is this?

_____

7. Find the gestation period for each animal:

   **a.** Dog: 63 days or _____ weeks

   **b.** Cat: _____ days or 8 weeks

© Scott Foresman Addison Wesley 4

# Exploring Even and Odd Numbers

**1.** How many odd numbers are there between 5 and 25 (not including 5 or 25)?

_____

List them:

_____

**2.** How many even numbers are there between 0 and 30 (not including 0 or 30)?

_____

List them:

_____

_____

**3.** What two even numbers can be added together to get a sum of 62?     _____

**4.** What two odd numbers can be added together to get a sum of 62?     _____

**5.** What kind of numbers can be added together to get a sum of 47? (Circle all correct answers.)

**a.** two even numbers

**b.** two odd numbers

**c.** one even number and one odd number

**6.** What kind of numbers can be added together to get a sum of 26? (Circle all correct answers.)

**a.** two even numbers

**b.** two odd numbers

**c.** one even number and one odd number

# Exploring Factors

**1. a.** List the factors of 12 and 24.

_____

_____

   **b.** What factors do 12 and 24 have in common?

_____

**2. a.** List the factors of 48, 50, and 63.

_____

_____

_____

   **b.** Which has the greatest number of factors? _____

   **c.** What factors do they all have in common? _____

**3.** Do any prime numbers end in 4? Explain.

_____

_____

**4.** How can a number have only 3 factors? Give examples of 3 numbers with only 3 factors.

_____

_____

**5.** List the dimensions of all the rectangles you could draw to show 60.

_____

_____

**GPS** PROBLEM 4, STUDENT PAGE 187

Sue, Leanne, and Ash made a total of 10 goals. Sue made 4 goals and Leanne made 2. Ash made twice as many goals as Leanne. How many goals did Ash make?

## — Understand —

1. Underline the question you need to answer.

2. Circle the sentence that tells you how to find the answer.

3. Look at the rest of the problem. What information do you need to find the answer? Draw a box around it.

## — Plan —

4. How will you find your answer? What operation will you use?

_____

## — Solve —

5. Write a number sentence and solve the problem.

_____

## — Look Back —

6. Did it help to know how many goals Sue made or how many total goals were made? _____

7. How can you check your answer?

_____

_____

SOLVE ANOTHER PROBLEM

Daniel slept 8 hours on Mon., 6 hours Tues., 7 hours Thurs., 8 hours Fri., 9 hours Sat., and 9 hours Sun. What is the *median* number of hours Daniel slept this week?

_____

**GPS** | **PROBLEM 4, STUDENT PAGE 189**

The Taneytown Cyclers put on a show. They used tricycles and bicycles. There were 12 tricycles and bicycles with a total of 27 wheels in the show. How many bicycles were there?

## ━ Understand ━

**1.** What do you know? _____

_____

**2.** What do you need to find out? _____

## ━ Plan ━

**3.** Name one number that would be too high of a guess of the number of bicycles. Name another number that would be too low. Explain.

_____

_____

_____

## ━ Solve ━

**4.** Check a guess of 6 bicycles. Are there too many or too few wheels? _____

**5.** How many bicycles were in the show? _____

## ━ Check ━

**6.** Describe another strategy you could use to check your work.

_____

| **SOLVE ANOTHER PROBLEM** |

Martha and Enrique brought 24 oranges to a picnic. Enrique brought 6 more oranges than Martha. How many oranges did they each bring?

_____

# Multiplying Tens

**Careers** Professional photographers take many pictures of events. Then they select the best pictures to sell.

**1.** Karen used 7 rolls of film to photograph the school's sports events. Each roll has 40 exposures. How many pictures did she take?

_____

**2.** Karen can develop 6 pictures an hour. If she works 40 hours a week, how many pictures can she develop?

_____

**3.** The best pictures will go in the school's photo album. The album has 20 pages. Each page in the album holds 8 pictures. How many pictures will the album hold in all?

_____

**4.** We drove to the Olympic games in 4 hours. Our speed averaged 60 miles per hour. We traveled another 3 hours at the same speed to visit a Civil War site.

**a.** How many miles did we travel to the Olympic games? _____

**b.** How many miles did we travel from there to the Civil War site? _____

**c.** We drove home from the Civil War site in 5 hours at 60 miles per hour. How many miles did we travel on the entire trip?

_____

**d.** Our car gets 20 miles to the gallon. If we bought 20 gallons twice on our journey, would we have enough for the whole trip?

_____

Name _____

# Exploring Multiplication Patterns

Find each product using place-value blocks.

**1.**

3 × 5 tens = _____ tens = _____

**2.**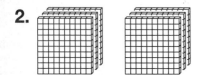

2 × 3 hundreds = _____ hundreds = _____

**3.** Linda says that the product of 3 and 700 has 2 zeros, and the product of 4 and 500 has 3 zeros. Is she correct? Explain.

_____

_____

Tell how many zeros will be in each product. Use place-value patterns to find each.

**4.** 4 × 700 _____   **5.** 9 × 3,000 _____

**6.** 8 × 4,000 _____   **7.** 7 × 50,000 _____

**8.** 3 × 30 _____   **9.** 6 × 70 _____

**10.** 5 × 200 _____   **11.** 8 × 50 _____

**12.** How are **10** and **11** different from **4–9**?

_____

_____

Solve using patterns.

**13.** A ream of paper is 500 sheets of paper. A case of paper has 2 stacks of 5 reams. How many sheets of paper are in a case of paper?

_____

## Estimating Products

**Science** It takes 24 hours (one full day) for the earth to make one complete turn. The earth makes 365 complete turns every year.

1. Estimate the number of hours it takes the earth to make 8 complete turns.

   _____

2. Estimate the number of times the earth turns in 5 years.

   _____

3. Does the earth turn more or less than 2,700 times in 9 years? Explain.

   _____

   _____

4. Which is the closest estimate for the number of hours it takes the earth to turn 7 times?

   A. 210 hours    B. 280 hours    C. 140 hours    D. 100 hours

   _____

Jake rented a video game system for 5 days. The system cost $18 for a 1-day rental. He also rented 2 games. Each game cost $12.00 for a 5-day period.

5. About how much did Jake pay to rent the system and the games for 5 days?          _____

6. Estimate the total cost of renting the video game system only for 6 days.          _____

7. About how much would it cost to rent the system only for 3 days?          _____

# Exploring Multiplication with Arrays

When you multiply a 2-digit number by a 1-digit number, remember to use your multiplication facts to help you multiply the tens columns.

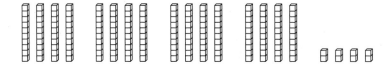

**1.** 42 × 4

   **a.** Write a number sentence to show the number of ones.

   _____

   **b.** Write a number sentence to show the number of tens.

   _____

   **c.** What is the number shown? _____

Write number sentences for the tens and the ones. Then find the total product.

**2.**     5 2
        ×    3
        ──────
           = _____ × _____ ones

       +___ = _____ × _____ tens

**3.**     2 3
        ×    3
        ──────
           = _____ × _____ ones

       +___ = _____ × _____ tens

**4.** Describe how multiplying with arrays is similar to how you solved **2** and **3**.

_____

_____

# Multiplying 2-Digit Numbers

**1.** Mr. Rodriguez bought 18 prizes for his school's storytelling contest. Each prize cost $4. How much money did he spend on the prizes?    _____

**2.** A dress costs $35. Sue bought 3 dresses. How much did Sue pay for the dresses?    _____

Maya bought the following items to stock her stationery store: 4 binders for $2 each, 25 boxes of notebook paper for $6 each, 24 boxes of pencils for $3 each, and 34 rubber stamps for $5 each.

**3.** How much money did Maya spend on the rubber stamps?    _____

**4.** How much money did Maya spend on notebook paper and pencils?    _____

**5.** What was the total cost of Maya's purchase?    _____

**6.** If Maya paid $500 for her purchases, how much change would she receive?    _____

**7. Choose a Strategy** Which costs more: The 34 rubber stamps, or the 4 binders, 25 boxes of paper, and 24 boxes of pencils combined?

- Use Objects/Act It Out
- Draw a Picture
- Look for a Pattern
- Guess and Check
- Use Logical Reasoning
- Make an Organized List
- Make a Table
- Solve a Simpler Problem
- Work Backward

**a.** What strategy would you use to solve the problem?

_____

_____

**b.** Answer the problem.

_____

# Multiplying 3-Digit Numbers

**History** The Egyptian pyramids were built almost 5,000 years ago. Of the three pyramids in Egypt, the Great Pyramid is the largest. The Great Pyramid is 480 feet tall and its base is about the size of ten football fields.

1. The stones that were used to build the pyramids often weighed about 3 tons. How much would 108 stones weigh?

   _____

2. Some of the pyramids' largest stones weighed 15 tons. If an elephant weighs 3 tons, how many elephants would it take to equal the weight of one stone?

   _____

3. If it took 25 minutes to prepare each stone for a pyramid, could 8 stones be finished in 3 hours? Explain.

   _____

4. A can of juice contains 354 mL. If Carl has 3 cans of juice and Brenda has 4, how many milliliters of juice do they have in all?

   _____

5. The distance from Merrimack to Hadley is 8 times as long as the distance from Merrimack to Amherst. The distance from Merrimack to Amherst is 146 km. How far is it from Merrimack to Hadley?

   _____

6. A movie lasts 117 minutes. Could a movie theater show the movie 4 times in 6 hours? Explain.

   _____

7. An ounce of Swiss cheese has 219 mg of calcium. How much calcium do 3 ounces of cheese contain?

   _____

# Decision Making

Suppose you and 7 friends went to a pizza parlor.
Each wanted 3 slices of pizza. A large pizza has
20 slices, a medium has 8 slices, and a small has
6 slices. Two friends wanted pepperoni, one wanted
sausage, three wanted only cheese, and two wanted
ham. What pizzas would you order?

1. What are you asked to do?

_____

2. How many slices of pizza do you need altogether?

_____

3. What size pizzas would you order? Describe two different orders that
   would provide enough slices of pizza.

_____

_____

4. What strategy can you use to help you determine the toppings for
   each pizza?

_____

5. What additional information would help you make your decision?

_____

_____

_____

6. Make a list of the pizzas you would order. List sizes and toppings.

_____

_____

7. Describe how you made your decision.

_____

_____

# Choosing a Calculation Method

**Geography** Charles lives in Boston. He often has to travel to other cities on business. He earns one frequent flier point for each mile he travels.

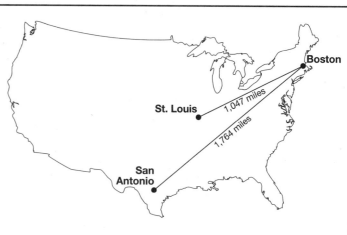

1. How many round trips between Boston and St. Louis would Charles need to take to earn 15,000 points? _____

2. **a.** How many fewer round trips to San Antonio would Charles need to take to earn 15,000 points? _____

   **b.** Explain how you found your answer.

   _____

   _____

   _____

3. Describe one combination of round trips Charles could take to St. Louis and to San Antonio to earn 15,000 points.

   _____

   _____

4. Maria, Jack, Cindy, and Ron each have jump ropes 187 centimeters long. If they lay their jump ropes end to end, how many centimeters in all will their jump ropes measure?

   _____

5. Maria uses her jump rope to jump 328 times. If each of the other students jumps half that number of times, how many jumps are made in all?

   _____

## Multiplying Money

**Social Studies** Use the table to answer **1–5**.

|  | **1970 price** | **1996 price** |
|---|---|---|
| **T-Shirt** | $3.15 | $15.35 |
| **Hat** | $1.29 | $7.86 |
| **Pennant** | $0.89 | $6.29 |

**1.** How much more did 7 T-shirts cost in 1996 than in 1970?

_____

_____

**2.** Would $6.00 have been enough to buy 5 hats in 1970? Explain.

_____

**3.** How much did 6 T-shirts cost in 1996?

_____

**4.** How much more would it cost to buy one T-shirt, one hat, and one pennant in 1996 than in 1970?

_____

**5.** Carlos bought 2 notebooks for $1.19 each and 3 pens for $0.79 each. Which cost more, 2 notebooks or 3 pens?

_____

**6.** What was the total that Carlos spent?

_____

**5.** How much change would he get from a $10 bill?

_____

# Mental Math: Special Products

**Science** Alligators, caimans, gharials, and crocodiles are all called crocodilians. There are 26 species of crocodilians.

1. There are 3 species of caimans. Use mental math to find the total number of caimans if there are 25 of each species sunning themselves.  _____

2. Many species of crocodilians are endangered. Today there may be only about 120 gharials in the wild. If there were 8 times that many today, how many gharials would there be all together?  _____

3. Crocodilians may lay as few as 12 eggs. How many crocodilians laid eggs if the total number of eggs is 84?  _____

4. How many minutes are there in 3 hours?  _____

5. How many seconds are in 9 minutes?  _____

6. How many weeks are there in 5 years? (There are 52 weeks in 1 year.)  _____

7. How many hours are there in 7 days?  _____

8. How many minutes are there in 7 days?  _____

9. How many days are in 5 years? (There are 365 days in a year. Ignore leap year.)  _____

Name _____

## Multiplying 3 Factors

Fine Art An artist is making collages. She
has the listed materials with which to work.

The artist wants to make a pattern and
duplicate the pattern 5 times for each
piece of artwork.

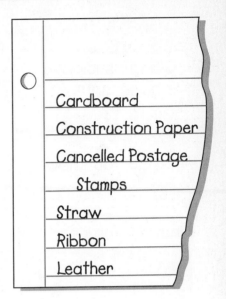

Cardboard
Construction Paper
Cancelled Postage
Stamps
Straw
Ribbon
Leather

1. If the artist uses 3 cancelled postage
   stamps in each pattern and makes
   4 copies of her artwork, how many
   postage stamps will she need?
   Explain.

   _____

   _____

2. Suppose the artist wants to use 2 strips of leather in each
   pattern and wants to make 2 copies of her artwork. How
   many strips of leather will she need? Explain.

   _____

3. If the artist has 20 pieces of straw will she have enough
   to use 1 piece on each pattern and make 4 copies of her
   artwork? Explain.

   _____

4. There are 31 floors in the Starr building. There are 3
   people in each office and 7 offices on each floor. How
   many people work in the building? Explain.

   _____

5. There are 5 windows on each of the 4 sides of the
   building. If this is true for each of the 31 floors, how
   many windows are there in all?

   _____

Name _____

PROBLEM 6, STUDENT PAGE 233

Joy has $50. She ordered 5 rainsticks. What is her change?

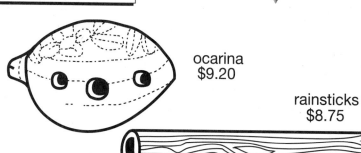

ocarina
$9.20

rainsticks
$8.75

## — Understand —

**1.** What do you know?

_____

**2.** What do you need to find out? _____

_____

## — Plan —

**3.** How will you begin?

_____

**4.** What's the next step?

_____

## — Solve —

**5.** How much change did Joy receive?

_____

## — Look Back —

**6.** How can you check if your answer makes sense?

_____

_____

| SOLVE ANOTHER PROBLEM |
|---|

Bill has $75. He ordered 8 ocarinas. What is his change? _____

Name _____

GPS | PROBLEM 4, STUDENT PAGE 236

If your pattern
has 4 squares,
how many pieces
will it have in all?

| Number of squares | Number of pieces |
|:---:|:---:|
| 1 | 4 |
| 2 | 9 |
| 3 | 14 |
| 4 |  |

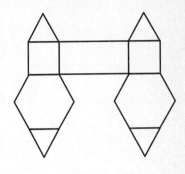

## — Understand —

**1.** If the pattern has 2 squares, how
many pieces will it have in all? _____

**2.** What do you need to find out?

_____

## — Plan —

**3.** Look at the table. What patterns do you see?

_____

**4.** Use the pattern to complete the table.
Fill in the table with the data you know.

## — Solve —

**5.** How many pieces will there be in a pattern with
4 squares? _____

## — Look Back —

**6.** What could you do to prove your answer is correct?

_____

SOLVE ANOTHER PROBLEM

If your pattern has 7 squares, how many pieces will it have
in all? _____

# Exploring Multiplication Patterns

Find the missing factors or products.

**1. a.** 30 × 4 = _____    **2. a.** 50 × 4 = _____

**b.** 300 × 40 = _____    **b.** 50 × _____ = 2,000

**c.** _____ × 400 = 120,000    **c.** _____ × 400 = 200,000

**d.** 3,000 × _____ = 120,000    **d.** 5 × _____ = 20,000

**3. a.** 9 × 30 = _____    **4. a.** 80 × 6 = _____

**b.** 90 × 30 = _____    **b.** 80 × 60 = _____

**c.** 900 × _____ = 27,000    **c.** 800 × _____ = 480,000

**d.** 90 × _____ = 270,000    **d.** 8,000 × _____ = 480,000

**5. a.** 70 × 8 = _____    **6. a.** 60 × 4 = _____

**b.** 700 × 80 = _____    **b.** 90 × 40 = _____

**c.** 70 × _____ = 56,000    **c.** _____ × 40 = 24,000

**d.** 7,000 × _____ = 56,000    **d.** 6,000 × _____ = 2,400,000

**7.** Describe the method you used to find the missing factors.

_____

_____

_____

_____

**8.** When multiplied by a one-digit number, what multiple of ten will always give a product with three zeros?  _____

**9.** What is a one-digit number that will give a product with three zeros when multiplied by 600?  _____

**10.** Which one-digit numbers will give a product with two zeros when multiplied by 500?

_____

## Estimating Products

**History** In 1873, Andrew Hallidge introduced the cable car system to San Francisco. At its peak just before 1900, there were over 600 cable cars and 100 miles of track. The great earthquake in 1906 caused extensive damage to the cars and cable lines. Today, there are 39 cars operating over a 10-mile network.

1. A round trip cable car ride is about 10 miles. A cable car makes about 27 round trips a day. Estimate how many miles the cable car travels each day. _____

2. If one cable car holds 48 people, estimate how many people 39 cable cars will hold. _____

3. Each cable car has a brake assembly made up of many small pieces. If each brake assembly costs about $600, is $24,500 enough to buy brake assemblies for 39 cars? _____

4. Each cable car is hand built by one skilled craftsperson. It takes about 18 months of work to build a cable car. About how many months of work would it take to build 39 cars? _____

5. Mr. Benson works an average of 42 hours a week. If he works for 48 weeks, about how many hours does he work?

   _____

6. Suppose Mr. Benson works an average of 48 hours a week, about how many more hours would he work in 48 weeks?

   _____

# Multiplying by Multiples of 10

**Recreation** Many people enjoy vacations that involve a sport. One popular sport vacation is a bicycle tour. Bicycle Adventures offers tours throughout the United States. You can take a tour based on your interests and your cycling ability.

1. There are 20 teams of bicyclists with 8 people on each team. How many bicyclists are there? _____

2. **a.** The bicyclists travel 40 miles a day. On a 12-day tour, how many miles will they bike? _____

   **b.** The bicyclists complete 22 miles of the tour before lunch. How many more miles must they bike that day? _____

3. The bicyclists drink water along the ride. They drink 20 cases of water. Each case contains 12 one-liter bottles. How many liters of water do they drink? _____

4. A van follows the bicyclists with luggage and safety equipment. The gas tank holds 20 gallons of gasoline. It can travel 15 miles on each gallon of gas. How many miles can the van travel on one tank of gas? _____

5. The bicycle tour costs $60 a day for each person. How much will it cost a family of four each day? _____

6. The average price for dinner at a local restaurant is $15. The restaurant serves about 40 dinners a night. About how much does the restaurant earn from dinners each day? _____

7. An auditorium has 30 rows with 15 seats in each row. Are there enough seats for 500 people? Explain.

_____

8. Alec wants to buy 30 pencils. The pencils cost $0.12 each. Alec has $3.00. Does he have enough money to buy the pencils?

_____

## Exploring Multiplying with 2-Digit Factors

Complete the multiplication.

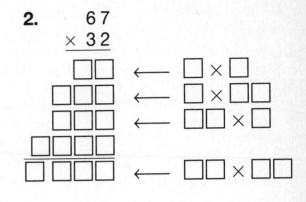

**1.**   3 2
       × 6 7

☐☐  ← 7 × 2
☐☐☐  ← 7 × 30
☐☐☐  ← ☐☐ × ☐
☐☐☐☐  ← ☐☐ × ☐☐
☐☐☐☐

**2.**   6 7
       × 3 2

☐☐  ← ☐ × ☐
☐☐☐  ← ☐ × ☐☐
☐☐☐  ← ☐☐ × ☐
☐☐☐☐
☐☐☐☐  ← ☐☐ × ☐☐

**3.** Compare **1** and **2**. Explain how they are alike and how they differ?

_____

_____

_____

**4.** Will 23 × 76 give the same product as 32 × 67? Explain.

_____

**5.** Will 47 × 52 give the same product as 57 × 42? Draw place-value blocks to show your answer.

_____

# Multiplying with 2-Digit Factors

1. The Mississippi Queen was built in 1976. How many years ago was it built?

   _____

2. The riverboat travels 55 miles a day up the river. How many miles will it travel in 43 days?

   _____

3. The average weight of a suitcase brought on board the riverboat is 27 pounds. How much will 35 suitcases weigh?

   _____

4. The riverboat has 2 crew members for every 10 passengers. If there are 100 passengers, how many crew members are there?

   _____

5. There are 208 cabins on the riverboat and 78 of them have balconies. How many cabins do not have balconies?

   _____

6. There are 4 passengers in line at the breakfast buffet. Earl is ahead of Kate. Edward is behind Kate. Earl is behind Tricia. Who is first in line?

   _____

7. Alan says if he reads 11 pages of his book every day for 21 days, he will finish it. How many pages are in his book?

   _____

8. **Choose a Strategy** A spaceship lands in the desert. Creatures exit the spaceship. Some of the creatures have 2 large eyes. Some have 1 very large eye in the middle of their forehead. There are 19 creatures with 29 eyes. How many creatures have 2 eyes? How many creatures have 1 eye?

   | • Use Objects/Act It Out |
   | • Draw a Picture |
   | • Look for a Pattern |
   | • Guess and Check |
   | • Use Logical Reasoning |
   | • Make an Organized List |
   | • Make a Table |
   | • Solve a Simpler Problem |
   | • Work Backward |

   a. What strategy would you use to solve the problem?

   _____

   _____

   b. Answer the problem. _____

Name _____

# Estimating Greater Products

**Science** The speed a planet travels around the Sun is measured in kilometers per second. The table shows the speed and the number of Earth days it takes a planet to revolve around the Sun.

| Planet | Speed around Sun (km/s) | Time to revolve around Sun |
|---|---|---|
| Mercury | 48 | 90 Earth days |
| Venus | 35 | 225 Earth days |
| Earth | 30 | 365 Earth days |
| Mars | 24 | 687 Earth days |

**1.** About how many kilometers will Venus travel in 185 seconds?

_____

**2.** About how many kilometers will Mercury travel in 14 minutes?

_____

**3.** About how many kilometers will Mars travel

in one minute? _____

in one hour? _____

in one Earth day? _____

**4.** About how many times will Mercury revolve around the

Sun in one Earth year? _____

**5.** About how much farther does Mercury travel in 195 seconds than Venus?

_____

**6.** The Jackson family spends $85 per week on food. About how much will they spend on food in one year?

_____

**7.** A school district has 38 school buses. Each bus seats 48 students. There are 2,300 students enrolled. Estimate to find if the district will have to purchase additional buses. Explain.

_____

_____

# Choosing a Calculation Method

**Sports** Suppose you are planning a long-distance biking trip of 1,733 miles. To find out how far you will travel, you make some comparisons with familiar lengths.

| Length | | Number in a Mile |
|---|---|---|
| **Football Field** | 120 yards | 15 |
| **Tennis Court** | 78 feet | 68 |
| **Basketball Court** | 28 meters | 57 |

1. How many football field lengths will you travel?

   _____

2. How many tennis court lengths will you travel?

   _____

3. How many more tennis court lengths than basketball court lengths will you travel? Explain.

   _____

5. The biking club reached Taos, New Mexico on September 12, 1998, after traveling 6 months. About when did they begin their trip?

   _____

6. The desert across North Africa grows about 6 miles per year. How many miles smaller was the desert 25 years ago? 50 years ago?

   _____

7. The temperature in Lyn's town in the winter may be as low as 12° F. In the summer it may reach 95 degrees F. What is the range of temperature?

   _____

8. Lilah worked on a painting 3 hours a day for 2 weeks. How many hours did it take her to complete it?

   _____

# Decision Making

You and a friend go to the local Play-A-Thon. The theater group is putting on 5 plays. You can use the table below to determine how long you must wait to see each show.

You and your friend want to see 2 plays together. You can stay for an hour.

| Play | People in Line | Room Capacity | Length of play (minutes) | Reviewer's Scores |
|------|------|------|------|------|
| *Time Travel* | 37 | 20 | 15 | good |
| *President* | 68 | 30 | 20 | excellent |
| *Campfire* | 63 | 35 | 15 | excellent |
| *Big Laugh* | 49 | 25 | 30 | good |
| *Cowpokes* | 72 | 40 | 10 | fair |

**1.** How long would have to wait in line to see *President* if there is a 10-minute wait before the next show? _____

**2.** Suppose the next run of each play will be starting in 5 minutes. Which plays would you be able to see without waiting any longer than 30 minutes?

_____

**3.** Would you wait in line longer than 30 minutes to see any of the plays? Why?

_____

_____

**4.** Can you see both of the plays that were rated excellent?

_____

_____

**5.** Which plays would you choose to see? Explain.

_____

_____

# Multiplying Money

**History** Life in 1900 was different from the way it is today. There were only 45 states. Women were not yet allowed to vote. Most people traveled by wagon. And prices were much lower. The chart shows the price of some grocery items.

| Item | Price in 1900 | Price Today |
|------|---------------|-------------|
| oranges (1 dozen) | $0.10 | $2.04 |
| sugar (1 lb) | $0.15 | $0.48 |
| turkey (1 lb) | $0.10 | $1.59 |
| beef (1 lb) | $0.10 | $2.49 |
| bread (1 loaf) | $0.05 | $2.49 |

Compare prices for the shopping list below.

|  | **a. Price in 1900** | **b. Price Today** |
|------|------|------|
| **1.** 4 dozen oranges | _____ | _____ |
| **2.** 20 lb of sugar | _____ | _____ |
| **3.** 22 lb of turkey | _____ | _____ |
| **4.** 12 lb of beef | _____ | _____ |
| **5.** 3 loaves of bread | _____ | _____ |

**5.** The chorus needs red T-shirts for its 24 members. They can buy 2 shirts for $7.92. How much will the T-shirts cost in all? _____

**6.** There are 28 students in the Science Club. Each student needs a notebook, which costs $2.59. How much will the notebooks cost in all? _____

**7.** An avocado costs $1.19. How much would a crate of 40 avocados cost? _____

**8.** One pen costs $1.09. A packet of 8 pens cost $7.79. Which is the better buy? Explain

_____

**GPS** | PROBLEM 3, STUDENT PAGE 279

You want to find about how long it will take to earn enough money to buy a skateboard. You earn $3.50 for mowing a lawn. You can mow 12 lawns a month.

**a.** Should you underestimate or overestimate? Why?
**b.** Estimate how much you might earn in a month.

## — Understand —

**1.** How much do you earn for mowing one lawn? _____

**2.** How many lawns can you mow in a month? _____

**3.** What do you need to find out?

_____

## — Plan —

**4.** Consider reasons why you should overestimate or underestimate.

_____

_____

## — Solve —

**5.** Should you overestimate or underestimate? Why?

_____

**6.** Estimate how much you might earn in a month. _____

## — Look Back —

**7.** How can you check your answer? _____

SOLVE ANOTHER PROBLEM

You purchase 5 new stamps each month for your collection. There are 37 stamps you want to add to it. About how many months will it take you to buy all the stamps? Did you overestimate or underestimate?

_____

**GPS** PROBLEM 2, STUDENT PAGE 281

Max lines up his baseball cards with the same number of cards in each row. The card in the middle of the array has 8 cards to its left, 8 to its right, 8 above, and 8 below.

**a.** How many cards are in each row?    **b.** How many are there in all?

## — Understand —

**1.** What do you need to find out?

_____

## — Plan —

**2.** Think of a picture that will help. What will it show?

_____

## — Solve —

**3.** Draw a picture.

**4.** How many cards are above, below, to the left, and to the right of the middle card?

_____

**5.** How many are in each row? _____

**6.** How many are there in all? _____

## — Look Back —

**7.** How can you check your answer?

_____

SOLVE ANOTHER PROBLEM

There are 56 members in a marching band. What are two ways they could line up in rows with the same number of members in each row?

_____

© Scott Foresman Addison Wesley 4

# Exploring Division Patterns

Find each quotient mentally. Then write the basic fact you
used to find the quotient.

**1.** 240 ÷ 3 = _____          Basic Fact: _____

**2.** 80 ÷ 4 = _____          Basic Fact: _____

**3.** 3,200 ÷ 4 = _____          Basic Fact: _____

**4.** 250 ÷ 5 = _____          Basic Fact: _____

**5.** 3,300 ÷ 3 = _____          Basic Fact: _____

**6.** 160 ÷ 4 = _____          Basic Fact: _____

**7.** 1,500 ÷ 3 = _____          Basic Fact: _____

**8.** 6,600 ÷ 11 = _____          Basic Fact: _____

Use basic facts to solve these word problems.

**9.** A natural food store orders 1,800 pounds of whole wheat
flour. It will come in 3 equal deliveries. How big will each
delivery be?

Basic Fact: _____          Answer: _____

**10.** A killer whale can eat 8,000 pounds of food in 4 days.
How many pounds of food is that each day?

Basic Fact: _____          Answer: _____

**11.** A forest has 7,200 trees. If there are 9 types of trees in
the forest, how many trees of each type are there?

Basic Fact: _____          Answer: _____

**12.** Frank has 280 stamps in his collection. If he puts 7
stamps on each page of his collector book, how many
pages will his book need?

Basic Fact: _____          Answer: _____

Name _____

# Estimating Quotients

**Recreation** Sometimes, before people play marbles, they divide the total evenly between them. Estimate how many marbles each player would get if there were:

1. 164 marbles and 3 players. _____ marbles

2. 354 marbles and 4 players _____ marbles

3. 309 marbles and 7 players _____ marbles

4. 276 marbles and 5 players _____ marbles

5. 251 marbles and 8 players _____ marbles

A recipe for Scrumptious Squash Soup calls for 7 pounds of squash. Estimate the answers to the following questions.

6. Mr. Winters has 129 pounds of squash. How many times could he make Scrumptious Squash Soup this winter?

_____

7. Mrs. Summers has 234 pounds of squash. How many times could she make Scrumptious Squash Soup this winter?

_____

8. The Food Market has 465 pounds of squash. How many times could they make Scrumptious Squash Soup this winter?

_____

Jason wants to arrange 172 books on shelves.

9. About how many books will be on each shelf if Jason uses 3 shelves?

_____

10. Jason wants to use 8 shelves. How many books will be on each shelf?

_____

# Exploring Division With Remainders

You bought 13 apples at the fruit market today. What will
you do with them? Your recipe book is full of ideas.

1. The recipe for a dozen apple bran muffins calls for 3 apples. How
   many dozens of muffins could you bake? How many apples would
   you have left over?

   **a.** How many groups of 3 apples are in 13 apples? _____

   **b.** How many apples are left over? _____

2. The recipe for a pint of applesauce calls for 6 apples.

   **a.** How many pints of applesauce could you make? _____

   **b.** How many apples would you have left over? _____

3. The recipe for a pan of apple crisp calls for 8 apples.

   **a.** How many pans of apple crisp could you make? _____

   **b.** How many apples would you have left over? _____

   **c.** Explain how you found the number of pans of apple crisp.

   _____

   _____

4. You want to make 4 batches of apple bread pudding.
   Explain how you would divide the apples equally among
   the 4 batches.

   _____

   _____

   _____

5. Which recipe or recipes would you make? Why?

   _____

   _____

# Exploring Division

There are 52 cards to be distributed equally among players
in a game. Draw pictures of place-value blocks to solve each
problem.

**1. a.** If there are 3 players, how many cards will each player get? _____

   **b.** How many cards will be left over after they are all dealt?    _____

**2. a.** If there are 5 players, how many cards will each player get? _____

   **b.** How many cards will be left over after they are all dealt?    _____

**3. a.** If there are 4 players, how many cards will each player get? _____

   **b.** How many cards will be left over after they are all dealt?    _____

**4.** Explain how you regrouped to solve **3**.

_____

_____

_____

# Dividing 2-Digit Dividends

**1.** An American toad can eat 48 flies in 3 minutes.
How many flies can it eat in 1 minute?                    _____

**2.** There are 50 states in the United States.
   **a.** If you divide them into 4 groups, how many
     states will be in each group?                          _____

   **b.** How many will be left over?                          _____

**3.** A poster with large type can fit about 9 words per line. If
you have a message that is 87 words long, how many
lines will your poster have?

_____

**4.** Keesha's book has 73 pages. If she reads 4 pages a day,
how many days will it take her to finish the book?
Explain.

_____

**5.** Patrick has 47 cans of soup. He can fit 8 cans in one
box. How many boxes will he need? Explain.

_____

**6. Choose a Strategy** A gardener has a garden space that
is 12 feet by 12 feet. He wants to plant flowers and
vegetables. He will use one row of flowers to divide the
garden into 2 equal parts. How many ways can he do
this?

   **a.** What strategy would you use to solve the
     problem?

    _____

   **b.** Answer the problem.

    _____

- Use Objects/Act It Out
- Draw a Picture
- Look for a Pattern
- Guess and Check
- Use Logical Reasoning
- Make an Organized List
- Make a Table
- Solve a Simpler Problem
- Work Backward

# Finding 3-Digit Quotients

**Geography** The Northeast part of the United States is often considered to be one of the most beautiful places to see the leaves change colors. The New England States and New York are easy to visit using different means of transportation.

| | Transportation | Time |
|---|---|---|
| Boston, MA to New York, NY | car airplane | 4 hours 1 hour |
| New York, NY to Burlington, VT | train airplane | 9 hours 2 hours |
| Burlington, VT to Portland, ME | airplane car | 2 hours 4 hours |

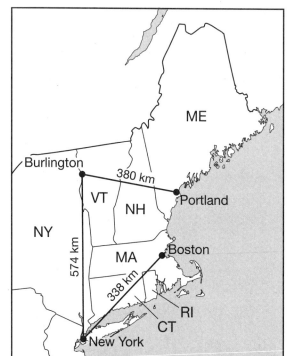

1. How fast would you need to fly to travel from New York to Burlington in 2 hours?

   _____

2. How fast would you need to fly to travel from Boston to New York to Burlington in 3 hours?

   _____

3. How fast would you need to fly to travel from Portland to Burlington in 2 hours? _____

4. A factory packs 8 reams of paper in one carton. How many cartons will they need to pack 976 reams of paper? _____

5. How many reams of paper can be packed in 450 cartons? _____

6. If 450 cartons are packed in 3 hours, how many cartons are packed per hour? _____

7. 8 paper workers work 896 hours in one month. On average, how many hours does each work? _____

## 2- or 3-Digit Quotients

**Geography**  North-south interstate highways have one or
two-digit odd numbers. Many end with the digit 5. I-55
runs 944 miles from Chicago, Illinois to La Place,
Louisiana. I-65 runs 888 miles from Gary, Indiana to
Mobile, Alabama.

1. You want to travel I-55 in 4 days. How
   many miles should you travel each day?    _____

2. You decide to take 8 days to travel I-55.
   How many miles should you travel each day?    _____

3. You want to travel I-65 in 3 days. How
   many miles should you travel each day?    _____

4. Perry had 492 baseball cards. He planned
   to put them in 4 albums. How many cards
   should be put in each album?

   _____

5. Joan rode her bicycle a total distance of
   84 miles this week. She spent 7 hours riding
   her bicycle. What was her average speed?

   _____

6. Li drove a distance of 378 miles. The trip
   took her 9 hours. What was her average speed?

   _____

7. Alex had 889 marbles which he packaged into
   7 bags. How many marbles were in each bag?

   _____

8. In a factory, 740 boxes are stacked 4 boxes high.
   How many stacks are there?

   _____

# Zeros in the Quotient

Write the answer to each question on the line.

**1.** Five medium-sized strawberries have about 1,000 seeds. About how many seeds does each strawberry contain?

_____

**2.** Three small jars of homemade jam cost $3.27. How much does one jar cost?

_____

**3.** Kevin picked 3 large baskets of strawberries. He picked 315 strawberries in all. How many strawberries were in each basket?

_____

**4.** Aisha picked 7 strawberries from each plant in one row. In all, she picked 763 berries. How many plants are in the row?

_____

**5.** Mary-Beth has 215 cranberries. She wants to make 2 loaves of cranberry bread with the same number of cranberries in each loaf.

**a.** How many cranberries will be in each loaf?

_____

**b.** How many will be left over? _____

**6. Choose a strategy** Miguel planted 4 different kinds of plants in his vegetable garden. The garden contains a total of 72 plants. Of the plants, 15 are tomato and 12 are squash. The remaining plants are either lettuce or cucumbers. The number of lettuce plants is twice the number of cucumber plants. How many lettuce plants are in Miguel's garden?

| |
|---|
| • Use Objects/Act It Out |
| • Draw a Picture |
| • Look for a Pattern |
| • Guess and Check |
| • Use Logical Reasoning |
| • Make an Organized List |
| • Make a Table |
| • Solve a Simpler Problem |
| • Work Backward |

**a.** What strategy would you use to solve the problem?

_____

**b.** Answer the problem. _____

© Scott Foresman Addison Wesley 4

Name _____

**GPS** **PROBLEM 6, STUDENT PAGE 317**

A gumbo recipe that serves 30 people calls for 45 ounces of canned tomatoes, 12 celery stalks, 3 green peppers, and 6 cups of okra, among other ingredients. Suppose you want to make enough for only 10 people.
 **a.** How much of each ingredient will you need?
 **b.** What strategy did you use to solve the problem?

## — Understand —

1. How many people does the original recipe serve? _____

2. How many people do you need to serve? _____

## — Plan —

3. Are you going to use less or more of each ingredient? _____

4. What part of the original ingredients will you need to serve 10 people? _____

## — Solve —

5. Divide each ingredient by 3. _____

_____

6. What strategy did you use to solve the problem?

_____

## — Look Back —

7. How can you check your answer? _____

_____

**SOLVE ANOTHER PROBLEM**

Rosa's fruit salad recipe serves 16 people. It calls for 8 pounds of grapes, 40 ounces of peaches, 4 pounds of melon, 12 oranges, and 32 strawberries. Suppose you wanted to make fruit salad for only 8 people. How much of each ingredient would you need?

_____

_____

Name _____

# Exploring Division with Money

Evan and three friends are sharing the cost of a pizza. The cost of the pizza is $6.80. To share the cost equally, how much should each person pay?

1. In the space below, draw a picture to show dollar bills and dimes totaling $6.80.

2. Divide the dollar bills into 4 equal groups. How many bills are in each group? _____

3. How many dollar bills are left over? _____

4. In the space below, draw dimes to represent the left over dollars. Include the original dimes in your drawing.

5. Divide the dimes into 4 equal groups. How many dimes are in each group? _____

6. How many dimes are left over? _____

7. In the space below, draw a picture to show how much each person should pay.

8. How much should each person pay? _____

9. Suppose the pizza cost $8.28. Explain how you can divide the cost by 4 people.

_____

_____

_____

# Dividing Money Amounts

**Careers** Tricia is a clerk at a costume jewelry store. She sells jewelry.

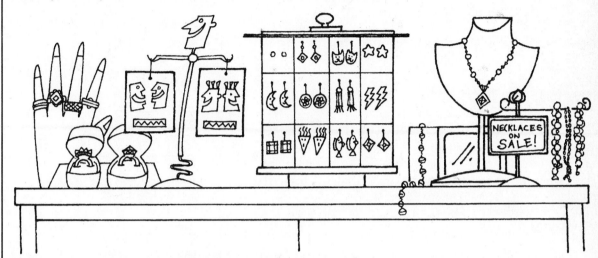

1. Tricia sells 4 rings. Each of the rings cost the same amount. The total cost is $21.00. How much does each ring cost? _____

2. Tricia sells 5 pairs of earrings. Each pair costs the same amount. If the total cost is $17.35, how much does each pair of earrings cost? _____

3. Tricia sells 3 necklaces for a total cost of $8.61. If each necklace costs the same amount, how much does each necklace cost? _____

4. John buys 6 blueberry muffins for $5.16. How much does each muffin cost? _____

5. José bought 8 bananas for $3.44. How much does each banana cost? _____

6. The school band collected $896 from ticket sales to the Spring Concert. If tickets cost $7 each, how many people bought tickets to the concert? _____

Name _____

# Exploring Mean

Find the typical length of four classmates' feet.

Measure the length of four of your classmates' feet and cut a strip of paper the length of each foot.

Tape the four strips together to form one long strip.

Now fold the long strip in half twice.

Open the long strip. Cut along the folds to get four equal lengths.

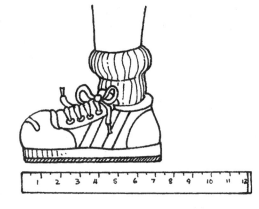

**1.** How long is one of these typical lengths of your classmates' feet?

_____

**2.** Using paper strips, how could you find the typical length of eight of your classmates' feet?

_____

_____

_____

**3.** What steps would you take to find the mean of 5, 8, 9, and 6? Explain.

_____

**4.** The mean of this set of numbers—4, 5, 6, 3, 2—is 4. What two numbers can you add to the set of numbers so the mean will still be 4?

_____

_____

**5.** The average of 4 numbers is 30. Three of the numbers are: 20, 25, and 40. Find the fourth number. _____

**6.** The average of 5 numbers is 15. If three of the numbers are 16, 17, and 18, what do you know about the other two numbers?

_____

© Scott Foresman Addison Wesley 4

# Exploring Divisibility

**1.** What is an **even** number? What is an **odd** number?

    **a.** Even: _____

    **b.** Odd: _____

**2.** When is a number **divisible** by another number?

_____

**3.** Is 130 divisible by 2, 5, or 10? Write Yes or No. What rule can you use to figure out if a number is divisible by 2, 5, or 10?

    **a.** by 2? _____ Rule: _____

    **b.** by 5? _____ Rule: _____

    _____

    **c.** by 10? _____ Rule: _____

    _____

**4.** Is 216 divisible by 3, 6, or 9? Write Yes or No. What rule can you use to figure out if a number is divisible by 3, 6, or 9?

    **a.** by 3? _____ Rule: _____

    _____

    **b.** by 6? _____ Rule: _____

    _____

    **c.** by 9? _____ Rule: _____

    _____

**5.** Write a number that is divisible by 3, 6 and 9.

_____

**7.** Without dividing, can you tell if you can share $5.19 equally among 3 people? Explain. _____

_____

Name _____

| **GPS** | PROBLEM 4, STUDENT PAGE 333 |

Wendy mixed 24 ounces of tomato sauce with some olive oil. She spread 3 ounces of the mixture on each of 6 pizzas. How much of the mixture did she have left over?

## ━ Understand ━

**1.** How much sauce with oil does she have? _____

**2.** What do you know?

_____

**3.** What are you asked to find?

_____

## ━ Plan ━

**4.** What do you need to do first?

_____

## ━ Solve ━

**5.** What is the amount of mixture used on each pizza? _____

**6.** How much mixture was used on all 6 pizzas? _____

**7.** How much mixture is left?

## ━ Look Back ━

**8.** How could you check your answer?



| SOLVE ANOTHER PROBLEM |

Fernando made a fruit punch. He divided the punch into three 8-ounce glasses and had 5 ounces left over. How much punch did he start with?

_____

## Exploring Solids

Complete the table.

| | Solid | Number of Flat Faces | Number of Edges | Number of Vertices |
|---|---|---|---|---|
| **1.** | sphere | 0 | | 0 |
| **2.** | cube | | | 8 |
| **3.** | square pyramid | 5 | | |

Most objects that we see around us are made up of combinations of these solids and cones and cylinders. The figure below is made up of several solids that have been joined together. Write the name of the solid used for each part of the figure.

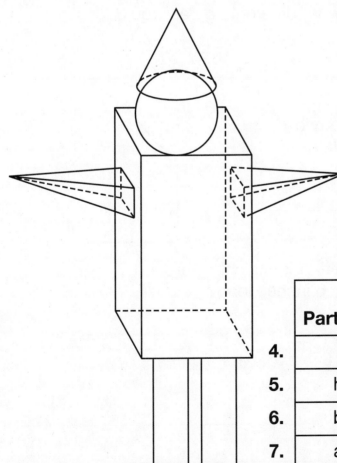

| | Part of Figure | Name of Solid |
|---|---|---|
| **4.** | hat | |
| **5.** | head | |
| **6.** | body | |
| **7.** | arms | |
| **8.** | legs | |

Name _____

# Exploring Polygons

1. On the right is a picture of a soccer ball. Although the object is a sphere, it has several polygon shapes on its surface. Use a colored pencil or highlighter to outline different polygons. Name the polygons that you find.

_____

2. How are all the black shapes on the soccer ball similar?

_____

3. How are all the black shapes on the soccer ball different from the white shapes?

_____

_____

4. If you cut a pentagon in half, what different figures would you make?

_____

5. Draw a line across the pentagon to show how one cut could make two completely different shapes. Name the shapes.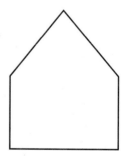

_____

6. What is the name of the figure that is 36 inches around and that has equal sides, each 6 inches long?

_____

7. If you were to cut the figure in **6** in two, what figures could you make?

_____

_____

## Exploring Triangles

Look at the polygons below. What is the smallest number of triangles it will take to cover each figure? Draw the triangles. Use a ruler if you want. The first one is started for you. Then label each triangle I for isosceles, E for equilateral, or S for scalene.

**1.**

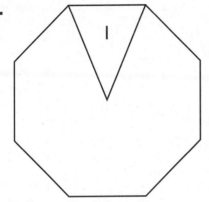

number of triangles: _____
names of triangles:

_____

**2.**

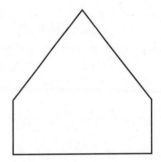

number of triangles: _____
names of triangles:

_____

**3.** Use 3 straight lines to divide the triangle on the right into equal sized smaller triangles.

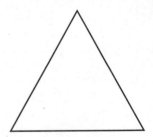

**a.** How many triangles are there? _____

**b.** What kind of triangles are they? _____

**4.** Name the kind of triangle shown on each flag.

**a.**

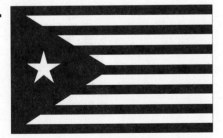

_____

**b.**

_____

# Triangles and Angles

**Fine Arts** Cubism is a type of
painting or drawing where
geometrical shapes and patterns
are used. Pablo Picasso was a
famous cubist painter. To the
right is a rough sample of a
cubist drawing.

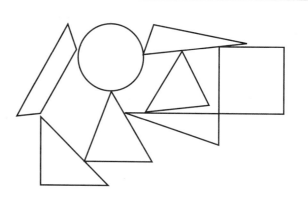

**1.** How many right triangles are in the drawing above? _____

**2.** How many acute triangles are in the drawing? _____

**3.** How many obtuse triangles are there? _____

Name the shaded angle between each clock's hands as
right, acute, or obtuse.

**4.**

**5.**

**6.**

_____        _____        _____

**7.** Make a drawing using right triangles,
obtuse triangles and acute triangles.

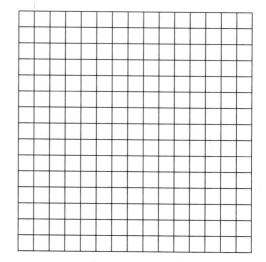

## Exploring Congruent Figures and Motions

Study the figures. Then decide what happens when they are
flipped, turned, or slid.

# I S H O X P B A

**1.** What do you see if you flip the capital letter I?

_____

**2.** Will the capital letter B appear the same if it is flipped?  _____

**3.** Name 3 other capital letters that you can flip and the
letter appears the same.

_____

**4.** What motions could these two figures show?

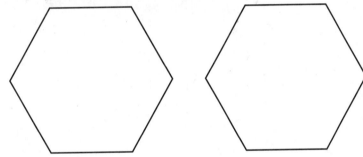

_____

**5.** Draw 3 polygons that you can flip, slide, and turn and the shape
appears the same.

# Exploring Similar Figures

Answer each question by finding the correct shapes in a box below. Write the letter or punctuation from each box in the blank above the question number.

    1      2      3      4      5      6

**1.** These two congruent shapes have 4 right angles each.

**2.** These two congruent shapes are right triangles.

**3.** These two similar shapes are octagons.

**4.** These two shapes are right triangles, but they are not similar or congruent.

**5.** These two shapes are octagons, but they are not similar or congruent.

**6.** These two shapes have 4 right angles, but they are not congruent.

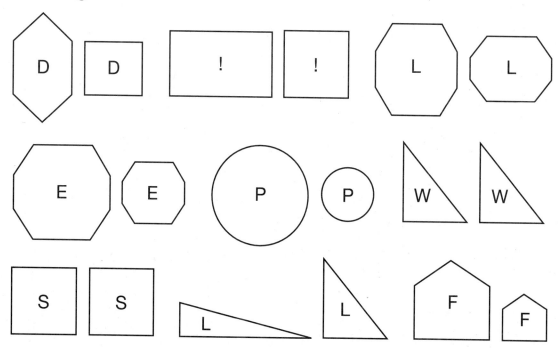

**7.** Ellen says that all pentagons are similar because they all have 5 sides. Is she right? Explain.

_____

_____

Name _____

# Lines and Line Segments

**Geography** A street map helps people find their way around a town or city. It provides a bird's-eye view so that the relationships of the street and the patterns they make become easier to remember. Use the street map below to answer the questions.

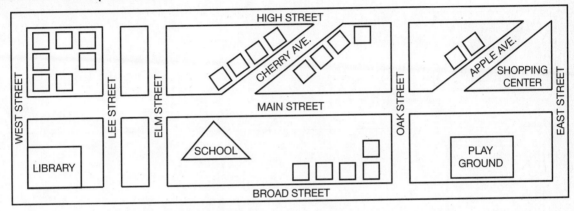

**1.** Which streets are parallel to Oak Street?

_____

**2.** Which street is parallel to Apple Avenue? _____

**3.** Elm Street is perpendicular to which streets? _____

**4.** Which building marks the point where Broad Street and West Street intersect?

_____

Write if the electrical wires for each pair of poles appear to be parallel or perpendicular.

**5.**

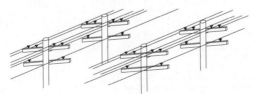

**6.**

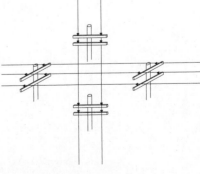

_____

Name _____

# Quadrilaterals

**Fine Arts** Quadrilaterals have often been used by artists who design signs that rely on a simple symbol, rather than on words, to communicate. (These signs are called "icons.") Below are some icons. Write which quadrilateral is used. Then explain where you might find each sign.

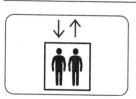

**1.** _____

**2.** _____

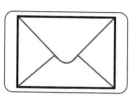

**3.** _____

Identify each quadrilateral.

**4.**  _____

**5.**  _____
_____

## Exploring Line Symmetry

Some of the figures below have 1 or more lines of symmetry.
Others have none. Explain why each is or is not symmetrical.

1.  _____

_____

2.  _____

_____

3.  _____

_____

_____

_____

4.  _____

_____

_____

5.  _____

_____

_____

6. 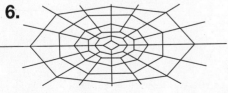 _____

Name _____

**GPS** | PROBLEM 3, STUDENT PAGE 365

Mark's birthday is before Alex's but after Beth's. Ellen's birthday is before Beth's but after Orlando's. Whose birthday is first?

## — Understand —

1. What do you need to find out? _____

## — Plan —

2. Choose five other objects to stand for the five people. What object will represent each person?

_____

## — Solve —

3. Look at the first clue. What is the order of Mark's, Alex's, and Beth's birthdays?   _____

4. Look at the second clue. Where should you put Ellen?

_____

5. What is the correct order? _____

_____

6. Whose birthday is first? _____

## — Look Back —

7. How can you check your answer?

_____

---

**SOLVE ANOTHER PROBLEM**

Tom finished the race before James but after Sue. Mary finished after James but before Henry finished. Who finished first?

_____

# Exploring Perimeter

**1.** One side of a square measures 3 cm. How can you use this information to find the perimeter of the square?

_____

**2.** Write a rule to find the perimeter of a square, using addition.

_____

**3.** What rule can you write for finding the perimeter of a square using multiplication?

_____

**4.** Each side of a square A is 2 units. What is the perimeter?

_____

**5.** Multiply each side of the square by 2 to get the measurements for square B.

   **a.** Draw and label square B.

   **b.** What is the perimeter of square B? _____

**6.** Multiply each side of square B by 2 to get the measurements for square C.

   **a.** Draw and label square C.

   **b.** What is the perimeter of square C? _____

**7.** Does the perimeter double each time you double

   the sides of the square? _____

**8.** How can you use the perimeter of square C to find the perimeter of a square with a side that measures 16 inches?

_____

# Exploring Areas of Rectangles

**1.** A rectangle has an area of 36 square inches. Write the dimensions of at least 3 different rectangles with this area.

_____

_____

**2.** A rectangle has an area of exactly 100 square meters. What are all the possible dimensions for this rectangle?

_____

**3.** A rectangle has an area of 48 square feet. Its width is 4 feet. How long is it?

_____

**4.** Find a rectangle whose area is greater than its perimeter. What are its dimensions?

_____

**5.** Find a rectangle whose perimeter is larger than its area. What are its dimensions?

_____

**6.** A rectangle has a length of 6 cm. What is its width if its perimeter and area are the same number?

_____

**7.** A square has an area of 36 square inches. What is the perimeter?

_____

Name _____

# Exploring Volume

**1.** List the dimensions of 3 solids that have a volume of 24 cubic cm.

_____

_____

**2.** A rectangular prism has a volume of 36 cubic inches. Its length is 2 inches, its depth 9 inches. How wide is it? Explain how you found your answer.

_____

_____

**3.** What is the volume of this cube? Explain how you know.

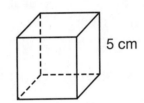

5 cm

_____

_____

**4.** Explain how you can divide this solid into two prisms to find the total volume. Then find the total volume of the solid.

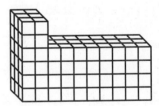

_____

_____

_____

**5.** This solid is made up of 2 prisms. Find the volume of the solid.

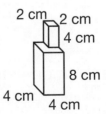

2 cm  2 cm
4 cm
8 cm
4 cm  4 cm

_____

# Decision Making

Your gardening club is planning to build compost bins. You have 10 metal posts and a 35 ft roll of fencing that is 3 feet tall. Group A in the club wants to build three separate bins each 3 ft by 3 ft by 3 ft. Group B wants to build one 9-foot long structure, divided into 3 sections.

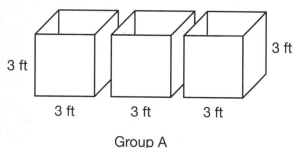

3 ft        3 ft
3 ft        3 ft        3 ft

Group A

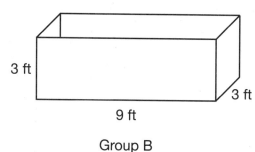

3 ft                    3 ft
9 ft

Group B

1. The fencing is used for the sides of the bins—not the tops and bottoms. How can you find the amount of fencing Group A will need? _____

2. **a.** How much fencing will Group A need for each bin? _____

   **b.** For all 3 bins? _____

3. **a.** What is the perimeter of Group B's design? _____

   **b.** They will need two 3-ft dividers. How much fencing will this use? _____

   **c.** How much total fencing will Group B need? _____

4. A post needs to hold the bins together at every corner.

   **a.** How many posts will Group A need to build 3 separate bins? _____

   **b.** How many posts will Group B need? _____

5. Do both designs hold the same amount of compost? Explain.

   _____

   _____

6. Which design do you think is the best choice? Explain your reasons.

   _____

   _____

# Exploring Fractions

1.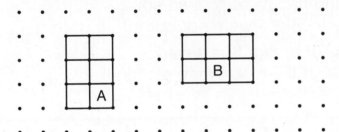

   **a.** Is the rectangle above divided into 4 equal parts? _____

   **b.** If you shade one of the parts, what
   fraction of the whole will be shaded? _____

2. These two dot-paper rectangles are the same size.

   **a.** What fraction of the first rectangle does A show? _____

   **b.** What fraction of the second rectangle does B show? _____

   **c.** How can you decide if A is the same size as B?

   _____

   _____

3. How can you tell whether parts of a whole are equal? Explain.

   _____

   _____

4. Can equal parts be the same shape but not the same size? Explain.

   _____

   _____

# Naming and Writing Fractions

> **Careers** Ms. Sparks is a baker. She owns her own bakery where she bakes all kinds of breads and pastries.
>
> 1. Ms. Sparks baked a vanilla sheet cake and cut it into 8 pieces. She sold 5 pieces of the cake in one day. What fraction of the cake was not sold?
>
> _____
>
> 2. Ms. Sparks made 10 raisin bagels at the beginning of the day. When she closed the bakery that day, there was 1 raisin bagel left. What fraction of the raisin bagels did she sell?
>
> _____
>
> 3. Ms. Sparks baked 12 oatmeal cookies. However, 5 of the cookies were burnt and had to be thrown out. What fraction of the oatmeal cookies were not burnt?
>
> _____
>
> 4. Ms. Sparks baked 16 loaves of bread. She saved 3 loaves for her family and sold the rest. What fraction of the loaves did she sell?
>
> _____

5. Together, Monday, Tuesday, and Wednesday form what fraction of the days in a week?

_____

6. Mona gave a bouquet of flowers to her Mother. There were 2 roses, 5 carnations, and 4 daisies in the bouquet. What fraction of the flowers in the bouquet were roses?

_____

7. Tony did yard work for 3 hours on Saturday afternoon. He spent 1 hour raking leaves and 2 hours trimming shrubs. What fraction of time he worked did he spend raking leaves?

_____

8. John has softball practice on Tuesday, Wednesday, Friday and Saturday. What fraction of the week does John have softball practice?

_____

## Estimating Fractional Amounts

**Technology** Computers have different amounts of
storage space for various things. This storage space is
called "memory" and is measured in "megabyte" or "meg"
units. The computer in Andy's classroom has 80 megs of
memory space. About 10 megs of memory space is taken
up by a word-processing program. System software, which
helps the computer run, takes up about 20 megs of
memory space. There is about 10 megs of unused memory
space in the computer.

| System Software 20 Megs |
| Word Processor 10 Megs |
| Other Software and Files |
| Unused 10 Megs |

1. About what fraction of the computer's memory space is
   taken up by the word-processing program?                _____

2. About what fraction of the computer's memory space is
   taken up by the system software?                        _____

3. About what fraction of the computer's memory space is
   unused?                                                  _____

Use the circle graph for **4–6.**

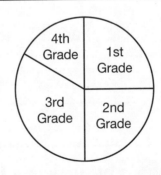

4. About what fraction of County Elementary School
   students are 2nd graders?                               _____

5. About what fraction of the students are 4th graders?    _____

6. The 1st, 2nd, and 3rd grades make up about what fraction
   of the total number of students?                        _____

# Exploring Mixed Numbers

1.

| 1 | $\frac{1}{3}$ |
|---|---|

| $\frac{1}{3}$ | $\frac{1}{3}$ | $\frac{1}{3}$ | $\frac{1}{3}$ |
|---|---|---|---|

  **a.** What mixed number is shown by the first group
  of fraction strips? _____

  **b.** What improper fraction is shown by the second
  group of fraction strips? _____

  **c.** Do the two groups of fraction strips show the
  same amount? Explain.

  _____

2. Is the fraction greater than 1? If yes, write the fraction as
   a mixed or whole number.

  **a.** $\frac{11}{10}$ _____

  **b.** $\frac{9}{10}$ _____

  **c.** $\frac{6}{3}$ _____

  **d.** $\frac{8}{5}$ _____

3. Describe how you would change $\frac{17}{4}$ to a mixed number.

  _____

4. Describe how you would change $3\frac{1}{2}$ to an improper fraction using
   fraction strips.

  _____

  _____

5. There are $\frac{13}{6}$ teaspoons of sugar in a 16-ounce serving of
   Sunshine Morning juice. There are 2 teaspoons of sugar
   in a 16-ounce serving of CJ juice. Which juice has more
   sugar per serving? Explain.

  _____

Name _____

## Decision Making

Take some lessons! The Aquatic Center offers several choices.

| Lessons | Days | Times | Prices |
|---------|------|-------|--------|
| Swimming | M–F | 1:00, 2:00, 3:00, 4:00, 5:00 | $25 per week |
| | Saturday | 10:00, 11:00, 12:00 | $7 per lesson |
| Diving | M–F | 4:00 | $50 per week |
| | Saturday | 12:00 | $12.50 per lesson |
| Water Aerobics | M–F | 3:00, 6:00 | $3 per session |
| | Saturday | 9:00, 2:00, 3:00 | $3.50 per session |

All activities are for one hour. The per week prices are for 5 lessons.

1. Which activities fit in with your schedule?

   _____

2. What is the difference in cost between a swimming lesson on a Thursday and on a Saturday? _____

3. What is the difference in cost between a diving lesson on a Monday and on a Saturday? _____

4. Write a fraction to show the cost of one swimming lesson during a week of lessons. _____

5. What fraction of the total number of water aerobics M–F lessons are the classes at 3:00? _____

6. If you had a 2-week vacation from school and $100 to spend on lessons, what could you take?

   _____

   _____

7. Describe how you made your decision.

   _____

   _____

# Exploring Equivalent Fractions

**1. a.** Write three fractions that name the same amount as 2.

_____

   **b.** What pattern do you see in the denominators and numerators of the fractions?

_____

**2. a.** List three fractions that name the same amount as $\frac{1}{4}$.

_____

   **b.** What pattern do you see in the denominators and numerators of the fractions that you have listed?

_____

**3.** How many $\frac{1}{5}$ fraction strips would you need to make a length that is $\frac{4}{5}$?

_____

**4.** How many $\frac{1}{3}$ fraction strips would you need to show $\frac{6}{9}$? _____

**5.** Suppose you were working with $\frac{1}{8}$ fraction strips and with $\frac{1}{4}$ fraction strips. Describe two ways you could show the fraction $\frac{3}{4}$.

_____

_____

**6.** Suppose you were working with $\frac{1}{10}$ strips and with $\frac{1}{5}$ strips. Describe two ways that you could show the fraction $\frac{3}{5}$.

_____

_____

# Naming and Writing Equivalent Fractions

**Careers** Often, when chefs are preparing a meal to feed hundreds of people, they have to work with fractions to know how much to make.

1. If 200 people are dining, and 40 salads are prepared, what fraction of the 200 guests can have a salad?

   **a.** $\frac{40}{200} = \frac{1}{\boxed{\phantom{0}}}$

   **b.** 1 out of every _____ guests can have a salad.

2. The head chef might decide that more of the guests will want a salad. She thinks that 3 out of every 5 guests will request a salad. How many salads need to be prepared?

   **a.** What fraction is equivalent to $\frac{3}{5}$ and has a denominator of 200?

   $\frac{3}{5} = \frac{\boxed{\phantom{0}}}{200}$

   **b.** _____ salads need to be prepared.

3. Tamsey's dad bakes 4 dozen muffins. 1 dozen of the muffins are blueberry muffins. Write a fraction that shows the number of muffins in the batch which are blueberry.

   _____

4. The combined kindergarten classes at Westbridge Elementary School have 60 students. Of the 60, 35 are girls. Write 2 fractions that show the portion of the class that are girls.

   _____

5. In America, 52 out of every 100 homes are heated by natural gas. Write 2 fractions that show this relationship.

   _____

6. Out of every 100 homes, 22 are heated by electricity. Write 2 fractions that show this relationship.

   _____

Name _____

# Simplest Form Fractions

**Social Studies** The map below shows the 10 states in which seat belts are used the most.

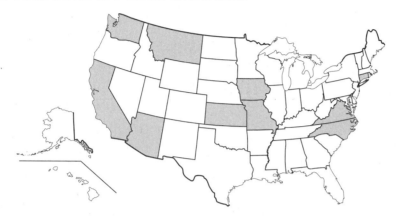

1. Washington and Arizona tie for the best record. Out of every 100 people, 73 use a seat belt. Write a fraction in simplest form to show the number of people who wear seat belts.

   _____

2. Of the mid-Atlantic states, Virginia has the best record. Out of every 100 people, only 28 do not use a seat belt. Write a fraction in simplest form to show the number of people who wear seat belts.

   _____

3. Some people have particular days of the week on which they prefer to shop. The most popular day is Saturday, but 6 out of every 50 people like Wednesdays best. Write a fraction in simplest form to show the number of people who shop on Wednesdays.

   _____

4. a. In a heart-shaped box of chocolates containing 30 pieces, 5 pieces are labeled as jellies. Write a fraction in simplest form to show the portion of chocolates that are not jellies.

   _____

   b. In the same box, 10 pieces are labelled as cream-filled. Write a fraction in simplest form to show the portion of the chococlates that are not jellies or cream-filled.

   _____

   c. Of the cream-filled chocolates, 8 were eaten. Write a fraction in simplest form to show the portion of the cream-filled chocolates that remain.

   _____

# Comparing and Ordering Fractions

**Social Studies**

**Children in U.S. Families**
(Percentage of families with children
under age 18 or no children)

3 children — ⌐ 4 or more children

2 children

No children

1 child

Number of Persons under
age 18 in U.S. Households

None: $\frac{51}{100}$

One: $\frac{1}{5}$

Two: $\frac{19}{100}$

Three: $\frac{7}{100}$

Four or More: $\frac{3}{100}$

1. Which are there more of, one-child
   households or two-children households? _____

2. How many one-child households are
   there in every 100 households? _____

3. Suppose that you answered 18 out of 22
   questions correctly on a Science test. On
   an English test, you answered 12 out of
   16 questions correctly. Your score for each
   test was written as a fraction of the number
   of questions you answered correctly. On
   which test did you score higher? _____

4. On March 28, $\frac{2}{7}$ of the students in the fourth
   grade were absent. On March 29, $\frac{1}{8}$ of the
   students were absent. Which day showed
   a higher absentee rate? _____

5. At lunchtime, $\frac{1}{3}$ of the students ordered
   pizza and $\frac{1}{6}$ ordered hamburgers. Which
   menu item was more popular? _____

# Exploring a Fraction of a Set

Solve.

1. A group of 8 people spent a total of 64 hours planning, shopping, and decorating for a dance. Each person put in the same amount of time.

   **a.** What fractional part of the time did 3 people work? _____

   **b.** How many hours was that? _____

2. Miriam used 12 of the 48 exercise machines at the gym. Her friend Sam used $\frac{1}{6}$ of the machines at the gym.

   **a.** What fractional part of the machines did Miriam use? _____

   **b.** Who used more machines? Explain.

   _____

3. Gabriella and Maxine ran for president of their class. Gabriella received $\frac{7}{10}$ of the vote. Maxine received the rest of the votes. If there are 30 students in the class, how many votes did each person receive? Explain your reasoning.

   _____

   _____

4. Aron has been into $\frac{2}{9}$ of the stores in the mall. There are 81 stores in the mall. How many stores has Aron not visited? Explain your reasoning.

   _____

5. Ryan said hello to $\frac{1}{5}$ of the people at the party. He said hello to 10 people. How many people were at the party? Explain your reasoning.

   _____

# Exploring Units of Length

Replace the false measurements below with more reasonable units of length. Replace with inches, feet, or yards. Follow the example.

Example: The table is 36 yards long. __36 inches__

1. The dictionary is about 4 yards thick. _____

2. The doorway is about 1 inch wide. _____

3. A child is 2 inches tall. _____

4. The soccer field is about 120 inches long. _____

5. The butterfly has a wingspan of 3 feet. _____

6. The kitchen is about 15 yards wide. _____

7. The flagpole is 18 inches tall. _____

8. A compact disc is about 5 yards wide. _____

9. The hamster is 4 feet long. _____

10. The length of the car is 10 yards. _____

11. The tallest giraffe ever recorded was almost 20 ft tall. Is this more or less than 250 in.? How much more or less? _____

12. The largest animal on the earth is the blue whale. The longest ever recorded was about 110 ft long. Is this more or less than 36 yd? How much more or less? _____

13. Would you choose inch, foot, or yard to measure these?

    a. length of a football field? _____

    b. length of a skateboard? _____

    c. width of this page? _____

    d. average cat? _____

# Measuring Fractional Parts of an Inch

**Careers** A mechanic must use the correct size wrench to loosen and tighten bolts. Use a ruler to measure the diameter of these bolts. Then match the bolt to the wrench that would be used to loosen or tighten it. (Hint: you'll have to measure the distance between the two open sides of the wrench.)

1. _____

2. _____

3. _____

4. _____

A.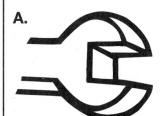

B.

C.

D.

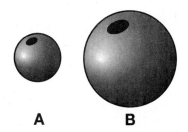

A          B

**5.** Which bead is closer to $\frac{3}{8}$ inch in diameter? _____

A          B

**6.** Which square is closer to one inch on each side? _____

# Exploring Feet, Yards, and Miles

The high school cross country team is participating in a
track meet. The map shows the seven sections of the
course, each measured in yards.

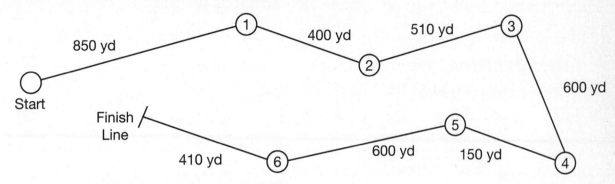

**1.** What is the total length of the course in yards? _____

**2.** How long is the course in miles? _____

in feet? _____

**3.** What course marker is 1 mile from the starting line? _____

**4.** If it takes about 1 minute to run 300 yds., how
long will it take to reach marker number 3? _____

**5.** How long will it take to run the entire course? _____

**6.** How would you describe how long a foot is without using numbers?

_____

**7.** If a room is 10 feet long, about how many of your steps would it take
to walk from one end to the other?

_____

_____

**GPS** PROBLEM 4, STUDENT PAGE 421

A group of 50 climbers took part in this year's mountain cleanup. For 29 climbers this was their second year helping. 10 had never helped before. How many of the 50 climbers had helped before last year?

## ── Understand ──

1. What do you know?

_____

_____

2. What do you need to find out? _____

_____

## ── Plan ──

3. Describe how you can solve the problem. _____

4. Of the 50 climbers, how many helped last year? _____

5. How many climbers had participated in a cleanup before? Write the number sentence. _____

## ── Solve ──

6. How many of the 50 climbers had helped before last year? Write the number sentence. _____

## ── Look Back ──

7. How can you check your answer?

_____

SOLVE ANOTHER PROBLEM

A crew of 28 people picked up trash in a local park. 18 people picked up trash along the hiking trails. 15 people picked up trash in the picnic areas. How many people helped in both areas?

_____

## Exploring Adding Fractions with Like Denominators

1. How many $\frac{1}{12}$ fraction strips does it take to make $\frac{12}{12}$?  _____

2. How many $\frac{1}{7}$ fraction strips would you need to show the sum of $\frac{2}{7}$ and $\frac{3}{7}$?  _____

3. Write 4 addition problems that have 2 fractions with a sum of $\frac{8}{9}$.

   _____        _____

   _____        _____

4. What fraction strips would you use to find the sum of $\frac{3}{8}$ and $\frac{4}{8}$? Explain.

   _____

Use fraction strips or draw pictures to solve each problem.

5. Bob ate $\frac{1}{4}$ of his sandwich at 10:15. He ate $\frac{1}{4}$ more at 11:30. How much of his sandwich did Bob eat?  _____

6. Laverne walked $\frac{1}{8}$ of a mile. Then she ran $\frac{3}{8}$ of a mile before stopping to catch her breath. How far did Laverne go before stopping?  _____

7. Kim did $\frac{1}{3}$ of her homework after school. She did $\frac{2}{3}$ of it after dinner. How much of her homework did Kim complete?  _____

8. James spent $\frac{1}{5}$ of his lunch money on a drink and $\frac{3}{5}$ of it on a sandwich. What fractional part of his lunch money did James spend on these 2 things?  _____

9. Shelley read $\frac{1}{6}$ of her magazine before lunch and $\frac{3}{6}$ after lunch. How much of her magazine did she read?  _____

# Exploring Adding Fractions with Unlike Denominators

**1.** $\frac{1}{3} + \frac{1}{6}$

    **a.** Which fraction would you rename to solve the problem? _____

    **b.** Rename the fraction. _____

    **c.** Use the renamed fraction to solve the problem. _____

    **d.** Simplify the sum, if possible. _____

**2.** $\frac{1}{2} + \frac{1}{4}$

    **a.** Which fraction would you rename to solve the problem? _____

    **b.** Rename the fraction. _____

    **c.** Use the renamed fraction to solve the problem. _____

    **d.** Simplify the sum, if possible. _____

**3.** $\frac{1}{3} + \frac{1}{4}$

    **a.** Explain why you cannot rename just one fraction to solve this problem.

    _____

    _____

    **b.** Rename both fractions as 12ths. _____

    **c.** Find the sum and simplify. _____

**4.** $\frac{1}{3} + \frac{1}{2}$

    **a.** What denominator could you use to rename these as equivalent fractions? _____

    **b.** Rename the fractions. _____

    **c.** Find the sum and simplify. _____

Name _____

# Adding Fractions

**Geography** New York City is made up of five boroughs (or parts). Some boroughs are large in size and some are small.

This table shows about how much of New York City's 319 square miles is contributed by each of its boroughs.

| Manhattan | $\frac{1}{15}$ |
| The Bronx | $\frac{1}{8}$ |
| Queens | $\frac{1}{3}$ |
| Brooklyn | $\frac{1}{4}$ |
| Staten Island | $\frac{1}{6}$ |

1. What fraction of New York City is Manhattan and Queens? _____

2. What fraction of New York City is Brooklyn and the Bronx? _____

3. What fraction of New York City is Staten Island and Queens? _____

4. What should the sum of all 5 fractions be? _____

Here are the ingredients for a batch of Zack's All-Natural Granola bars:

$\frac{1}{2}$ cup raisins          $\frac{2}{3}$ cup chocolate chips

$\frac{3}{4}$ cup of oats          $\frac{1}{4}$ cup coconut

$\frac{1}{3}$ cup peanuts          $\frac{1}{8}$ cup maple syrup

5. How many cups of peanuts and chocolate chips are used? _____

6. How many cups of oats and maple syrup are used? _____

7. You asked your classmates to name their favorite writer. $\frac{2}{3}$ of the class chose Jack Prelutsky. $\frac{1}{6}$ of the class chose Shel Silverstein. The rest chose other writers. What fraction of your class chose either Prelutsky or Silverstein? _____

# Decision Making

Your class wants to paint a mural on the wall of the school gymnasium. The wall is large, about 800 square feet. One gallon of paint will cover about 100 square feet.

After getting permission from the school board, the class collected paint from people in the neighborhood on two different days last week. Here is what they got:

| Color | Amount Collected on Monday | Amount Collected on Friday |
|-------|----------------------------|----------------------------|
| White | 1 gallon | 1 gallon |
| Black | $\frac{1}{2}$ gallon | $\frac{1}{2}$ gallon |
| Blue | $\frac{1}{6}$ gallon | $\frac{1}{3}$ gallon |
| Red | $\frac{1}{4}$ gallon | $\frac{1}{2}$ gallon |
| Green | $\frac{1}{8}$ gallon | $\frac{1}{8}$ gallon |
| Purple | 3 gallons | 1 gallon |
| Brown | $\frac{1}{3}$ gallon | $\frac{1}{6}$ gallon |

**1.** How much paint of each color was collected?

_____

_____

_____

**2.** Do you have enough paint after 2 collection days to start your mural? Explain.

_____

**3.** Some students want the mural to show people playing basketball. Another group of students wants to paint a pattern in the team's colors, which are purple and white. Which mural would you choose? Explain your reasoning.

_____

## Exploring Subtracting Fractions

1. $\frac{1}{2} - \frac{1}{6}$

   **a.** Which fraction would you rename to solve the problem? _____

   **b.** Rename the fraction. _____

   **c.** Solve the problem. _____

   **d.** Simplify, if possible. _____

2. $\frac{3}{10} - \frac{1}{5}$

   **a.** Which fraction would you rename to solve the problem? _____

   **b.** Rename the fraction. _____

   **c.** Solve the problem. _____

   **d.** Simplify, if possible. _____

3. $\frac{2}{3} - \frac{1}{2}$

   **a.** Explain why you cannot rename just one fraction to solve this problem.

   _____

   _____

   **b.** Rename both fractions as 6ths. _____

   **c.** Find the difference and simplify. _____

4. $\frac{1}{3} - \frac{1}{4}$

   **a.** What denominator could you use to rename these as equivalent fractions? _____

   **b.** Rename both fractions. _____

   **c.** Find the difference and simplify. _____

# Subtracting Fractions

A certain city gets its electricity from several different sources:

| Source of power | Fraction of total energy |
|---|---|
| Wind power | $\frac{1}{10}$ |
| Nuclear power | $\frac{1}{2}$ |
| Solar power | $\frac{1}{5}$ |
| Hydroelectric power | $\frac{1}{5}$ |

**1.** What is the greatest source of electricity in this city?

_____

**2.** How much of the city's electricity comes from
hydroelectric power and wind power?          _____

**3.** How much more of the city's electricity comes from
nuclear power than from wind power?          _____

**4.** Compare the amount of electricity coming from nuclear
power to the total amount coming from all the other
sources.

_____

_____

**5. Choose a strategy** $\frac{1}{2}$ of a city park is being
planted with trees. Another $\frac{1}{4}$ of the park is
being used for a baseball field. Another $\frac{1}{8}$ of
the park is being used for a wading pool. How
much of the park is still unplanned?

- Use Objects/Act It Out
- Draw a Picture
- Look for a Pattern
- Guess and Check
- Use Logical Reasoning
- Make an Organized List
- Make a Table
- Solve a Simpler Problem
- Work Backward

**a.** What strategy would you use to solve the
problem?

_____

**b.** Answer the problem. _____

How much longer is the wingspan of the Western pipistrelle bat than the wingspan of hog-nosed bat?

| Smallest Bats |
| --- |
| World record: Hog-nosed bat<br>Location: Thailand<br>Wingspan: $\frac{13}{24}$ ft |
| U.S. record: Western pipistrelle<br>Wingspan: $\frac{2}{3}$ ft |

## — Understand —

1. What do you know?

   _____

   _____

   _____

2. What do you need to find out? _____

## — Plan —

3. What operation should you use? _____

4. What words in the problem tell you this operation is needed?

   _____

## — Solve —

5. Rename $\frac{2}{3}$ so the fractions have like denominators. _____

6. Solve the problem. _____

## — Look Back —

7. How can you check your answer? _____

   _____

---

**SOLVE ANOTHER PROBLEM**

Seth has two pieces of wire. One piece is $\frac{1}{10}$ ft long and the other piece is $\frac{3}{5}$ ft long. What is the total length of the two pieces of wire? _____

Name _____

# Exploring Weight

**1.** You have learned that a slice of bread weighs about 1 oz. Look around the classroom. Name one object that weighs about as much as a slice of bread. What is your item?

_____

**2.** How many oz are in 1 lb? _____

**3.** How many slices of bread would weigh 1 lb? _____

Use the weight of a loaf of bread to estimate the weight of each object below. Write whether each object weighs *less than*, *greater than*, or *about the same as* a loaf of bread.

**4.**

_____

**5.**

_____

**6.**

_____

**7.**

_____

**8.**

_____

**9.**

_____

**10.**

_____

**11.**

_____

**12.**

_____

# Exploring Capacity

List two things you might measure with each unit of capacity.

**1.** teaspoon _____

**2.** tablespoon _____

**3.** cup _____

**4.** pint _____

**5.** quart _____

**6.** gallon _____

**7.** Joan says she served 50 gallons of fruit punch at a party.

   **a.** If there were 50 people at the party, could this be true? Explain.

   _____

   _____

   **b.** Suppose there were 25 people at the party. Complete the following sentence with a reasonable unit of measure.

   Joan served 50 _____ of fruit punch.

   **c.** How many people do you think could have been at the party for Joan to serve 50 gallons of fruit punch? How much did each person drink on average?

   _____

   _____

   _____

   _____

# Changing Units: Length, Weight and Capacity

**Health** The table shows serving sizes of some foods that are rich in calcium.

| Item | Serving Size |
|---|---|
| Sardines, with bones | 3 oz |
| Yogurt | 1 c |
| Oysters | $\frac{3}{4}$ c |
| Cottage cheese | $\frac{1}{2}$ c |
| Swiss cheese | 1 oz |

Use the table to help solve the problems.

1. Stacy bought a pound of sardines.

   **a.** How many servings is that? _____

   **b.** How many ounces would be left over? _____

2. This week, Jerome ate a pint of cottage cheese. How many servings is that? _____

3. How many servings of yogurt are in a quart? _____

4. Suppose you purchased 1 lb of Swiss cheese. If you ate 2 servings of Swiss cheese per day, how long would it last? _____

5. **a.** How many cups of oysters should Karla buy to make 24 servings? _____

   **b.** How many quarts is that? _____

Solve.

6. Quincy ran 45 yds. How many feet is that? _____

7. Roger's table is 3 ft long. How many inches is that? _____

**GPS** | PROBLEM 1, STUDENT PAGE 463

A school required three adult leaders for every 24 students. If 168 students signed up for a field trip to the Alamo, how many adults were needed?

| Students | 24 | 48 | 72 | 96 | | 144 | 168 | 192 |
|---|---|---|---|---|---|---|---|---|
| Adult leaders | 3 | | | 12 | 15 | | | |

## — Understand —

**1.** What do you know? _____

_____

**2.** What do you need to find out? _____

## — Plan —

**3.** How are the numbers in the top row of the table changing?

_____

## — Solve —

**4.** Describe the pattern in the table.

_____

**5.** Complete the table.

**6.** How many adults are needed for the trip? _____

## — Look Back —

**7.** How could you use a picture to solve the problem?

_____

| SOLVE ANOTHER PROBLEM |
|---|

In Karen's photo album, there are 4 photographs per page. If there are 24 pages in the album, how many photographs does Karen have? _____

# Exploring Algebra: Using a Balance Scale Model

1. These two equations mean the same thing. Explain how you know.

   $n + n = 12$      $12 = n + n$

   _____

   _____

2. If you start with a balanced scale and subtract the same amount of weight from each side, what happens to the scale?

   _____

   _____

3. If you start with a balanced scale and add 4 counters to the right side and 2 counters to the left side, what happens to the scale?

   _____

   _____

4. Suppose you start with a balanced scale that has an unknown weight on one side and 2 one-pound weights on the other side. What is the unknown weight? How do you know?

   _____

   _____

5. Suppose you start with a balanced scale that has an unknown weight and 3 one-pound weights on one side. On the other side are 5 one-pound weights. What could you do to the scale to show the unknown weight?

   _____

   _____

# Reading and Writing Decimals

**Careers** Ms. Alonzo is a professional gardener. She runs a nursery in the country.

**1.** Look at the picture of the garden plot above.

   **a.** Write the decimal showing the number of pumpkins compared to the total number of plants in the garden plot. _____

   **b.** Write the decimal for broccoli compared to the total. _____

**2.** Ms. Alonzo has a garden plot of 100 rose bushes. Forty-one of the bushes are yellow rose bushes. Fifty-nine of the bushes are red rose bushes.

   **a.** Write the decimal showing red rose bushes compared to the total number of bushes in the garden plot. _____

   **b.** Write the decimal for yellow rose bushes compared to the total number of bushes in the garden plot. _____

**3.** Four out of the ten orange trees in Ms. Alonzo's nursery died due to a long frost. Write the decimal for the number of orange trees that survived the frost, compared to the original number of trees. _____

**4.** Complete the number line. Write the missing decimals.

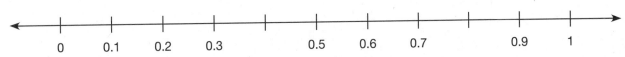

0    0.1    0.2    0.3        0.5    0.6    0.7        0.9    1

**5.** Write the decimal for the number of shaded figures below compared to the total number of figures. _____

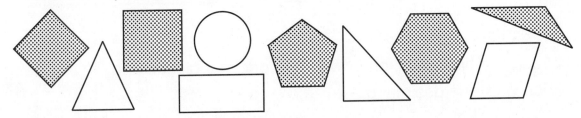

# Exploring Decimal Place-Value Relationships

**1.**

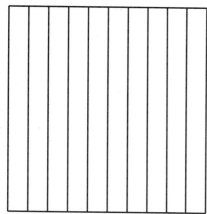
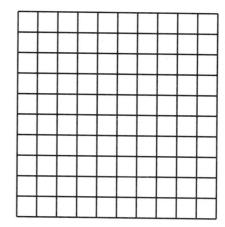

**a.** Shade the tenths grid to show 4 tenths. Write the decimal amount below the grid.

**b.** Shade the hundredths grid to show 40 hundredths. Write the decimal amount below the grid.

**c.** Is 4 tenths the same as 40 hundredths? Explain.

_____

_____

**2.** Is 11.43 greater or less than eleven and five tenths? Explain how you know.

_____

**3.** Write the word names for 13.20 in tenths and hundredths.

_____

**4.** John said that since 7 is less than 70, 2.7 is less than 2.70. Is he right? Explain.

_____

_____

**5.** Write $\frac{1}{10}$ in two ways, once with two decimal places and once with one decimal place.

_____ , _____

© Scott Foresman Addison Wesley 4

**GPS** PROBLEM 3, STUDENT PAGE 481

Suppose you have the same number of pennies and dimes. The coins total $1.21. How many of each coin do you have?

## — Understand —

1. What do you know? _____

_____

2. What do you need to find out? _____

_____

## — Plan —

3. Will you make an organized list or use objects to solve the problem?

_____

## — Solve —

4. Use your strategy to solve the problem.

   a. If you decided to make an organized list, write the list on another sheet of paper. If you decided to use objects, draw a picture of the objects you used.

   b. How many of each coin do you have?

_____

## — Look Back —

5. Use a different strategy to check your answer. Is your answer reasonable? Explain.

_____

_____

SOLVE ANOTHER PROBLEM

Renee has 1 dollar, 6 quarters, and 5 nickels. Does she have enough to buy a book that costs $2.95? Explain.

_____

# Comparing and Ordering Decimals

**Physical Education** Nadia's gym class practiced their distance running. They decided to see how far they could run in 20 minutes. Here are the results:

| Student | Distance in 20 Minutes |
|---------|------------------------|
| Karen | 1.67 miles |
| Neil | 1.98 miles |
| Patricia | 1.7 miles |
| Antonio | 1.76 miles |
| Nadia | 1.90 miles |

1. Who ran the longest distance in 20 minutes? _____

2. Who ran the shortest distance in 20 minutes? _____

3. Who ran farther, Patricia or Antonio? _____

4. Order the distances the students ran from shortest to longest.

_____

5. In the high school women's gymnastics meet, five students competed on the balance beam. Bonnie got a score of 9.89, Fiona got 8.98, Alison got 9.8, Cindy got 9.08, and Mia got 9.19.

   a. Who got the highest score on the balance beam? _____

   b. Who got the lowest score? _____

   c. Order of the scores of the balance beam competition from 1st place to 5th place.

_____

# Rounding Decimals

**Careers** Mr. Kowalski is a cartographer. A cartographer is a person who makes maps. Most maps have a key telling the distances between different places on the map. Sometimes the distances are given to the nearest mile. The cartographer rounds to the nearest mile to make the map convenient and easy to use.

1. Mr. Kowalski is drafting a map of Livingston County in New York State. The exact distance between the villages of Avon and Geneseo is 11.31 miles. What is the distance between the two villages rounded to the nearest mile? _____

2. The distance between the villages of Dansville and Livonia is 29.88 miles. What is the distance rounded to the nearest mile? _____

3. Mr. Kowalski wrote that the distance between Lakeville and Mount Morris is 17 miles, rounded to the nearest mile. Write the greatest and least possible distances between the two villages, in decimals to hundredths.

_____

4. Circle the two decimals in each set that round to the same whole number. Write the whole number.

   **a.** 2.52, 2.49, 2.60 _____

   **b.** 0.61, 1.51, 1.06 _____

   **c.** 3.45, 3.02, 3.53 _____

5. John has $1.50, Alice has $1.75, and Akheem has $1.45.

   **a.** Who has an amount that rounds to $2.00?

   _____

   **b.** Who has an amount that rounds to $1.00?

   _____

# Exploring Fractions as Decimals

**1.**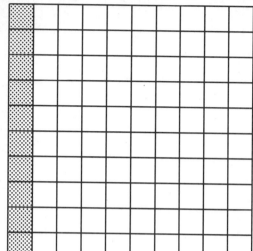

    **a.** What fractional amount do the shaded squares show? _____

    **b.** What decimal amount do the shaded squares show? _____

**2.** How would you find a decimal amount for $\frac{3}{5}$? Explain the process step by step.

_____

_____

**3.** Which is greater, $\frac{6}{25}$ or 0.25? Explain.

_____

**4.** What fraction of a dollar is 70 pennies? Write the fraction. Then write the amount using a decimal point.

_____

**5.** Explain how knowing that $\frac{1}{4} = 0.25$ can help you find the decimal for $\frac{3}{4}$. What is the decimal?

_____

# Estimating Sums and Differences

**Recreation** Do your sneakers weigh more than you think?
Use the table to solve the problems.

| Shoe | Weight of 1 shoe |
|------|------------------|
| Brand A | 19.5 oz |
| Brand B | 11.1 oz |
| Brand C | 15.8 oz |

**1.** Estimate how much a pair of Brand B sneakers weighs.

_____

**2.** Estimate how much a pair of Brand A sneakers weighs.

_____

**3.** Estimate the difference in weight between a pair of
Brand A and a pair of Brand C sneakers.

_____

Use the table to solve **4–7.**

| Ring | Bracelet | Necklace |
|------|----------|----------|
| $1.55 | $2.06 | $4.34 |

**4.** Estimate the cost of a bracelet and a ring. _____

**5.** Venise bought a bracelet with a $5 bill. About how
much money does she have left? _____

**6.** Alanna has $10. Can she buy a ring, a bracelet, and a
necklace? Explain.

_____

**7.** Becky has $5. Can she buy a ring and a necklace?
Explain.

_____

# Exploring Adding and Subtracting Decimals

**1.** Shade the grid to show 0.09 + 0.42. What is the sum? _____

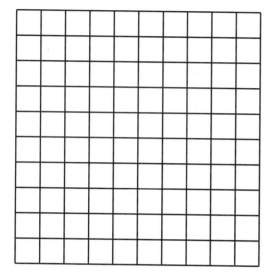

**2.** Shade the grid to show 0.56 − 0.2. What is the difference? _____

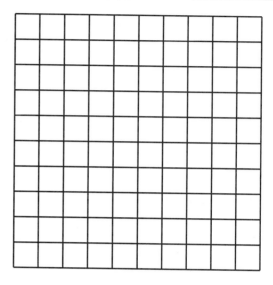

**3.** Compare these problems. How are they the same? How are they different?

$$\begin{array}{r} 0.36 \\ +\ 0.18 \\ \hline 0.54 \end{array} \qquad \begin{array}{r} 36 \\ +\ 18 \\ \hline 54 \end{array}$$

_____

_____

_____

**4.** Compare the problems. How are the methods used to solve the problems the same? How are the methods different?

$$\begin{array}{r} 0.42 \\ -\ 0.07 \\ \hline 0.35 \end{array} \qquad \begin{array}{r} 42 \\ -\ 7 \\ \hline 35 \end{array}$$

_____

_____

_____

**5.** Victor subtracted 0.03 from 0.7 and got 0.4. Is he correct? Explain.

_____

# Adding and Subtracting Decimals

Gerry and Liz went shopping for bargains. They priced
t-shirts with logos at three different stores. Here's what
they found.

| Store | Price |
|---|---|
| Shirts Ahoy! | $24.99 |
| Bargain Basement | $19.99 |
| Your Store | $21.49 |

Use the table for **1–3.**

1. How much more was the most expensive
   shirt than the least expensive shirt?          _____

2. How much would 2 shirts from the Bargain
   Basement cost?                                 _____

3. Estimate the difference in price between a
   shirt from Your Store and one from Shirts
   Ahoy!                                          _____

4. Adam has $10. He bought a paint brush for
   $1.99 and a tube of paint for $2.25. How
   much money does he have left?                  _____

5. Tyron ran 0.86 of a mile. Mariah ran 0.57 of
   a mile. How much further did Tyron run?        _____

6. **Choose a Strategy.** Mikhail wants to make punch for
   everyone in his class. There are 25 students. If each
   student gets 1 cup of punch, how many quarts of punch
   will he need? Will there be any punch left over?

   a. What strategy would you use to solve the
      problem?

      _____

      _____

   b. Answer the problem.

      _____

   • Use Objects/Act It Out
   • Draw a Picture
   • Look for a Pattern
   • Guess and Check
   • Use Logical Reasoning
   • Make an Organized List
   • Make a Table
   • Solve a Simpler Problem
   • Work Backward

Name _____

# Exploring Centimeters, Decimeters, and Meters

Complete the table.

| | Centimeters | Decimeters | Meters |
|---|---|---|---|
| 1. | 100 cm | 10 dm | 1 m |
| 2. | 200 cm | 20 dm | |
| 3. | 300 cm | | |
| 4. | 400 cm | | |
| 5. | 500 cm | | |
| 6. | 600 cm | | |
| 7. | 700 cm | | |
| 8. | 800 cm | | |
| 9. | 900 cm | | |
| 10. | 1,000 cm | | |

**11.** What pattern do you see in the centimeter column?

_____

**12.** What pattern do you see in the decimeter column?

_____

**13.** What pattern do you see in the meter column?

_____

**14.** What pattern do you see in each row?

_____

_____

_____

# Meters and Kilometers

**Geography** The table shows the highest mountain on each continent.

| Continent | Highest Point on Each Continent | Mountain Height |
|-----------|--------------------------------|-----------------|
| Africa | Kilimanjaro | 5,895 m |
| Asia | Everest | 8,854 m |
| Antarctica | Vinson Massif | 4,897 m |
| S. America | Aconcagua | 6,960 m |
| Europe | Blanc | 4,810 m |
| Australia | Kosciusko | 2,231 m |

1. Which continent has the highest mountain? _____

2. How much higher is Kilimanjaro than
Vinson Massif? _____

3. About how high is Aconcagua in kilometers? _____

4. About how many kilometers higher is Blanc
than Kosciusko? _____

5. The swim team has to swim the following laps at
practice today: 400 m, 600 m, 200 m, 800 m, with
a rest between each set of laps. How many
kilometers will they swim in all? _____

6. Mary stayed in the pool from 11:00 A.M. to 3:30 P.M.
How many hours did she stay in the pool? _____

7. On the first day of practice, Rick could only swim
225 meters without stopping. Now he can swim
1 kilometer. How much further can he swim now? _____

8. The boys' swimsuits cost $17 each. There are 12 boys.
The coach has received $187. Have all the boys paid?
Explain.

_____

# Exploring Length and Decimals

A cubit is a unit of length used by many early civilizations. It is based on the length of a person's arm from the elbow to the tip of the middle finger.

1. Name one advantage of using the length of a person's arm as a unit of measurement. Name one disadvantage.

   _____

   _____

2. The length of the English cubit is 46 cm. What is the length in meters?  _____

3. Mark used the English cubit to measure a picture that he wanted to frame. The picture was 1.5 cubits by 2 cubits. What are the picture's dimensions in centimeters? Explain how you solved the problem.

   _____

4. The Egyptian cubit is 53 cm. How many more meters is it than the English cubit?  _____

5. Suppose a rug measured 2.2 English cubits by 1.4 English cubits. If you used Egyptian cubits, would the measures be greater or less? Explain your reasoning.

   _____

   _____

6. Why do you think the Egyptian cubit is larger than the English cubit?

   _____

7. Suppose an English company is building in Egypt. The planners used cubits for all the measurements. If you were in charge of the construction, what is the first question you would ask? Explain your answer.

   _____

   _____

# Exploring Mass

Labels on packaged foods contain nutrition information. The amount of nutrients are given in grams. Use the cereal box label to answer **1–4**.

1. How many grams of protein are in 5 servings? _____

2. If you eat a serving each day for 7 days, how many grams of carbohydrates will you consume? _____

    How many kilograms? _____

3. **a.** A box of cereal weighs 390 g. How many servings are in one box? _____

    **b.** A family of four each has a cereal serving every day. Will 2 boxes of cereal be enough for the week? Explain.

    _____

    _____

4. Sue bought 4 loaves of bread. Each loaf weighed 700 g. How many kilograms did the bread weigh all together? _____

5. Write g or kg to complete the sentence. Katrina went grocery shopping; she bought one 200 _____ bar of soap, a 5 _____ turkey, a 310 _____ can of soup, and a 2 _____ pork roast.

6. Samuel and his father bake bread. To make 5 loaves, they need 2.5 kg of flour. They have a 1 kg bag and 250 g of flour in a container. How many more kilograms of flour do they need? _____

7. A bag of popcorn is twice the size of a bag of oranges. Will the popcorn have the greater mass? Explain.

    _____

8. Does a larger object always weigh more than a smaller object? Explain.

    _____

## WHEAToaties

| | |
|---|---|
| Serving Size ..................30 g | |
| Nutrition Information per serving | |
| Calories ......................115 | |
| Protein ..........................4 g | |
| Carbohydrates ..............24 g | |
| Fat .................................0 g | |
| Cholesterol ....................0 g | |

Ingredients: oat bran, wheat, corn, raisins, honey

# Exploring Capacity

The basketball team has a party to celebrate a winning season. They serve lemony punch. Use the recipe to answer questions **1–5**.

> ## Lemony Punch
>
> | | |
> |---|---|
> | 360 mL | Lemonade |
> | 1 L | Pinneapple juice |
> | 1.4 L | Cranberry juice |
> | 5 L | Ginger ale |
> | 945 mL | Lemon sherbet |
>
> Place liquids in punch bowl.
>
> Add sherbet before serving.

1. How much more pineapple juice than

   lemonade is used? _____

2. How many milliliters of ginger ale
   is used?

   _____

3. How many more liters of ginger ale
   than cranberry juice is used? _____

4. How many milliliters of ingredients are in the punch? _____

   How many liters? _____

5. A punch cup holds 225 mL. Is there enough punch to serve one cup
   of punch to 40 people? Explain.

   _____

6. Marcie has to put eyedrops in her eyes twice a day for a week. Do
   you think the bottle the medicine comes in is measured in liters or
   milliliters? Explain your reasoning.

   _____

7. Marcie puts 2 drops in each eye twice a day. If a drop is 1 mL, about
   how many milliliters will she use in a week? Explain how you know.

   _____

8. At a rate of 2 milliliters a day, how long would a one-liter bottle of
   eyedrops last? Why do you think eyedrops are not sold in liter
   containers? Give two reasons.

   _____

   _____

   _____

© Scott Foresman Addison Wesley 4

# Temperature

**Science** Meteorology is the study of the atmosphere, weather, and climate. A meteorologist studies atmospheric conditions and makes predictions about the weather, based on the data.

| Record Temperatures | | | | |
|---|---|---|---|---|
| | High | | Low | |
| **State** | °C | °F | °C | °F |
| Washington | 47.7 | 118 | −44.4 | −48 |
| North Dakota | 48.8 | 121 | −51.1 | −60 |
| California | 56.6 | 134 | −42.8 | −45 |
| Florida | 42.7 | 109 | −18.8 | −2 |
| Georgia | 44.4 | 112 | −27.2 | −17 |

1. What is the difference between the highest and lowest temperatures

    in degrees Fahrenheit? _____ in degrees Celsius? _____

2. What is the difference between the highest and lowest temperatures for the state of Washington

    in degrees Fahrenheit? _____ in degrees Celsius? _____

3. Which state has the greatest difference
    between the high and low temperature?   _____

4. Order the states from the greatest to least difference between the high and low temperatures.

    _____

5. Ramón has a fever. His body temperature is 40°C.
    Normal body temperature is 37°C. How many
    degrees will his body temperature have to drop to
    reach normal body temperature?                          _____

6. A freezer cools itself down 8°F per minute until it
    reaches the correct temperature. If the freezer is
    72°F now, how many minutes will it take before
    the freezer can make ice cubes?                          _____

7. If it is snowing, is the temperature more likely to be
    30°F or 30°C?                                                   _____

# Decision Making

A carousel has horses on an inside ring, one or more middle rings, and an outside ring. If you want to ride one of the fastest horses, which ring should you select?

1. Think about a carousel ride. Does any horse ever pass another one?                    _____

2. Does any horse go around the track more times than any other horse?                    _____

3. Does any horse cover more distance than any other horse? Explain.

   _____

4. Think about a way to demonstrate the speed of various horses on a carousel. Explain how you would do it.

   _____

   _____

   _____

   _____

5. Which horse would you choose if you wanted to go the fastest possible speed on a carousel?

   _____

6. Explain how you decided which horse would be the fastest.

   _____

   _____

   _____

Name _____

## Exploring Division Patterns

Show place-value patterns to the millions for the following
basic facts. Follow the example.

**Example:**

Basic fact: 49 ÷ 7 = 7

490 ÷ 70 = 7

4,900 ÷ 70 = 70

49,000 ÷ 70 = 700

490,000 ÷ 70 = 7,000

4,900,000 ÷ 70 = 70,000

**1.** Basic fact: 8 ÷ 2 = 4

    80 ÷ 20 = _____

    _____ ÷ 20 = 40

    8,000 ÷ _____ = 400

    _____ ÷ 20 = 4,000

    800,000 ÷ 20 = _____

**2.** Basic fact: 12 ÷ 4 = 3

    120 ÷ _____ = 3

    1,200 ÷ 40 = _____

    _____ ÷ 40 = 300

    120,000 ÷ _____ = 3,000

    1,200,000 ÷ 40 = _____

**3.** Basic fact: 36 ÷ 6 = 6

_____

_____

_____

_____

_____

**4.** Basic fact: 9 ÷ 3 = 3

_____

_____

_____

_____

_____

**5.** Will has a recipe for potato salad which serves 4. It uses
24 potatoes. He is making the salad for a party and he
has 240 potatoes. How many people will the salad
serve?

_____

# Estimating Quotients with 2-Digit Divisors

**Geography** Use the table to solve the problems.

| Road Mileage Between Selected U.S. Cities | |
|---|---|
| Boston to Chicago | 963 miles |
| Denver to Dallas | 781 miles |
| Indianapolis to Atlanta | 493 miles |
| Minneapolis to Cincinnati | 692 miles |
| Kansas City to Cleveland | 770 miles |

**1.** If Kahlil drives 65 miles per hour, about how much driving time will it take to get from Boston to Chicago?

_____

**2.** Denise left Indianapolis at 6:00 A.M., driving 60 miles per hour. About what time will she arrive in Atlanta if she stops for an hour for lunch?

_____

**3.** About how many hours of driving time would it take to get from Kansas City to Cleveland at an average rate of 55 miles per hour?

_____

**4.** About how many hours would it take to drive from Denver to Dallas, at 65 miles per hour, if you stop every 4 hours to take a 20-minute break?

_____

Estimate before you answer yes or no.

**5.** At 35 miles per hour, can you go 150 miles in 4 hours? _____

**6.** At 55 miles per hour, can you go 150 miles in 2 hours? _____

**7.** At 65 miles per hour, can you go 120 miles in 2 hours? _____

**8.** At 45 miles per hour, can you go 200 miles in 4 hours? _____

**9.** At 50 miles per hour, can you go 240 miles in 5 hours? _____

## Dividing by Tens

**Careers** Fishermen go out on their boats very early in the morning, in order to get fish to the market by the time it opens. Use the table to solve the problems.

| Fish Market: Today's Catch | |
|---|---|
| Salmon | 586 |
| Halibut | 819 |
| Petrale Sole | 733 |
| Crabs | 986 |
| Trout | 648 |

The Fish Market has 40 regular customers who are buyers for local restaurants. Each customer buys the same amount of fish.

**1.** About how many salmon can each customer buy? _____

**2.** About how many halibut can each customer buy? _____

**3.** About how many petrale sole can each customer buy? _____

**4.** 10 customers are not interested in crabs. How many crabs can each of the remaining 30 customers buy? _____

**5.** 20 customers do not want trout. How many trout can each of the remaining 20 customers buy? _____

**6.** Clancy the Clown has 198 balloons to give out equally to 60 children. How many balloons will each child get? _____

**7.** Pricilla has to type 148 pages. She can usually type about 10 pages an hour. How many hours will it take her to finish? _____

**8.** An auditorium can hold 348 people. There are 20 full rows of seats.

  **a.** How many people are in each full row? _____

  **b.** How many people are in the one shorter row? _____

# Dividing with 2-Digit Divisors

**Careers** The table shows the maximum weight allowed by the U.S. Post Office for packages sent by air to some other countries. Use the table to solve the problems.

| Country | Maximum Weight Limit |
|---|---|
| Argentina | 44 |
| Denmark | 66 |
| Ireland | 50 |
| Israel | 33 |
| Lebanon | 11 |
| Portugal | 22 |

For each situation, answer these questions:

   **a.** How many boxes will be needed?

   **b.** Will every box be full?

1. Corinne, a shipping clerk, has to send 892 pounds of computer parts to Argentina.　　a. _____ b. _____

2. The Portuguese branch of Marvin's company needs 547 pounds of denim to complete an order.　　a. _____ b. _____

3. A customer in Israel ordered 264 pounds of chocolate from Abe's Chocolate Factory.　　a. _____ b. _____

4. Tadashi must send 426 pounds of iris bulbs to a customer in Denmark.　　a. _____ b. _____

5. A customer in Ireland ordered 750 pounds of coffee beans from Mick's company.　　a. _____ b. _____

6. Fateema is sending 40 copies of her company's 3-pound catalog to Lebanon.　　a. _____ b. _____

7. 936 pairs of shoes will go on 26 long shelves in the back room of your shop. How many pairs will go on each shelf? _____

8. You need to store 882 zippers in 14 drawers. How many zippers will go in each drawer? _____

Name _____

# Decision Making

There are two main routes to get from Daniel's house to
his grandparents' house by car. Here are the pros and cons
of each.

| Route | Pros | Cons |
|---|---|---|
| Scenic route<br><br>(530 miles) | • Some ocean views and interesting towns<br>• Varied choice of restaurants for lunch<br>• Easy access to service stations | • Takes about 10 hours<br>• Towns slow you down because of stop lights and traffic<br>• Occasional stop-and-go traffic |
| Direct route<br><br>(406 miles) | • No traffic jams<br>• All freeway driving<br>• Takes about $6\frac{1}{2}$ hours | • Boring drive<br>• Very few places to stop for lunch<br>• Service stations can be up to 30 miles apart |

**1.** How many miles longer is the scenic route? _____

**2.** Which route would be better if Daniel's car has some problems? Why?

_____

**3.** Which route would be better if Daniel is in a hurry to get there? Why?

_____

**4.** At 35 miles per gallon, about how many
gallons would the direct route take? _____

**5.** At 27 miles per gallon, about how many
gallons would the scenic route take? _____

**6.** Why might you choose the direct route?

_____

**7.** Why might you choose the scenic route?

_____

**8.** Make a decision. Which route would you choose?
Explain.

_____

# Exploring Likely and Unlikely

Read each statement about the numbers
in the box. Suppose you put your finger on one
number in the box without looking. For each
statement, write impossible, unlikely, equally
likely as unlikely, likely, or certain.

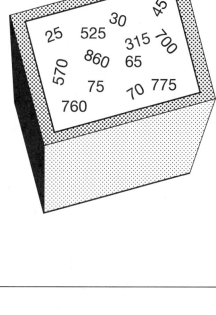

25   525   30   315   700   45
570   860   65
75   70   775
760

1. The number has 4 digits.

   _____

2. The number has two or three digits.

   _____

3. The number has a 0 in the ones place.

   _____

4. The number has an 8 in it.          _____

5. The number has a 9 in it.           _____

6. The number has a 4 in it.           _____

7. The ones digit is a 0 or 5.         _____

8. You can count by 2s to reach the number.  _____

9. You can divide the number by 5.     _____

Suppose you choose 1 number from the hat without looking.

10. The number is evenly divided by 3.

    _____

11. The number is a 2-digit number.

    _____

3   18   9
15   6   12

12. The number is a 3.

    _____

13. The number is evenly divided by 10.

    _____

14. The number is greater than 8.

    _____

# Exploring Fairness

Write whether each situation is fair or unfair.

1. Isaiah and Ismael want to play a game. They have to decide who plays first. To do so, they place one hand behind their back. On the count of three, they face their hand palm up or palm down. If both hands are palm up or palm down, Isaiah plays first. If one palm is up and the other is down, Ismael plays first. Is this fair or unfair? Explain.

_____

_____

2. You want to watch a movie on TV. Your brother wants to watch a baseball game. You say to your brother, "I'll write "movie" on 3 slips of paper and "baseball" on 2 slips of paper. I'll put the papers in a hat, and without looking, I'll let you choose a paper from the hat. We'll watch whatever you choose." Is this fair or unfair? Explain

_____

_____

3. **a.** Flora and Marisol make a game to practice their division facts. They label a number cube with the numbers 3, 4, 6, 8, 9, and 12. In turn, they roll the number cube. If the number can be evenly divided by 3, Flora wins 1 point. If it can be evenly divided by 4, Marisol wins 1 point. Is this a fair or unfair game? Explain.

_____

_____

**b.** Suppose Flora and Marisol use the same rules but with a number cube numbered 8, 16, 18, 20, 21, and 27. Is this a fair or unfair game? Explain.

_____

_____

Name _____

**Problem Solving
12-8**

# Listing Possible Outcomes

 tiger = frog      tiger = squirrel

**Fine Arts** An artist likes to create crazy animal pictures by combining two different animals into one.

The artist uses a tiger, gorilla, frog, squirrel, and giraffe to create the crazy animals. One animal is used in front; the other in the back.

**1.** What are the possible outcomes if the front animal is a tiger?

_____

**2.** Is a tiger-giraffe picture different from a giraffe-tiger picture? _____

**3.** How many possible crazy animal pictures are there using the five animals? _____

**4.** If a camel is added to the list of animals, how many more pictures can be created? _____

**5.** Suppose you roll a pair of number cubes. One of them is labeled 1, 3, 5, 7, 9, 11 and the other is labeled 2, 4, 6, 8, 10, 12.

 **a.** How many different sums are possible? _____

 **b.** What is the greatest possible sum? _____

   the least possible sum? _____

 **c.** How many ways can you roll a sum of 13? _____

 **d.** How many ways can you roll a sum of 9? _____

 **e.** Which outcome is more likely, 7 or 17? _____

 **f.** Which sums are least likely to occur? _____

**158**  Use with pages 544–545.

# Exploring Probability

1. The probability of rolling a 3 on a number cube is $\frac{1}{2}$. How many faces on the cube have a 3? _____

2. A sack contains 15 marbles. The probability of drawing a red marble without looking is $\frac{3}{5}$. How many red marbles are in the sack? _____

3. A spinner is divided into 6 equal parts. The probability of spinning yellow is 1. How many of the 6 parts are colored yellow? _____

4. A box contains 18 markers. The probability of picking a green marker without looking is $\frac{2}{9}$. How many green markers are in the box? _____

5. A sock drawer contains 15 pairs of socks. The probability of pulling out a pair of white socks without looking is $\frac{1}{5}$. How many pairs of white socks are in the drawer? _____

6. There are 6 teddy bears in a toy chest filled with stuffed animals. The probability of pulling out a teddy bear without looking is $\frac{3}{10}$. How many stuffed animals are in the toy chest? _____

7. Lauren has 12 coins in her pocket. The probability of her pulling out a penny is $\frac{1}{2}$. How many pennies are in her pocket? _____

8. Shawn has 2 nickels in his pocket. The probability of him pulling out a nickel is $\frac{1}{3}$. How many coins are in his pocket? _____

9. Ronnie has less than 12 nickels, dimes, and quarters in his pocket. The probability of pulling out a nickel or a quarter is $\frac{1}{4}$. The probability of pulling out a dime is $\frac{1}{2}$.
   a. How many coins could Ronnie have in his pocket? _____
   b. How many of each coin could Ronnie have?

_____

_____

# Exploring Predictions

Andrea passed out a survey which asked people to choose their favorite color from a list of five different colors. From her results, Andrea concluded that she could make the following predictions:

$\frac{1}{2}$ of all people would choose blue as their favorite color.

$\frac{1}{12}$ of all people would choose yellow as their favorite color.

$\frac{1}{8}$ of all people would choose green as their favorite color.

$\frac{1}{4}$ of all people would choose red as their favorite color.

$\frac{1}{24}$ of all people would choose orange as their favorite color.

**1.** Evan says "I think Andrea gave the survey to 10 students." Could Evan be right? Why or why not?

_____

_____

**2.** Suppose Andrea made her predictions from 48 completed surveys. How many people do you think chose each color as their favorite?

Red _____    Yellow _____    Blue _____

Green _____    Orange _____

**3.** Suppose Andrea gave her original survey to 24 people. She wants to check the reasonableness of her predictions by giving the survey to either 120 people or 240 people. Which number of people would best show whether Andrea's original predictions were reasonable? Explain.

_____

_____

_____

GPS PROBLEM 3, STUDENT PAGE 551

A 2-letter group has A, B, C, or D as its first letter, and E or F as its second letter.

**a.** Write all possible 2-letter groups.   **b.** How many possibilities are there?

## — Understand —

1. How many letters make a group? _____

2. What letters can be used as the first letter? _____

   second? _____

## — Plan —

3. Solve a Simpler Problem. Suppose a 2-letter group has either A or B as its first letter and E as its second letter.

   **a.** Write a 2-letter group that starts with A. _____ with B. _____

   **b.** How many 2-letter groups in this simpler problem

   are possible? _____

## — Solve —

4. Make an organized list of arrangements with letter A as the first letter. Continue with arrangements using B, C, and D. How many arrangements are possible?

   _____

## — Look Back —

5. Look for a pattern in your list. How can you use the pattern to check your answer?

   _____

   _____

SOLVE ANOTHER PROBLEM

Stephen's little sister has 1 red, 1 green, 1 blue, and 1 yellow block. She randomly grabs 2 blocks. How many different combinations of blocks could she pick up? _____

## Pictographs and Bar Graphs

**Science** The deepest places on earth are trenches beneath the ocean. The deepest trench is the Mariana Trench. It is close to 7 miles deep!

Below is a bar graph that shows the depths of some trenches:

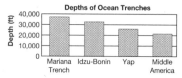

**Depths of Ocean Trenches**

1. Which trench in the graph is the shallowest? **Middle America**

2. About how deep is the deepest trench? **About 36,000 ft**

3. Which trenches shown in the graph are deeper than the Yap trench? **Mariana Trench, Idzu-Bonin**

Use the pictograph to answer **4–5**.

4. List the number of pets from the pictograph in order from most to least.
**Cats, dogs, rodents**

| Number of Pets Cleveland Elementary School Students Have | |
|---|---|
| Cats | 🐱🐱🐱🐱🐱 🐱🐱🐱 |
| Dogs | 🐶🐶🐶🐶🐶 🐶🐶 |
| Rodents | 🐭 |

🐱 = 10
🐭 = 5

5. Students at Cleveland Elementary have 40 pet birds. How many pictures would you draw to show the number of birds?
**4 pictures**

---

## Ordered Pairs

**Geography** Knowing how to use ordered pairs to locate points on a coordinate grid is helpful for reading a map. Below is a coordinate grid map of a town.

Give the ordered pair for these points on the map:

1. The Library **(4,2)**
2. The Post Office **(5,5)**
3. The Hardware Store **(1,2)**
4. The Town Hall **(3,3)**
5. The Bank **(6,6)**
6. The School **(2,3)**

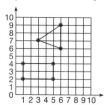

Use the grid to locate the points to answer the questions.

7. Use the grid to locate the points (1,2), (1,4), (5,4), (5,2), and (1,2). Connect them in this order: (1,2), (1,4), (5,4), (5,2), and back to (1,2). What shape do they make? **a rectangle**

8. Use the grid to locate the points (3,6), (6,9), (6,6), and (3,7). Connect them in order: (3,7), (6,9), (6,6), and back to (3,7). What shape do they make? **a triangle**

---

## Reading Line Graphs

**Geography** The temperature in Portland, Maine remains relatively cool throughout the year because it is so far north. This graph shows the average temperature in Portland, Maine.

**Average Temperature in Portland, ME**

1. Estimate the average temperature in Portland in January. **About 22°F**

2. In which month is the average temperature about 70 degrees? **July**

3. About how many degrees warmer is it in Portland in April than in January? **About 20°F warmer**

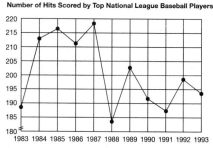

**Number of Hits Scored by Top National League Baseball Players**

Use the line graph to answer **4–5**.

4. About how many hits were made in 1990? **About 192**

5. About how many more hits were made in 1987 than in 1988? **About 34 more hits**

---

## Reading Line Plots

**Geography** Most of the snowiest cities in the U.S. are in the North. This line plot shows the amount of snowfall that falls on some of the snowiest cities in the country.

```
    x   x
    x   x   x
    x   x   x   x
  +---+---+---+---+
    8   9   10  11
```
**Greatest Average Snowfall in Some U.S. Cities (ft)**

Use the line plot to answer **1–4**.

1. How many cities get about 11 feet of snow in one year? **1 city**

2. How many cities get about 9 feet of snow in one year? **3 cities**

3. Syracuse, New York gets about 10 feet of snow in a typical year. How many cities shown on the line plot get that much snow or more in one year? **3 cities**

4. What are the two most common amounts of snow shown on the line plot? **8 or 9 feet of snow**

Use the line plot to answer **5–8**.

```
  x
  x   x
  x   x
  x   x   x
  x   x   x   x   x
+---+---+---+---+---+
  0   1   2   3   4
```
**Number of Pets Students Have**

5. How many students do not have any pets? **5**

6. How many students have 4 pets? **1**

7. How many students have 1 or more pets? **8**

8. Do most of the students have pets? Explain.
**Yes; 8 students have pets, 5 students do not.**

**Problem Solving**
**1-5**

## Reading Stem-and-Leaf Plots

**Science** The largest animals known were dinosaurs. From their skeletons, scientists can estimate how long they were.

**Lengths of the Largest Dinosaurs (meters)**

| Stem | Leaf |
|------|------|
| 1 | 5  2  2 |
| 2 | 7  5  5  1 |
| 3 | 6  0  0 |

Use the stem-and-leaf plot to answer **1–4.**

**1.** The Seismosaurus is the longest known dinosaur. About how many meters long was a Seismosaurus?    **About 36 meters**

**2.** The Tyrannosaurus and Spinosaurus were the same length. How many meters long could they have been?
**About 12 meters, 25 meters, or 30 meters long**

**3.** How many types of dinosaurs were longer than 15 meters?    **7 types**

**4.** Suppose a new dinosaur was discovered tomorrow. If its length is 10 meters, would it be one of the 9 largest dinosaurs? Explain.
**Possible answer: No; There are 10 dinosaurs shown in the stem-and-leaf plot and all are greater than 10 meters long.**

Use the stem-and-leaf plot to answer **5–7.**

**Lengths of the Longest Snakes (ft)**

| Stem | Leaf |
|------|------|
| 1 | 1  2  4  6 |
| 2 | 4 |
| 3 | 3 |

**5.** The python is the longest snake. What is its length?    **33 feet**

**6.** How many snakes are longer than 16 feet?    **2**

**7.** How many snakes are between 11 and 24 feet long?    **3**

---

**Guided Problem Solving**
**1-6**

**GPS PROBLEM 6, STUDENT PAGE 21**

What is the difference in length between the San Francisco garter snake and the Texas blind snake?

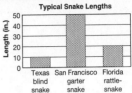

**Typical Snake Lengths**

— **Understand** —

**1.** What facts do you know? **Length of San Francisco garter snake: 50 in., and Texas blind snake: 10 in.**

**2.** What do you need to find out?
**The difference in the length between the 2 snakes**

— **Plan** —

**3.** What operation do you use to find a difference? **Subtraction**

— **Solve** —

**4.** Find the difference. **50 − 10 = 40**

**5.** Write your answer. **The San Francisco garter snake is 40 inches longer than the Texas blind snake.**

— **Look Back** —

**6.** How can you check to see if your answer makes sense?
**Add to check. 40 + 10 = 50**

**SOLVE ANOTHER PROBLEM**

Find the difference in length between the Florida rattlesnake and the Texas blind snake.    **10 inches**

---

**Guided Problem Solving**
**1-7**

**GPS PROBLEM 5, STUDENT PAGE 23**

Fennecs, the smallest kind of foxes, are about 16 inches long. A red fox is about 25 inches long. What is the difference in length between a fennec and a red fox?

— **Understand** —

**1.** What do you know?
**The length of a fennec and a red fox**

**2.** What is the length of a fennec? **16 in.**

**3.** What is the length of a red fox? **25 in.**

**4.** What are you asked to find?
**The difference in length between a fennec and a red fox**

— **Plan** —

**5.** Which operation is used to find the *difference* between two numbers?
**Subtraction**

**6.** Looking at the two numbers, can you estimate their difference?
**Yes, about 10 inches**

— **Solve** —

**7.** Write the number sentence. **25 − 16 = 9**

**8.** What is the difference in length between a fennec and a red fox?
**9 inches**

— **Look Back** —

**9.** How can you check your answer?
**Add 16 + 9 to see if you get 25.**

**SOLVE ANOTHER PROBLEM**

On Monday morning, there were 12 dogs at the city animal shelter. During the day, 9 more dogs were brought in. How many dogs are at the shelter now?    **21 dogs**

---

**Problem Solving**
**1-8**

## Exploring Making Bar Graphs

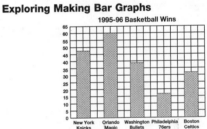

**1995-96 Basketball Wins**

**1.** What does this bar graph compare?
**The win records of basketball teams**

**2.** What scale does the graph use? **5**

**3.** Which team won between 45 and 50 games? **Knicks**

**4.** If you wanted to add the Chicago Bulls (72 wins) to the bar graph, how would you change the graph? **Possible answer: Make it higher so the scale includes numbers up to 72.**

**5.** Describe how the graph would look using a scale of 10.
**Possible answer: The bars would be shorter and closer in height.**

**6.** Use this grid to make the graph with a scale of 10.

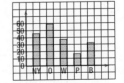

## Exploring Making Line Plots

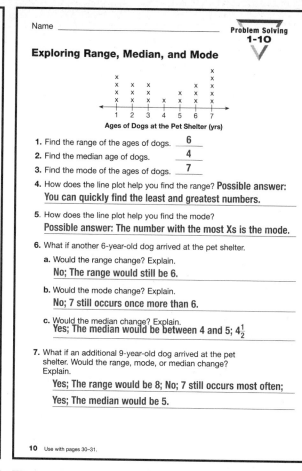

x
x
x   x   x
x   x   x   x
x   x   x   x
x   x   x   x   x
x   x   x   x   x
x   x   x   x   x

15   18   21   24   27   30

**Hamsters' Lifespans (Months)**

**1.** What does this line plot compare?
**The lifespans of hamsters**

**2.** Based on the line plot, would you say most hamsters live to 30 months? Explain.
**No; Only 4 of the hamsters lived to be 30 months. Most lived about 24 months.**

**3. a.** If two more hamsters that lived 21 months each were included in the data, how would you change the line plot?
**Add 2 Xs above 21 on the line plot.**

   **b.** How would your answer in Part **a** change your answer to **2**?
**Most hamsters live to 21 or 24 months.**

**4.** Why are there no Xs at 15?
**No hamsters died at 15 months.**

**5.** Write a question that can be answered by the line plot.
**Sample question: How many hamsters lived 21 months?**

**6.** Answer your question.
**Sample answer: 7 hamsters**

---

## Exploring Range, Median, and Mode

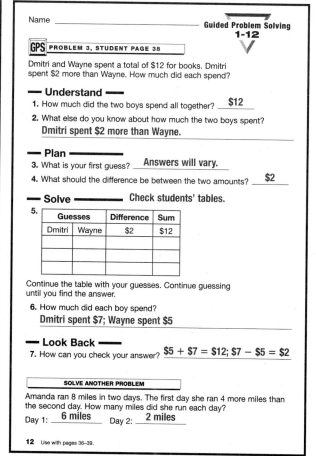

x
x   x
x   x   x                           x
x   x   x           x   x   x   x
x   x   x   x   x   x   x   x

1   2   3   4   5   6   7

**Ages of Dogs at the Pet Shelter (yrs)**

**1.** Find the range of the ages of dogs.  **6**

**2.** Find the median age of dogs.  **4**

**3.** Find the mode of the ages of dogs.  **7**

**4.** How does the line plot help you find the range? **Possible answer: You can quickly find the least and greatest numbers.**

**5.** How does the line plot help you find the mode?
**Possible answer: The number with the most Xs is the mode.**

**6.** What if another 6-year-old dog arrived at the pet shelter.

   **a.** Would the range change? Explain.
**No; The range would still be 6.**

   **b.** Would the mode change? Explain.
**No; 7 still occurs once more than 6.**

   **c.** Would the median change? Explain.
**Yes; The median would be between 4 and 5; $4\frac{1}{2}$**

**7.** What if an additional 9-year-old dog arrived at the pet shelter. Would the range, mode, or median change? Explain.
**Yes; The range would be 8; No; 7 still occurs most often; Yes; The median would be 5.**

---

## Exploring Algebra: What's the Rule?

A rule can use addition or subtraction. It can also use multiplication or division.

| In | 4 | 1 | 6 | 7 | 2 |
|----|----|----|----|----|----|
| Out | 12 | 3 | 18 | 21 | 6 |

**1. a.** Write the table's rule in words.  **Multiply by 3.**

   **b.** Write the table's rule with a variable.  **$n \times 3$**

   **c.** Complete the table.

   **d.** Describe how you discovered the rule.
**Possible answer: Looked at what was done to the first number to get the second and checked to see if this worked for all pairs of numbers.**

| In | 8 | 10 | 14 | 6 | 18 | 20 |
|----|----|----|----|----|----|----|
| Out | 4 | 5 | 7 | 3 | 9 | 10 |

**2. a.** Write a rule for the first pair of numbers that doesn't work for the second pair.  **Subtract 4.**

   **b.** Write a rule with a variable that works for all pairs of numbers.  **$n \div 2$**

   **c.** Complete the table.

**3.** Make your own table. Your rule can use addition, subtraction, multiplication, or division. Leave some spaces blank. Give your table to a classmate to complete. **Check students' tables. Look for a consistent rule.**

| In | | | | | |
|----|----|----|----|----|----|
| Out | | | | | |

Rule: **Rule should match table.**

---

**GPS** PROBLEM 3, STUDENT PAGE 38

Dmitri and Wayne spent a total of $12 for books. Dmitri spent $2 more than Wayne. How much did each spend?

— **Understand** —

**1.** How much did the two boys spend all together?  **$12**

**2.** What else do you know about how much the two boys spent?
**Dmitri spent $2 more than Wayne.**

— **Plan** —

**3.** What is your first guess?  **Answers will vary.**

**4.** What should the difference be between the two amounts?  **$2**

— **Solve** —  **Check students' tables.**

**5.**

| Guesses | | Difference | Sum |
|---------|---------|------------|------|
| Dmitri | Wayne | $2 | $12 |
| | | | |
| | | | |
| | | | |

Continue the table with your guesses. Continue guessing until you find the answer.

**6.** How much did each boy spend?
**Dmitri spent $7; Wayne spent $5**

— **Look Back** —

**7.** How can you check your answer?  **$5 + $7 = $12; $7 − $5 = $2**

SOLVE ANOTHER PROBLEM

Amanda ran 8 miles in two days. The first day she ran 4 more miles than the second day. How many miles did she run each day?

Day 1: **6 miles**   Day 2: **2 miles**

## Place Value Through Thousands

**Careers** Here are the number of Americans who work in each career. Write the word name for each number.

**1.** Actors/directors/producers—129,000 people

One hundred twenty-nine thousand

**2.** Aircraft pilots—85,000 people

Eighty-five thousand

**3.** Auto mechanics—739,000 people

Seven hundred thirty-nine thousand

**4.** Bank tellers—525,000 people

Five hundred twenty-five thousand

**5.** All these numbers have been rounded to what place?

The thousands place

**Patterns** What number comes next?

**6.** 23; 230; 2,300 _23,000_   **7.** 439; 4,390; 43,900 _439,000_

**8.** 124; 1,240; 12,400 _124,000_   **9.** 309; 3,090; 30,900 _309,000_

**10.** 31; 313; 3,131 _31,313_   **11.** 472; 1,472; 10,472 _100,472_

**12.** 100; 1,000; 10,000 _100,000_

**13.** 700; 700,000; 700,000,000 _700,000,000,000_

**14.** The letters of the word "wonderful" have been assigned a number. Using the chart, write the number for each word below, then write its word name.

| W | O | N | D | E | R | F | U | L |
|---|---|---|---|---|---|---|---|---|
| 1 | 2 | 3 | 4 | 5 | 6 | 7 | 8 | 9 |

a. FOLDER _729,456; seven hundred twenty-nine thousand,
four hundred fifty-six_

b. LOWER _92,156; ninety-two thousand, one hundred fifty-six_

---

## Exploring Place-Value Relationships
Complete the table. Use place-value blocks.

| | Number | Ones | Tens | Hundreds |
|---|---|---|---|---|
| **1.** | 1 | 1 | 0 | 0 |
| **2.** | 10 | 10 | 1 | 0 |
| **3.** | 100 | 100 | 10 | 1 |
| **4.** | 1,000 | 1,000 | 100 | 10 |

**5.** What pattern(s) do you see in the table?

Possible answers: Vertical pattern: each number has 10 times

more ones than the number above it; Horizontal pattern: in

3–4 as you go from left to right, the numbers decrease by

powers of ten.

**6.** How many tens are in 6,000? _600_

**7.** How many hundreds are in 5,000? _50_

**8.** How could you find the number of hundreds in 9,000 without using place-value blocks or paper and pencil?

Take 2 zeros from 9,000. There are 90 hundreds in 9,000.

**9.** Michael has 2,400 comics in his collection. How many stacks would he have if he stacked them in

a. hundreds? _24_

b. tens? _240_

c. thousands? _3, 2 stacks with 1,000 each and 1 stack
with 400_

---

## Place Value Through Millions

**Science** The Earth is $4\frac{1}{2}$ billion years old. Scientists divide the Earth's history into time periods according to the fossils they find in rocks. Use the table of periods in Earth's history to solve the problems.

| Time Period | When It Began |
|---|---|
| Late Triassic Period | 225,000,000 years ago |
| Jurassic Period | 213,000,000 years ago |
| Cretaceous Period | 144,000,000 years ago |
| Tertiary Period | 65,000,000 years ago |

**1.** Write the word name for the number that tells when the Tertiary period began. — Sixty-five million

**2.** Which period began one hundred forty-four million years ago? — Cretaceous period

**3.** Which two periods began more than two-hundred million years ago?

Jurassic and Late Triassic periods

Solve the riddles.

**4.** I'm a seven-digit number with digits from 1 to 7. Each digit is used once. From left to right the digits go from least to greatest. What number am I? _1,234,567_

**5.** I'm an odd six-digit number whose tens digit is less than the tens digit in 345,211. My ones digit is greater than the ones digit in 345,208. The rest of my digits are the same as these two numbers. What number am I? _345,209_

**6.** I'm a number that ends in 0 or 5. I have exactly three 1s and three 0s for digits. What number could I be?

Possible answers: 111,000; 110,100; 100,110; 1,000,115

---

**GPS** PROBLEM 3, STUDENT PAGE 60

Suppose you have 5 neon markers: green, purple, blue, yellow, and pink. You choose 2 markers to make a drawing.

**a.** How many different choices do you have?

**b.** If one color must be green, how many choices do you have?

**— Understand —**

**1.** What do you know?

Part a. _5 markers of different colors, you choose 2_

Part b. _1 marker must be green._

**2.** What must you find?

Part a. _Number of choices you have_

Part b. _Number of choices you have if one must be green_

**— Plan —**

How can you organize your answers? _Make an organized list._

**— Solve —**

List your choices. How many are there?

Part a. _G Pu, G B, G Y, G Pi; Pu B, Pu Y, Pu Pi; B Y, B Pi; Y P; 10_

Part b. _G Pu, G B, G Y , G Pi; 4_

**— Look Back —**

How can you check your answers? _Use markers or crayons._

SOLVE ANOTHER PROBLEM

What if the same set of 5 markers had 2 blue markers and no green markers? What are your choices?

B Pu, B Pi, B Y, B B; Pu Pi, Pu Y; Pi Y

## Comparing Numbers

**Literature** In a library, the Dewey Decimal System groups books by subjects. Here are the first five categories.

| Number | Category |
|---|---|
| 000-099 | Encyclopedias, magazines, almanacs, bibliographies |
| 100-199 | Philosophy, psychology, ethics |
| 200-299 | Religion and myths |
| 300-399 | Sociology (Civics, economics, education) |
| 400-499 | Language, dictionaries, grammar |

**1.** In which category does a book with the number 317 belong?

**sociology**

**2.** What is the greatest number a book could have if it were an encyclopedia?

**99**

**3.** Could a book with the number 452 be a dictionary? Explain.

**Yes; 452 is between 400 and 499.**

**4.** What is the least number a book could have if it was about Native American myths?

**200**

Solve the riddles.

**5.** I am greater than 23,451 by 1,000. What number am I?

**24,451**

**6.** I am less than 34,211 by 2 hundreds. What number am I?

**34,011**

**7.** I'm the number between 9,999 and 10,001.  **10,000**

---

## Ordering Numbers

**Social Studies** Groups of years are sometimes given names. Some of these are:

Decade: 10 years     Century: 100 years     Millennium: 1,000 years

Place the groups of years in order from shortest to longest.

**1.** 3 centuries, 1 millennium, 9 decades

**9 decades, 3 centuries, 1 millennium**

**2.** 18 decades, 1 century, 5 millenniums

**1 century, 18 decades, 5 millenniums**

**3.** 47 centuries, 2 millenniums, 89 decades

**89 decades, 2 millenniums, 46 centuries**

**4.** In Abraham Lincoln's Gettysburg Address he said "four score and seven years ago." He could have said "eight decades and seven years ago." How many years was Lincoln referring to in this quote?

**87 years**

Solve.

**5.** Use the digits 1, 2, and 3. Create as many 3-digit numbers as you can. Order the numbers from least to greatest.

**123; 132; 213; 231; 312; 321**

**6.** Use the digits 5, 5, 5 and 1. Create as many 4-digit numbers as you can. Order the numbers from greatest to least.

**5,551; 5,515; 5,155; 1,555**

**7.** Write three numbers in order from least to greatest that are greater than 21,894 but less than 42,189.

**Check students' answers**

---

## Exploring Rounding

Show the height of each of these famous mountains on a number line. On each number line, show the number that is the mountain's height rounded to the nearest thousand. Then answer the questions. **Check students' answers.**

**Famous Mountains of the World**

| Mountain | Height in feet | |
|---|---|---|
| Mt. Everest | 29,028 | 0  5,000  10,000  15,000  20,000  25,000  30,000 |
| Mt. McKinley | 20,320 | 0  5,000  10,000  15,000  20,000  25,000  30,000 |
| Mt. Ararat | 16,946 | 0  5,000  10,000  15,000  20,000  25,000  30,000 |
| Mt. Olympus | 9,550 | 0  5,000  10,000  15,000  20,000  25,000  30,000 |
| Mt. Rushmore | 5,725 | 0  5,000  10,000  15,000  20,000  25,000  30,000 |

**1.** How did you decide where to show Mt. Ararat's rounded height on the number line?

**Possible answer: 16,946 rounded to 17,000 which is less than halfway between 15,000 and 20,000.**

**2.** You are climbing Mt. Olympus, and are at 6,405 ft high. Round this number to the nearest 1,000. Show your position on the Mt. Olympus number line. About how far from the mountain top are you? How do you know?

**6,000 feet; point (on number line) should be close to 5,000; About 4,000, since the difference between my point and Mt. Olympus' point at 10,000 is 4,000.**

**3.** Explain how to decide if Mt. Rushmore's height is closer to 5,000 feet or 10,000 feet.

**Possible answer: 7,500 is halfway between 5,000 and 10,000. 5,725 is less than 7,500, so it is closer to 5,000.**

---

## Telling Time

**Careers** A work schedule shows when certain things happen every day, such as starting times and work breaks.

Use the clocks to write the missing times.

**1.** ___**8:00 A.M.**___ Work begins.

**2.** ___**10:15 A.M.**___ Morning break ends.

**3.** ___**1:00 P.M.**___ Lunch break ends.

**4.** ___**3:45 P.M.**___ Afternoon break ends.

**5.** ___**5:00 P.M.**___ Work ends.

**6.** Doreen's dentist appointment is at half past two in the afternoon. She arrives at 2:15 P.M. Is she early or late? Explain.

**She is early. 2:15 P.M. is fifteen minutes before 2:30 P.M.**

**7.** Ron and Will met to go ice skating. Ron arrived at quarter to three. Will arrived at 2:55. Who arrived first? Explain.

**Ron arrived first. 2:45 is ten minutes before 2:55.**

## Exploring Time: Exact or Estimate?

Read the following story. Change all the inappropriate units of time to make a sensible story. Write the correct sentences below.

Mrs. Spoon woke up at 6:20 A.M. It took her 1 minute to get ready for work. On her way out to the car, she noticed her neighbor, Emily, was having car trouble. She told Emily she would go inside in a few days and call the tow truck. The tow-truck service said they would be there in 15 years. Mrs. Spoon slipped on a patch of ice as she walked back to her car. She looked around for an hour before getting up, so she could find a less slippery place to walk. In a couple of months she was in her car. It usually took her 30 seconds to get to work, but today it took her a week. Mrs. Spoon finally arrived at the office. She had been working there since she left college 5 hours ago.

It took her 1 hour to get ready for work.

She told Emily she would go inside in a few minutes and call the tow truck.

The tow truck service said they would be there in 15 minutes.

She looked around for a second before getting up, so she could find a less slippery place to walk.

In a couple of minutes she was in her car.

It usually took her 30 minutes to get to work, but today it took her an hour.

She had been working there since she left college 5 years ago.

_____

_____

---

## Elapsed Time

**Careers** Flight attendants and pilots may fly between many cities in a day. Karyn is a pilot. Her schedule for Monday is shown below. Use the schedule to answer the questions.

| Departure | Arrival |
| --- | --- |
| St. Louis 7:35 A.M. | Chicago - O'Hare 8:25 A.M. |
| Chicago - O'Hare 9:40 A.M. | Houston 2:55 P.M. |

1. How long is Karyn's flight from St. Louis to Chicago?
**50 minutes**

2. How long is Karyn's break between flights?
**1 hour and 15 minutes**

3. On Monday, how many hours will Karyn be flying the plane?
**5 hours and 5 minutes**

4. Sam and his dad start to play checkers at 7:57 P.M. They play until 8:22 P.M. How long does their game last? **25 minutes**

5. A play begins at 7:30 P.M. and lasts for 2 hours and 17 minutes. What time does the play end? **9:47 P.M.**

Use the bus schedule to answer the questions below.

| Leave Station | Arrive | | | | |
| --- | --- | --- | --- | --- | --- |
| | A St. | B St. | 3rd Ave. | Pier St. | Mall |
| 11:55 a.m. | 12:00 p.m. | 12:05 p.m. | 12:11 p.m. | 12:15 p.m. | 12:25 p.m. |
| 12:15 p.m. | 12:20 p.m. | 12:25 p.m. | 12:31 p.m. | 12:35 p.m. | 12:45 p.m. |
| 12:35 p.m. | 12:40 p.m. | 12:45 p.m. | 12:51 p.m. | 12:55 p.m. | 1:05 p.m. |

6. If you take the 12:15 bus and get off 20 minutes later, where will you be? **Pier St.**

7. How long does it take to go from the station to the mall? **30 minutes; Half an hour**

---

## Exploring the Calendar

June is a busy month! It's time to fill in the calendar!

| Sunday | Monday | Tuesday | Wednesday | Thursday | Friday | Saturday |
| --- | --- | --- | --- | --- | --- | --- |
| | | | | | | 1 |
| P 2 | 3 | 4 | S 5 | 6 | 7 | C 8 |
| 9 | 10 | 11 | 12 | 13 | OFF 14 | ● 15 |
| P FD 16 | 17 | B 18 | 19 | ☼ 20 | 21 | 22 |
| 23 | 24 | 25 | 26 | K 27 | 28 | 29 |
| P ○ 30 | | | | | | |

Find the correct date for each Special Day listed below and follow the *What to do* directions to mark it on the calendar.

| Special Day | When | What to do |
| --- | --- | --- |
| Swimming pool opens | the first Wednesday | Write an "S." |
| Craft Fair | the second Saturday | Write a "C." |
| Puppet Show | every other Sunday, starting June 2 | Write a "P." |
| Bike Race | the third Tuesday | Write a "B." |
| Camera Day at Park | 9 days after bike race | Write a "K." |
| Flag Day | 1 day before new moon | Draw a flag. |
| The full moon | 4 weeks after the first puppet show | Draw a circle. |
| The new moon | 1 week after craft fair | Draw a dark circle. |
| Summer begins! | 1 week before camera day | Draw a sun. |
| Father's Day | the third Sunday | Write "FD." |

If Flag Day falls on a weekend, workers are given Friday and Monday off. Otherwise, workers just get Flag Day off. Write "off" on the calendar on each day workers will have off.

---

## Decision Making

Your class is making a fifteen-minute video about your school for new students. The video will include an introduction, information about the teachers, students, after-school activities, and a tour of the building.

You need to plan your video so that you cover all your information in the time allowed.

1. What do you need to decide?
**Possible answer: How many parts to have and how long to make each part**

2. How many different kinds of information will you have in your video?
**5**

3. Do you think you should have a separate part for each kind of information, or combine some of them together? Why?
**Check answers; Answers will vary.**

4. Do you think all the parts should be the same length, or should some parts be longer than other? Why?
**Check answers; Answers will vary.**

5. Make a schedule for your video and write it in the space below.
**Schedule should include information needed and total 15 minutes**

_____

_____

_____

## Exploring Addition and Subtraction Patterns

1. Oakdale School is collecting cans for a recycling center. Fourth grade students collected 800 cans. Third grade students collected 500 cans. Josh wants to know the total number of cans collected by the third and fourth grade students.

   a. Explain how Josh can add 800 and 500 mentally.
   **He can use addition patterns.**

   b. What basic fact could help him find the sum? **8 + 5**

   c. What is the total number of cans collected by the third and fourth grade students? **1,300**

   d. How many more cans were collected by fourth grade students than by third grade students? **300**

2. Students at the Wilson School also collected cans for the recycling center. The third grade students collected 700 cans. Fourth grade students collected 400 cans.

   a. How can you use mental math to find the total number of cans collected by students at Wilson School?
   **Use addition patterns.**

   b. What basic fact could help you find the sum? **7 + 4**

   c. What is the total number of cans collected by the third and fourth grade students at Wilson School? **1,100**

   d. How many more cans were collected by third grade students than by fourth grade students? **300**

   e. How did you use 7 − 4 to solve 700 − 400?
   **Used the basic fact of 7 − 4 and added the two zeros to the answer**

3. Which school collected the most cans? How many more cans did they collect? **Oakdale School, 200**

---

## Exploring Adding and Subtracting on a Thousand Chart

Marty saves baseball cards. He has a total of 730 cards in his collection. He wants to give 180 cards to his friend Marie.

1. Marty wants to know how many cards he will have left in his collection after he gives Marie 180 cards.

   a. How could Marty use a thousand chart to find his new card total?
   **Start at 730 and move back 1 hundred and 8 tens.**

   b. How could Marty use mental math to find his new card total?
   **730 − 200 = 530; 530 + 20 = 550**

   c. Use mental math or a thousand chart to find Marty's new card total. **550**

2. Marie had 260 of her own cards. Then Marty gave her 180 cards from his collection.

   a. Describe two ways Marie could use a thousand chart to find her new card total.
   **Possible answers: Start at 260 and move forward 1 hundred and 8 tens; start at 180 and move forward 2 hundreds and 6 tens.**

   b. How could Marie use mental math to find her new card total?
   **260 + 100 = 360; 360 + 80 = 440**

   c. Use mental math or a thousand chart to find Marie's new card total. **440**

3. Who has more cards, Marty or Marie? How many more? **Marty; 110 more**

4. Marty buys another 170 cards and Marie buys another 90. Now how many do each have? **Marty: 720, Marie: 530**

---

## Estimating Sums and Differences

**Social Studies** The chart shows the number of inventions registered in the United States between 1800 and 1860. Use the chart to answer the questions below.

| Year | Number of Inventions |
|------|----------------------|
| 1800 | 41 |
| 1810 | 223 |
| 1820 | 155 |
| 1830 | 544 |
| 1840 | 458 |
| 1850 | 883 |
| 1860 | 4,357 |

1. About how many more inventions were created in 1850 than in 1820? **700**

2. About how many inventions were created from 1810 through 1820? **400**

3. About how many more inventions were created in 1860 than from 1810 through 1830? **3,000**

4. In which years were there almost the same number of inventions? **1810, 1820; 1830, 1840**

The Zigot company makes bicycles. The chart shows how many bicycles were made over a five-day period.

| Day | Monday | Tuesday | Wednesday | Thursday | Friday |
|-----|--------|---------|-----------|----------|--------|
| Bicycles Made | 1,745 | 2,319 | 2,832 | 1,601 | 1,459 |

5. About how many bicycles were made during the first two days of the week? **4,000**

6. What is the approximate difference between the greatest and the least number of bicycles made during the week? **About 2,000**

---

**GPS** **PROBLEM 5, STUDENT PAGE 101**

The table shows the number of school lunches served in a week.

| Day | Lunch | Number Served |
|-----|-------|---------------|
| Monday | Hamburgers | 285 |
| Tuesday | Baked chicken | 189 |
| Wednesday | Spaghetti | 329 |
| Thursday | Chicken nuggets | 423 |
| Friday | Pizza | 397 |

The cafeteria provides milk with each meal. It also sells milk to students who bring bag lunches. Last Wednesday, 20 students bought milk. How many cartons of milk did the cafeteria need that day?

— **Understand** —

1. What do you know?
   **How many students bought milk**

2. What do you need to know? **How many cartons of milk the cafeteria needed on Wednesday**

— **Plan** —

3. Do you need an exact answer or will an estimate do? **Exact answer**

— **Solve** —

4. What operation will you use? **Addition**

5. How many cartons of milk did the cafeteria need on Wednesday? **349**

— **Look Back** —

6. Is your answer reasonable? Explain why.
   **Yes, because 330 + 20 = 350; 349 is close to 350.**

| SOLVE ANOTHER PROBLEM |
|---|

Last Friday, the cafeteria sold 28 more pizza lunches than it did this Friday. How many pizza lunches were sold last Friday? **425**

## Adding

**Sports** This table shows how many games were won and lost by five NBA head coaches. Use the table to answer **1–4**.

| Coach | Won | Lost | Teams |
|---|---|---|---|
| Pat Riley | 533 | 194 | Los Angeles Lakers (1981–90) |
| K.C. Jones | 463 | 193 | Washington Bullets (1973–76)<br>Boston Celtics (1983–88) |
| Billy Cunningham | 454 | 196 | Philadelphia 76ers (1977–85) |
| Red Auerbach | 938 | 479 | Washington Capitols (1946–49)<br>Tri-Cities Blackhawks (1949–50)<br>Boston Celtics (1950–66) |
| Tom Heinsohn | 427 | 263 | Boston Celtics (1969–77) |

1. Red Auerbach was the head coach of three different teams. How many games did he coach?  **1,417 games**

2. What is the total number of games won by Pat Riley and Billy Cunningham?  **987 games**

3. What is the total number of games lost by Tom Heinsohn and K.C. Jones?  **456 games**

4. What is the total number of games won by all five coaches?  **2,815 games**

5. Frieda makes beaded necklaces. She has 325 blue beads and 219 red beads. How many beads does she have in all?  **544 beads**

6. **Choose a strategy** For the high school football games on Saturday and Sunday, 257 and 394 tickets were sold. How many more tickets were sold for the Sunday game than the Saturday game?

   • Use Objects/Act It Out
   • Draw a Picture
   • Look for a Pattern
   • Guess and Check
   • Use Logical Reasoning
   • Make an Organized List
   • Make a Table
   • Solve a Simpler Problem
   • Work Backward

   a. What strategy would you use to solve the problem?  **Strategies will vary.**

   b. Answer the problem.  **137 games**

---

## Column Addition

**History** Marco Polo is known for his 4-year journey from Italy to China in the 13th century. He returned to Italy 24 years later where he shared his knowledge of useful Chinese customs. The map below shows the approximate path of Marco Polo's trip.

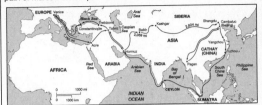

1. Marco Polo began his journey in Venice. How far did he travel to arrive at Hormuz? The distance from Acre to Hormuz is 3,029 miles.  **4,794 miles**

2. How far did Marco Polo travel to arrive at Kashgar?  **6,853 miles**

3. Was the distance from Venice to Hormuz greater or less than the distance from Hormuz to Cambaluc? Explain.

   **The distance is greater from Hormuz to Cambaluc. 2,059 + 2,824 = 4,883 miles; 1,765 + 3,029 = 4,794 miles; 4,883 mile > 4,794 miles**

5. Landon has a coin collection with 789 pennies, 231 nickels, 408 dimes, and 149 quarters. How many coins does he have in his collection?  **1,577 coins**

6. Patti's school library has 27 encyclopedias, 14 dictionaries, 348 fiction books, and 13 atlases. How many books are in the library?  **402 books**

---

## Subtracting

Use the table for **1–4**.

| Average Snowfall | |
|---|---|
| **Place** | **Snowfall in Inches** |
| Buffalo, NY | 92 |
| Caribou, ME | 113 |
| Juneau, AK | 103 |
| Mt. Washington, NH | 247 |

1. Which place gets the least snowfall?  **Buffalo, NY**

2. How much more snowfall does Juneau get than Buffalo?  **11 inches**

3. How much more snow does the place with the most snowfall get than the place with the least snowfall?  **155 inches**

4. What is the total amount of snowfall in the places listed in the table?  **555 inches**

5. Michael had 397 stickers in his collection. He gave away 49 and lost 126. How many stickers does Michael have left?  **222 stickers**

6. **Choose a strategy** Suppose you offered juice or milk to 10 guests. Three guests said, "I would like juice, but only if you have apple juice. Otherwise, I would like milk." Two guests said, "I would like milk, but only if you have chocolate milk. Otherwise, I would like juice." Five guests said, "I would like juice, but only if you have orange juice. Otherwise, I would like milk." If you had only orange juice and regular milk, how many guests would have juice?

   • Use Objects/Act It Out
   • Draw a Picture
   • Look for a Pattern
   • Guess and Check
   • Use Logical Reasoning
   • Make an Organized List
   • Make a Table
   • Solve a Simpler Problem
   • Work Backward

   a. What strategy would you use to solve the problem?  **Possible answers: Make an Organized List; Draw a Picture.**

   b. Answer the problem.  **7 guests**

---

## Subtracting with Middle Zeros

**Science** Scientists have discovered about 500 active volcanoes on Earth. A few are listed below.

| Volcano | Height |
|---|---|
| Kilauea, USA | 4,090 feet |
| Mt. Katmai, Alaska | 6,700 feet |
| Mt. Melbourne, Antarctica | 9,000 feet |
| Mt. Saint Helens, USA | 9,677 feet |
| Mt. Tarawera, New Zealand | 3,645 feet |

1. Which of these volcanoes is the tallest?  **Mt. St. Helens**

2. What is the difference in height between the tallest volcano and the shortest volcano?  **6,032 ft**

3. How much taller is Mt. Katmai than Mt. Tarawera?  **3,055 ft**

4. How much taller is Mt. St. Helens than Mt. Melbourne?  **677 ft**

5. One mile is 5,280 feet.

   a. Which volcanoes are under 1 mile in height?  **Kilauea and Mt. Tarawera**

   b. How many feet less than 2 miles is Mt. St. Helens?  **883 ft**

6. Felicia has 2,003 animals on her farm. The only animals she has are sheep and goats. She has 1,379 sheep. How many goats does she have?  **624 goats**

7. Arthur made 205 scones for a school bake sale. Joe bought 28 scones. How many scones were left?  **177 scones**

8. A stationery store had 4,000 greeting cards. If they sold 2,750, how many cards are left?  **1,250 cards**

**GPS** PROBLEM 3, STUDENT PAGE 119

Kyle's first published story is 117 words long. His second story is 42 words longer. His third story is 56 words shorter than his second story. How long is his third story?

## — Understand —

**1.** How long is Kyle's first story? __117 words__

**2.** What do you need to know to answer the question?

__The length of the second story and the third story__

## — Plan —

**3. a.** How will you find the length of the second story? Explain.

__Add 42 to 117 because the second story is 42 words__
__longer than the first story.__

**b.** Write the number sentence. __117 + 42 = 159__

**4. a.** How will you find the length of the third story? Explain.

__Subtract 56 from 159 because the third story is 56 words__
__shorter than the second story.__

**b.** Write the number sentence. __159 − 56 = 103__

## — Solve —

**5.** How long is Kyle's second story? __159 words__

**6.** How long is Kyle's third story? __103 words__

## — Look Back —

**6.** What strategy could you use to check your answer?

__Possible answer: Work Backward__

SOLVE ANOTHER PROBLEM

Keesha's first draft of a story was 223 words long. When she edited the story, she crossed out 51 words and added 74 new ones. How long was the edited story? __246 words__

---

## Using Mental Math

**Health** Different activities burn different amounts of calories. Here is a chart showing about how many calories Alex burned doing various things on Saturday and Sunday.

| Activity | Time | Calories Burned |
|---|---|---|
| Light housework | $1\frac{1}{4}$ hours | 248 |
| Sitting at the movies | $3\frac{3}{4}$ hours | 375 |
| Riding a bike | $4\frac{3}{4}$ hours | 997 |
| Playing tennis | $1\frac{1}{4}$ hours | 552 |
| Walking | 1 hour | 298 |
| Studying | 2 hours | 230 |

Add or subtract mentally. Use any method you choose.

**1.** How many fewer calories did Alex burn doing housework than playing tennis? __304 calories__

**2.** It took Alex 1 hour to walk to the library to study. He studied for 2 hours. How many calories did this burn? __528 calories__

**3.** Alex spent Saturday afternoon riding his bike and played tennis on Sunday. Together, how many calories did these activities burn? __1,549 calories__

**4.** Donna bought a book for $24.95. She bought a CD for $16.99. About how much more did the book cost than the CD? __$8.00__

**5.** Donna read 136 pages of her 434-page book. How many pages are left? __298 pages__

**6.** Joanne was exercising. She did 255 push-ups and 347 sit-ups. About how many more sit-ups did she do? __90__

---

## Choosing a Calculation Method

**Social Studies** Information about four American cities is shown in the table.

| City | Population in 1994 | Tallest Building | Height of Building |
|---|---|---|---|
| Boston | 547,725 | John Hancock Tower | 790 feet |
| Atlanta | 396,052 | Nation's Bank Tower | 1,050 feet |
| Denver | 493,559 | Republic Plaza | 714 feet |
| San Francisco | 734,676 | Transamerica Pyramid | 853 feet |

Use the data to solve. Choose any method.

**1.** How many more people lived in San Francisco than in Denver in 1994? __241,117__

**2.** What was the total population of Boston and Atlanta in 1994? __943,777__

**3.** How many more people lived in the two cities with the greatest population than the two cities with the least population? __392,790__

**4.** How much taller is the Transamerica Pyramid than the John Hancock Tower? __63 ft__

**5.** How much taller is the tallest building listed than the shortest one? __336 ft__

**6.** The Toddler Toy Factory produced 57,327 toys on Monday and 62,571 toys on Tuesday.

**a.** How many more toys did it produce on Tuesday than on Monday? __5,244 toys__

**b.** How many toys did it produce all together on Monday and Tuesday? __119,898 toys__

**7.** Caroline had 236 building bricks, and her sister had 264. How many did they have in total? __500 bricks__

---

## Counting Money

**Careers** Mr. Conte, the clerk at the music store, processed the following two orders:

piano lesson books for $30.99

sheet music for $67.95

**1.** Mr. Conte received only five-dollar bills for the books.

**a.** How many bills did he receive? __7__

**b.** Should he give change? __Yes__

**c.** If so, how much? __$4.01__

**2.** Mr. Conte received 6 bills and 5 coins to pay for the sheet music. He received the exact amount. What were the bills and coins?

__3 twenty-dollar bills, 1 five-dollar bill, 2 dollars, 3 quarters,__
__and 2 dimes__

**3.** What is the least number of bills and coins you could use to make a $15.27 purchase?

__1 ten-dollar bill, 1 five-dollar bill, 1 quarter, and 2 pennies__

**4. a.** If you have 3 ten-dollar bills, 8 dollars, 16 dimes, and 21 pennies, could you make a $47.56 purchase? Explain.

__No; $39.81 < $47.56__

**b.** What is the least number of bills and coins you could use to make the $47.56 purchase?

__2 twenty-dollar bills, 1 five-dollar bill, 2 dollars, 2 quarters,__
__1 nickel, and 1 penny__

**5.** If you only had 10-dollar bills how many would you use to pay for an item that costs $56.15? __6__

## Adding and Subtracting Money

**History** In November 1929, during the time in American History known as the Great Depression, you could buy a candy bar for as little as 3¢! But a worker earned only about $25 a week.

Here are some typical Depression Age prices for items you would buy today. Find the difference in prices.

| | Item | Price in 1929 | Price in 1997 | Difference |
|---|---|---|---|---|
| 1. | Hamburger | $0.05 | $0.69 | $0.64 |
| 2. | Ice cream cone | $0.03 | $1.19 | $1.16 |
| 3. | Ticket to the movies | $0.10 | $5.50 | $5.40 |
| 4. | Bus fare | $0.08 | $1.00 | $0.92 |

5. How much would a hamburger and an ice-cream cone combined cost in
   a. 1929? __$0.08__
   b. 1997? __$1.88__

6. If you pay $20 for a shirt that costs $12.79, how much change should you receive?    __$7.21__

7. Sue went to a movie that cost $5.50. Her popcorn cost $2.50 and her soda cost $2.25.
   a. How much did Sue spend?    __$10.25__
   b. If Sue brought $15 to the movies with her, did she have enough money left to buy a book that cost $3.29 on the way home? Explain.
   __Yes; $15.00 − $10.25 = $4.75; $4.752 < 3.29__

8. Write your own subtraction problem about money. Use $30.76 and $41.80. Be sure to include the answer.
   __Check students' problems. $41.80 − $30.76 = $11.04__

---

## Exploring Making Change

1. When you give change to a customer, you usually count on from the price of the purchase to the amount which the customer has given to you. Write what the cashier should say when counting change from a $43.27 purchase paid for with a $50 dollar bill.
   __Possible answer: $43.27, $43.28, $43.29, $43.30, $43.40,__
   __$43.50, $43.75, $44, $45, $50__

2. Have you ever noticed that in some stores, next to the cash register, there is a small container of pennies? Customers are allowed to take pennies out to pay for their purchase.
   a. Why is this helpful?
   __Possible answer: Some people take pennies out so that__
   __they can give the clerk an amount closer to exact change.__
   __Then they can receive higher-value coins or bills in change.__
   b. Suppose there are 10 pennies in the container. If your purchase was $12.27 and you paid with a 20-dollar bill, how many pennies would you take from the container? Why? How would this affect your change?
   __Possible answer: Take 2 pennies from the container; this__
   __will reduce the coin part of the change to 3 quarters,__
   __instead of 2 quarters, 2 dimes, and 3 pennies.__

3. If a customer paid for a $4.89 purchase with a $20-dollar bill, what is the least number of coins and bills they could get in change?
   __1 ten-dollar bill, 1 five-dollar bill, 1 dime and 1 penny.__

4. If you had no bills, what is the least number of coins you could use for the customer in change?
   __60 quarters, 1 dime and 1 penny.__

---

## Exploring Algebra: Balancing Number Sentences

1. a. Write the following problem as a number sentence:
   106
   + n
   ___
   178        __106 + n = 178__
   b. What is the value of n? __72__

2. a. Write the number sentence each workmat shows. __14 = n + 8__
   b. What is the value of n? __6__

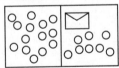

3. a. Draw a number sentence workmat that shows 6 + n = 13.
   b. What is the value of n? __7__

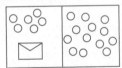

4. Write three number sentences with the same meaning as n + 5 = 12.
   __5 + n = 12; 12 = 5 + n; 12 = n + 5__

5. a. Draw a number sentence workmat that shows n + n = 10.
   b. What is the value of n? __5__

---

**GPS** PROBLEM 6, STUDENT PAGE 137

Continue the pattern. Describe the rule.

2,001; 1,901; 1,811; 1,731; 1,661; ____; ____; ____

**— Understand —**

1. What does the problem ask you to find?
   __The next 3 numbers and the pattern__

2. Would it seem reasonable to assume your answer would begin with:
   a. About 3,000    b. About 1,751    c. About 1,600

**— Plan —**

3. Write the difference between:
   a. The first 2 numbers __100__
   b. The second and third numbers __90__
   c. The third and fourth numbers __80__

**— Solve —**

4. a. What is the pattern so far? __Minus: 100, 90, 80, 70__
   b. What will you do to continue the pattern? __Minus: 60, 50, 40__

5. a. What are the next 3 numbers? Describe the rule?
   __1,601; 1551; 1511; Subtract 100, then 90, then 80, and so on.__

**— Look Back —**

6. Describe one way you can check your answer.
   __Start with the last number and add 40, then 50, then 60, and__
   __so on. The sums should be the numbers in the pattern.__

SOLVE ANOTHER PROBLEM

Continue the pattern. Describe the rule.

Z, X, Y, W, X, __V__, __W__, __U__

__Move back 2 letters, then forward 1 letter.__

Name _____

Problem Solving
4-1

## Reviewing the Meaning of Multiplication

**Science** Earth is not the only planet that has a moon. Most of the other planets in our solar system also have moons. In many cases, they have more than one moon.

1. In 1610, Galileo discovered 4 moons on Jupiter. Today, scientists believe that Jupiter has 4 times as many moons as Galileo saw. How many known moons does Jupiter have?
**16 moons**

2. Mars has 2 known moons. Saturn is known to have 9 times as many moons as Mars. How many known moons does Saturn have?
**18 moons**

3. Until 1989, scientists had only discovered 2 of Neptune's moons. Since then, scientists have found 4 times as many moons orbiting Neptune as they originally thought. How many known moons does Neptune have?
**8 moons**

4. Uranus is known to have 5 times as many moons as Earth. How many known moons does Uranus have?
**5 moons**

5. Suppose you go to soccer practice 5 days a week. How many days would you go to practice in 4 weeks?
**20 days**

6. Suppose you work on homework 2 hours a day. How many hours would you work in 5 days?
**10 hours**

7. A magazine costs $3. How much would you pay for 6 magazines?
**$18**

8. A tray of blueberry muffins contains 2 cups of blueberries. How many blueberries are in 3 trays?
**6 cups**

Use with pages 148–149. **41**

---

Name _____

Problem Solving
4-2

## Exploring Patterns in Multiplying by 0, 1, 2, 5, and 9

| 51 | 52 | 53 | 54 | 55 | 56 | 57 | 58 | 59 | 60 |
|----|----|----|----|----|----|----|----|----|-----|
| 61 | 62 | 63 | 64 | 65 | 66 | 67 | 68 | 69 | 70 |
| 71 | 72 | 73 | 74 | 75 | 76 | 77 | 78 | 79 | 80 |
| 81 | 82 | 83 | 84 | 85 | 86 | 87 | 88 | 89 | 90 |
| 91 | 92 | 93 | 94 | 95 | 96 | 97 | 98 | 99 | 100 |

Use the half of a hundred chart above to answer **1–3** below.

1. Do you think that 10 would have more or fewer multiples than 5 on a hundred chart? Explain.
**Fewer multiples; Possible answer: They are spaced farther apart, so there are fewer of them.**

2. How many multiples does 1 have on the half of a hundred chart above? Explain.
**50; Every number is a multiple of 1.**

3. How many multiples does 0 have on the half of a hundred chart above? Explain.
**None; only 0 is a multiple of 0.**

4. How do you know that $45 \times 23 = 23 \times 45$ without finding their products?
**Two numbers can be multiplied in any order.**

5. Tell if each number is a multiple of 2, 5, both, or neither.
a. 714 _____**2**_____
b. 1,850 _____**Both**_____
c. 30 _____**Both**_____
d. 765 _____**5**_____

**42** Use with pages 150–151.

---

Name _____

Problem Solving
4-3

## Multiplying with 3 and 4 as Factors

**History** Presidential elections happen every 4 years. This 4-year cycle is called a term.

1. Franklin D. Roosevelt served a little more than 3 full terms as president. About how long was he president?
**About 12 years**

2. In 1944, Roosevelt was elected to serve a 4th term, which he never completed. How many years would Roosevelt have been in office if he had completed a 4th term?
**16 years**

3. Because Roosevelt won so many elections, Congress passed a law. It states that presidents can only serve 2 terms. How many years can a president remain in office today?
**8 years**

4. Adrienne and Derrick each bought 4 comic books.
a. How many comic books did they buy in all?
**8 comic books**
b. Each comic book they bought cost $3. How much did they spend in all?
**$24**

5. Aaron practices the piano 7 days a week. How many days does he practice in 4 weeks?
**28 days**

6. Joel made 3 roundtrips to the next town. The roundtrip is a total of 6 miles. How many miles did he travel?
**18 miles**

7. Keith went swimming 3 days a week during his summer vacation. His summer vacation was 9 weeks long. How many days did he go swimming?
**27 days**

8. It takes Alan 4 minutes to complete a puzzle. How long will it take him to complete 5 puzzles?
**20 minutes**

Use with pages 152–153. **43**

---

Name _____

Problem Solving
4-4

## Multiplying with 6, 7, and 8 as Factors

1. Niles multiplied two numbers. The product was 32. One factor was 8. What was the other factor?
**4**

2. Dawn multiplied two numbers. The product was 63. One factor was 9. What was the other factor?
**7**

3. Tickets to the movie cost $7.00 each. How much money would you need to buy 6 tickets?
**$42.00**

4. Kenneth paid $4.00 each for himself and 7 other people to see a show. How much did all the tickets cost?
**$32.00**

5. Notebooks cost $6.00 each. How much money would you need to buy 4 notebooks?
**$24.00**

6. Suppose a pool has 8 lanes for lap swimming. Each lane is 5 feet wide. How wide is the pool?
**40 feet**

7. Steve can cook only 2 eggs at a time in his saucepan. He wants to boil 6 eggs for 7 minutes each. How long will it take?
**21 minutes**

8. **Choose a strategy** Garden A has 6 rows. Each row in Garden A has 8 heads of lettuce growing in it. Garden B has 4 rows. There are the same number of heads of lettuce in Garden A as there are in Garden B. How many heads of lettuce are there in each row in Garden B?

- Use Objects/Act It Out
- Draw a Picture
- Look for a Pattern
- Guess and Check
- Use Logical Reasoning
- Make an Organized List
- Make a Table
- Solve a Simpler Problem
- Work Backward

a. What strategy would you use to solve the problem?
**Possible answer: Use Logical Reasoning.**

b. Answer the problem.
**12 heads of lettuce**

**44** Use with pages 154–157.

**172**

## Exploring Patterns in Multiples of 10, 11, and 12

Use a hundred chart to help you answer each question.

**1.** List the multiples of 10 in order.
**0, 10, 20, 30, 40, 50, 60, 70, 80, 90, 100**

**2.** Write a rule using addition for the multiples of 10.
**Add 10.**

**3.** List the multiples of 11 in order.
**0, 11, 22, 33, 44, 55, 66, 77, 88, 99**

**4.** Write a rule using addition for the multiples of 11.
**Add 11.**

**5.** List the multiples of 12 in order.
**0, 12, 24, 36, 48, 60, 72, 84, 96**

**6.** Write a rule using addition for the multiples of 12.
**Add 12.**

**7.** Write a rule using addition to find the multiples of any number.
**Add the number to each previous multiple.**

**8.** What other patterns do you see on a hundred chart?
**Possible answers: Rows increase by 10, all numbers in a column have the same ones digit.**

**9.** What patterns can you find in the sums of digits in a column?
**They increase by 1.**

**10.** What patterns do you notice in the diagonal from 1 to 100?
**Numbers increase by 11.**

Use with pages 158–159. **45**

---

## Decision Making

The cross country ski club is planning a weekend trip to Manchester, Vermont. They are leaving for the trip in 6 weeks. They need to raise about $40 per person for the trip. There are 12 students in the club, so they need to raise $480 in 6 weeks. How should the club raise money?

**Facts and Data**
6 students are not free on Tuesdays.
4 students are not free on Thursdays.

Possible jobs:

| Day | Job | Number of Hours per Student | Pay |
|-----|-----|-----|-----|
| Tuesday | Shoveling Snow | 2 hours | $5 per hour |
| Thursday | Walking Dogs | 2 hours | $4 per hour |

**1.** How many students are available to work on Tuesdays? **6 students**
**2.** How many students are available to work on Thursdays? **8 students**
**3.** How much can the club earn in a week shoveling snow? **$60**
**4.** How much can the club earn in a week walking dogs? **$64**
**5.** How many weeks will it take to earn $480 shoveling snow? walking dogs?
**8 weeks shoveling snow; $7\frac{1}{2}$ weeks walking dogs**

**6. a.** If the club members worked at both jobs each week, how much would they earn per week? **$124**

**b.** About how many weeks would it take to earn $480?
**About 4 or 5 weeks working at both jobs**

**7.** What do you think the club should do to earn the money they need for the trip? Explain.
**Possible answer: 6 of the students should shovel snow each week and 6 of the students should walk dogs each week, because they will make over $480 in 6 weeks.**

**46** Use with pages 162–163.

---

## Reviewing the Meaning of Division

**Language Arts** Books are often divided into sections called chapters. Sometimes chapters are grouped together to form parts. *Gulliver's Travels*, by Jonathan Swift, is divided into 4 parts, and each one of those parts is divided into chapters.

**1.** Mark is reading Part I (A Voyage to Lilliput) of *Gulliver's Travels*. He has 63 pages to read. If he reads 7 pages each day, how long will it take him to read Part I? **9 days (nights)**

**2.** Part I of *Gulliver's Travels* has 8 chapters. If your class spends 16 days studying Part I, how many days will you spend on each chapter? **2 days**

**3.** Chapter 1 of Part I is 9 pages long. If you want to read the chapter in 3 days, how many pages should you read each day? **3 pages**

**4.** Lila, who is planning on competing in a spelling bee, needs to study the spelling of 72 frequently misspelled words. She has 9 days to get ready. How many words should she study each day? **8 words**

**5.** Gary is assigned a role in a play on May 1st. He has 36 lines to memorize. He needs to know all of his lines by heart by May 6th.

**a.** If he studies the same number of lines each day, how many should he memorize each day? **6 lines**

**b.** Suppose Gary forgets to study his lines on May 1st and 2nd. How many lines does he need to memorize each of the remaining days? **9 lines**

**6.** Graham is backpacking with his family. They have 56 miles to cover in a week. How many miles should they walk in a day? **8 miles**

Use with pages 166–167. **47**

---

## Exploring Multiplication and Division Stories

**1.** Suppose you wanted to write a multiplication and division story with the numbers 4, 20, and 5. Write the number sentences you could use.
**$4 \times 5 = 20, 20 \div 4 = 5, 5 \times 4 = 20, 20 \div 5 = 4$**

**2.** Some fact families only have 2 number sentences.

**a.** Write four fact families that have only 2 number sentences.
**Possible answers: $1 \times 1 = 1, 1 \div 1 = 1; 2 \times 2 = 4,$**
**$4 \div 2 = 2; 3 \times 3 = 9, 9 \div 3 = 3; 4 \times 4 = 16; 16 \div 4 = 4$**

**b.** What do the fact families with 2 number sentences have in common? Explain.
**Possible answer: Each family includes a number multiplied by itself.**

**3.** Suppose you want to write a multiplication or division story with the number 36. Write all of the possible basic facts (using factors under 10) you could use.
**$4 \times 9 = 36, 9 \times 4 = 36, 36 \div 4 = 9, 36 \div 9 = 4;$**
**$6 \times 6 = 36, 36 \div 6 = 6$**

**4.** Describe a situation with money where you could use multiplication and division facts.
**Possible answer: Tan mowed his neighbor's lawn for 2 hours and was paid $4 per hour. How much did Tan make an hour?**

**5.** Write a multiplication or division story using the basic facts $4 \times 3$ and $12 \div 3$.
**Check students' answers.**

**48** Use with pages 168–169.

## Worksheet 4-9 (top left)

**Problem Solving 4-9**

### Dividing with 2, 5, and 9

> **Physical Education** Mike's gym teacher, Ms. Whitman, formed a bicycle club in the spring. Nine students joined the club. The club goes biking every day after school and sometimes on the weekends.

> 1. One day after school, everybody on the bike team rode the same number of miles. If the total number of miles the team rode was 36 miles, how many miles did each team member ride that day?   **4 miles**

> 2. Mike rode 40 miles over five days. If he traveled the same numbers of miles each day, how many miles did Mike ride each day?   **8 miles**

> 3. Mike rode for 2 hours each day for an entire week. How many hours did he ride during that week?   **14 hours**

4. Angie gets paid $5 per hour mowing lawns. If Angie makes $45 one week, how many hours did she work?   **9 hours**

5. There are 27 students in Mr. Morelli's 4th grade class. He asks the students to split into groups of 3 for a math lesson. How many groups of 3 students will there be?   **9 groups**

6. Joyce bought 18 marbles. She gave each of her 2 children an equal number of marbles. How many marbles did each child get?   **9 marbles**

7. Nora bought 2 shirts. Each shirt was the same price. If she paid $24.00, how much was each shirt?   **$12.00**

8. Ben is playing a game with 5 friends. 25 counters are divided equally among them. How many counters does each one get?   **5 counters**

---

## Worksheet 4-10 (top right)

**Problem Solving 4-10**

### Special Quotients

> **Fine Arts** The City Museum is putting on a small exhibit of paintings by famous European artists. A curator at the museum, Mrs. Hanson, had to research, select, and obtain the paintings for the exhibit.

> 1. Mrs. Hanson obtained 6 different paintings by the French artist, Claude Monet. How many Monet paintings were in the exhibit? Write a number sentence for this problem.   $6; 6 \div 1 = 6$

> 2. Mrs. Hanson obtained 9 different paintings from 9 different artists. How many paintings did each artist have in the exhibit? Write a number sentence for this problem.   $1; 9 \div 9 = 1$

> 3. Mrs. Hanson wanted to get 3 paintings by Matisse for the exhibit. The 3 Matisse paintings are being shared by 3 museums including the City Museum. How many paintings by Matisse were in the exhibit? Write a number sentence for this problem.   $1; 3 \div 3 = 1$

4. If the dividend of a number sentence is 0, and the divisor is greater than 0, what do you know about the quotient?

**The quotient is also 0.**

5. John gets paid $5 per hour for his job stocking shelves at the hardware store. If he makes $5 one day, how many hours did he work?   **1 hour**

6. Karen has 3 flower beds. She has planted 3 different types of flowers in each bed. How many different types of flowers did Karen plant?   **9**

7. Jim is playing a game of tiddlywinks with Cathy. Cathy says she will add 3 counters to Jim's winnings, or multiply Jim's winnings by 3. If Jim is not likely to win anything, which choice do you think he should make? Explain.

**Possible answer: Jim should choose to have Cathy add to his winnings, because $3 \times 0 = 0$.**

---

## Worksheet 4-11 (bottom left)

**Problem Solving 4-11**

### Dividing with 3 and 4

> **Fine Arts** When a composer writes a piece of music, he or she divides the music into *measures*. A measure is a part of a song. Each measure has the same number of beats. Composers sometimes write music with 3, 4 or 6 beats per measure.

> 1. A composer writes a short children's song with 27 beats, total. If there are 3 beats per measure, how many measures does the song contain?   **9**

> 2. Another song contains 32 beats, total. If there are 4 beats per measure, how many measures does this song contain?   **8**

> 3. If a third song is 11 measures long and has 44 beats total, how many beats per measure are there?   **4**

4. Jason played 9 quarters during 3 football games.

   a. If he played the same number of quarters in each game, how many quarters did he play per game?   **3**

   b. If one of the games went into overtime, and continued to 5 quarters, how many quarters did Jason spend on the bench?   **4**

5. Complete the table. Write the rule.

| In  | 16 | 21 | 24 | 27 | 32 | 33 | 36 |
|-----|----|----|----|----|----|----|----|
| Out | 4  | 7  | 6  | 9  | 8  | 11 | 9  |

Rule: **Alternate dividing by 4 and then by 3.**

6. Mark is having 3 guests to visit. He makes 12 sandwiches.

   a. How many sandwiches can each guest have?   **4**

   b. Another guest joins them. How many sandwiches will each guest have now?   **3**

---

## Worksheet 4-12 (bottom right)

**Problem Solving 4-12**

### Dividing with 6, 7 and 8

> **Science** Don't call a spider an insect! A spider is an *arachnid*. Insects have 6 legs while arachnids have 8 legs.
>
> Some insects: flies, beetles, mosquitoes, ants
>
> Some arachnids: spiders, scorpions, mites, aphids

> 1. A very careful scientist was studying photographs of her ant farm. In one picture, she counted 54 individual ant legs. How many ants were in the picture?   **9**

> 2. The same scientist came across some bug tracks in the sand. She decided the tracks were made by a scorpion. If there were 56 individual footprints in the sand, how many times did each of the scorpion's legs touch the ground?   **7**

> 3. Eight scientists on the project agreed to share the research time equally. If 40 hours are needed, how many hours is each scientist responsible for?   **5**

4. It takes 14 days for a canary egg to incubate (get ready to hatch). How many weeks is this?   **2**

5. Find the incubation period for each bird:

   a. Chickens: 21 days or __**3**__ weeks

   b. Turkeys: __**28**__ days or 4 weeks

6. It takes 28 days for a squirrel to gestate (get ready to be born). How many weeks is this?   **4**

7. Find the gestation period for each animal:

   a. Dog: 63 days or __**9**__ weeks

   b. Cat: __**56**__ days or 8 weeks

---

## Exploring Even and Odd Numbers

**1.** How many odd numbers are there between 5 and 25 (not including 5 or 25)?

9

List them:

7, 9, 11, 13, 15, 17, 19, 21, 23

**2.** How many even numbers are there between 0 and 30 (not including 0 or 30)?

14

List them:

2, 4, 6, 8, 10, 12, 14, 16, 18, 20, 22, 24, 26, 28

Possible answers:

**3.** What two even numbers can be added together to get a sum of 62?

30 + 32

**4.** What two odd numbers can be added together to get a sum of 62?

31 + 31

**5.** What kind of numbers can be added together to get a sum of 47? (Circle all correct answers.)

a. two even numbers

b. two odd numbers

(c.) one even number and one odd number

**6.** What kind of numbers can be added together to get a sum of 26? (Circle all correct answers.)

(a.) two even numbers

(b.) two odd numbers

c. one even number and one odd number

---

## Exploring Factors

**1. a.** List the factors of 12 and 24.

12: 1, 2, 3, 4, 6, 12

24: 1, 2, 3, 4, 6, 8, 12, 24

**b.** What factors do 12 and 24 have in common?

1, 2, 3, 4, 6, 12

**2. a.** List the factors of 48, 50, and 63.

48: 1, 2, 3, 4, 6, 8, 12, 16, 24, 48

50: 1, 2, 5, 10, 25, 50

63: 1, 3, 7, 9, 21, 63

**b.** Which has the greatest number of factors? 48

**c.** What factors do they all have in common? 1

**3.** Do any prime numbers end in 4? Explain.

No, if a number ends in 4, it is an even number. The only even prime number is 2.

**4.** How can a number have only 3 factors? Give examples of 3 numbers with only 3 factors.

Possible answer: When a number is a square number, it could have only 3 factors: 4, 9, 25

**5.** List the dimensions of all the rectangles you could draw to show 60.

1 by 60, 2 by 30, 3 by 20, 4 by 15, 5 by 12, 6 by 10

---

**GPS** PROBLEM 4, STUDENT PAGE 187

Sue, Leanne, and Ash made a total of 10 goals. Sue made 4 goals and Leanne made 2. Ash made twice as many goals as Leanne. How many goals did Ash make?

**— Understand —**

**1.** Underline the question you need to answer.

**2.** Circle the sentence that tells you how to find the answer.

**3.** Look at the rest of the problem. What information do you need to find the answer? Draw a box around it.

**— Plan —**

**4.** How will you find your answer? What operation will you use?

Multiply Leanne's goals by 2; Multiplication

**— Solve —**

**5.** Write a number sentence and solve the problem.

$2 \times 2 = 4$; Ash made 4 goals.

**— Look Back —**

**6.** Did it help to know how many goals Sue made or how many total goals were made?

No

**7.** How can you check your answer?

Possible answer: Divide my answer by 2. The result should be the number of goals Leanne made.

SOLVE ANOTHER PROBLEM

Daniel slept 8 hours on Mon., 6 hours Tues., 7 hours Thurs., 8 hours Fri., 9 hours Sat., and 9 hours Sun. What is the *median* number of hours Daniel slept this week?

Too little information; don't know the number of hours Daniel slept on Wed.

---

**GPS** PROBLEM 4, STUDENT PAGE 189

The Taneytown Cyclers put on a show. They used tricycles and bicycles. There were 12 tricycles and bicycles with a total of 27 wheels in the show. How many bicycles were there?

**— Understand —**

**1.** What do you know? The number of tricycles and bicycles together and the total number of wheels

**2.** What do you need to find out? The number of bicycles

**— Plan —**

**3.** Name one number that would be too high of a guess of the number of bicycles. Name another number that would be too low. Explain.

Possible answers: 12 bicycles would be too many because there would be no tricycles. 3 bicycles would be too few because there would be over 27 wheels.

**— Solve —**

**4.** Check a guess of 6 bicycles. Are there too many or too few wheels?

Too many

**5.** How many bicycles were in the show?

9

**— Check —**

**6.** Describe another strategy you could use to check your work.

Possible answer: Draw a Picture.

SOLVE ANOTHER PROBLEM

Martha and Enrique brought 24 oranges to a picnic. Enrique brought 6 more oranges than Martha. How many oranges did they each bring?

Enrique—15, Martha—9

## Multiplying Tens

**Careers** Professional photographers take many pictures of events. Then they select the best pictures to sell.

**1.** Karen used 7 rolls of film to photograph the school's sports events. Each roll has 40 exposures. How many pictures did she take?

**280 pictures**

**2.** Karen can develop 6 pictures an hour. If she works 40 hours a week, how many pictures can she develop?

**6 × 40 = 240**

**3.** The best pictures will go in the school's photo album. The album has 20 pages. Each page in the album holds 8 pictures. How many pictures will the album hold in all?

**8 × 20 = 160 pictures**

**4.** We drove to the Olympic games in 4 hours. Our speed averaged 60 miles per hour. We traveled another 3 hours at the same speed to visit a Civil War site.

**a.** How many miles did we travel to the Olympic games?

**240 miles**

**b.** How many miles did we travel from there to the Civil War site?

**180 miles**

**c.** We drove home from the Civil War site in 5 hours at 60 miles per hour. How many miles did we travel on the entire trip?

**300 + 240 + 180 = 720 miles**

**d.** Our car gets 20 miles to the gallon. If we bought 20 gallons twice on our journey, would we have enough for the whole trip?

**Yes; (20 × 2) × 20 = 800**

---

## Exploring Multiplication Patterns

Find each product using place-value blocks.

**1.**

3 × 5 tens = ____**15**____ tens = ____**150**____

**2.**

2 × 3 hundreds = ____**6**____ hundreds = ____**600**____

**3.** Linda says that the product of 3 and 700 has 2 zeros, and the product of 4 and 500 has 3 zeros. Is she correct? Explain.

**Yes; 4 × 5 = 20. The zero in 20 increases the number of zeros in the product by 1.**

Tell how many zeros will be in each product. Use place-value patterns to find each.

**4.** 4 × 700 ____**2; 2,800**____   **5.** 9 × 3,000 ____**3; 27,000**____

**6.** 8 × 4,000 ____**3; 32,000**____   **7.** 7 × 50,000 ____**4; 350,000**____

**8.** 3 × 30 ____**1; 90**____   **9.** 6 × 70 ____**1; 420**____

**10.** 5 × 200 ____**3; 1,000**____   **11.** 8 × 50 ____**2; 400**____

**12.** How are **10** and **11** different from **4–9**?

**The basic facts used to solve 10 and 11 have zeros. This adds 1 more zero to the product.**

Solve using patterns.

**13.** A ream of paper is 500 sheets of paper. A case of paper has 2 stacks of 5 reams. How many sheets of paper are in a case of paper?

**5,000 sheets of paper**

---

## Estimating Products

**Science** It takes 24 hours (one full day) for the earth to make one complete turn. The earth makes 365 complete turns every year.

**1.** Estimate the number of hours it takes the earth to make 8 complete turns.

**160 hours**

**2.** Estimate the number of times the earth turns in 5 years.

**2,000**

**3.** Does the earth turn more or less than 2,700 times in 9 years? Explain.

**More; 9 × 300 = 2,700, so 9 × 365 must be greater than 2,700.**

**4.** Which is the closest estimate for the number of hours it takes the earth to turn 7 times?

A. 210 hours   B. 280 hours   C. 140 hours   D. 100 hours

**C**

Jake rented a video game system for 5 days. The system cost $18 for a 1-day rental. He also rented 2 games. Each game cost $12.00 for a 5-day period.

**5.** About how much did Jake pay to rent the system and the games for 5 days?

**About $120**

**6.** Estimate the total cost of renting the video game system only for 6 days.

**About $120**

**7.** About how much would it cost to rent the system only for 3 days?

**About $60**

---

## Exploring Multiplication with Arrays

When you multiply a 2-digit number by a 1-digit number, remember to use your multiplication facts to help you multiply the tens columns.

**1.** 42 × 4

**a.** Write a number sentence to show the number of ones.

**4 × 2 = 8**

**b.** Write a number sentence to show the number of tens.

**4 × 40 = 160**

**c.** What is the number shown? ____**168**____

Write number sentences for the tens and the ones. Then find the total product.

**2.**
```
   5 2
 ×   3
 ─────
     6  =  __3__ × __2__  ones
+ 150  =  __3__ × __5__  tens
 ─────
   156
```

**3.**
```
   2 3
 ×   3
 ─────
     9  =  __3__ × __3__  ones
 + 60  =  __3__ × __2__  tens
 ─────
    69
```

**4.** Describe how multiplying with arrays is similar to how you solved **2** and **3**.

**Possible answer: In problems 2 and 3 I wrote the steps I did mentally when using an array.**

## Multiplying 2-Digit Numbers

**1.** Mr. Rodriguez bought 18 prizes for his school's storytelling contest. Each prize cost $4. How much money did he spend on the prizes?  $72

**2.** A dress costs $35. Sue bought 3 dresses. How much did Sue pay for the dresses?  $105

Maya bought the following items to stock her stationery store: 4 binders for $2 each, 25 boxes of notebook paper for $6 each, 24 boxes of pencils for $3 each, and 34 rubber stamps for $5 each.

**3.** How much money did Maya spend on the rubber stamps?  $170

**4.** How much money did Maya spend on notebook paper and pencils?  $222

**5.** What was the total cost of Maya's purchase?  $400

**6.** If Maya paid $500 for her purchases, how much change would she receive?  $100

**7. Choose a Strategy** Which costs more: The 34 rubber stamps, or the 4 binders, 25 boxes of paper, and 24 boxes of pencils combined?

> • Use Objects/Act It Out
> • Draw a Picture
> • Look for a Pattern
> • Guess and Check
> • Use Logical Reasoning
> • Make an Organized List
> • Make a Table
> • Solve a Simpler Problem
> • Work Backward

**a.** What strategy would you use to solve the problem?
Possible answers: Make an
Organized List; Guess and Check.

**b.** Answer the problem.
The binders, paper, and pencils cost more.

---

## Multiplying 3-Digit Numbers

**History** The Egyptian pyramids were built almost 5,000 years ago. Of the three pyramids in Egypt, the Great Pyramid is the largest. The Great Pyramid is 480 feet tall and its base is about the size of ten football fields.

**1.** The stones that were used to build the pyramids often weighed about 3 tons. How much would 108 stones weigh?
**324 tons**

**2.** Some of the pyramids' largest stones weighed 15 tons. If an elephant weighs 3 tons, how many elephants would it take to equal the weight of one stone?
**5 elephants**

**3.** If it took 25 minutes to prepare each stone for a pyramid, could 8 stones be finished in 3 hours? Explain.
**No. 25 × 8 = 200 minutes; 60 × 3 = 180 minutes**

**4.** A can of juice contains 354 mL. If Carl has 3 cans of juice and Brenda has 4, how many milliliters of juice do they have in all?
**2,478 mL**

**5.** The distance from Merrimack to Hadley is 8 times as long as the distance from Merrimack to Amherst. The distance from Merrimack to Amherst is 146 km. How far is it from Merrimack to Hadley?
**1,168 kilometers**

**6.** A movie lasts 117 minutes. Could a movie theater show the movie 4 times in 6 hours? Explain.
**No; 117 × 4 = 468 minutes; 60 × 6 = 360 minutes**

**7.** An ounce of Swiss cheese has 219 mg of calcium. How much calcium do 3 ounces of cheese contain?
**219 × 3; 657 mg**

---

## Decision Making

Suppose you and 7 friends went to a pizza parlor. Each wanted 3 slices of pizza. A large pizza has 20 slices, a medium has 8 slices, and a small has 6 slices. Two friends wanted pepperoni, one wanted sausage, three wanted only cheese, and two wanted ham. What pizzas would you order?

**1.** What are you asked to do?
Decide what pizzas to order.

**2.** How many slices of pizza do you need altogether?
8 × 3 = 24 slices

**3.** What size pizzas would you order? Describe two different orders that would provide enough slices of pizza.
Possible answers: 1 large and 1 small; 3 medium; 1 medium
and 3 small; 4 small

**4.** What strategy can you use to help you determine the toppings for each pizza?
Possible answers: Draw a picture.

**5.** What additional information would help you make your decision?
Possible answers: cost of pizzas; will those who want single
toppings want to eat pizza with more than one topping?

**6.** Make a list of the pizzas you would order. List sizes and toppings.
Answers will vary. Possible answer: 5 small, 1 with pepperoni,
1 with ham, 1 with sausage, 2 with cheese

**7.** Describe how you made your decision.
Answers will vary. Possible answer: This way everyone
can have the topping they want.

---

## Choosing a Calculation Method

**Geography** Charles lives in Boston. He often has to travel to other cities on business. He earns one frequent flier point for each mile he travels.

**1.** How many round trips between Boston and St. Louis would Charles need to take to earn 15,000 points?  8

**2. a.** How many fewer round trips to San Antonio would Charles need to take to earn 15,000 points?  3

**b.** Explain how you found your answer.
Possible answer: I found the number of round trips
Charles would have to take to San Antonio to earn 15,000
points. Then I subtracted from 8.

**3.** Describe one combination of round trips Charles could take to St. Louis and to San Antonio to earn 15,000 points.
Possible answer: 2 trips to San Antonio and 4 trips to
St. Louis

**4.** Maria, Jack, Cindy, and Ron each have jump ropes 187 centimeters long. If they lay their jump ropes end to end, how many centimeters in all will their jump ropes measure?
**748 centimeters**

**5.** Maria uses her jump rope to jump 328 times. If each of the other students jumps half that number of times, how many jumps are made in all?
**820 jumps**

## Multiplying Money

**Social Studies** Use the table to answer **1–5**.

|  | 1970 price | 1996 price |
|---|---|---|
| T-Shirt | $3.15 | $15.35 |
| Hat | $1.29 | $7.86 |
| Pennant | $0.89 | $6.29 |

**1.** How much more did 7 T-shirts cost in 1996 than in 1970?

$7 \times \$15.35 = \$107.45$; $7 \times \$3.15 = \$22.05$;

$\$107.45 - \$22.05 = \$85.40$

**2.** Would $6.00 have been enough to buy 5 hats in 1970? Explain.
No; $5 \times \$1.29 = \$6.45$

**3.** How much did 6 T-shirts cost in 1996?
$92.10

**4.** How much more would it cost to buy one T-shirt, one hat, and one pennant in 1996 than in 1970?
$24.17 more

**5.** Carlos bought 2 notebooks for $1.19 each and 3 pens for $0.79 each. Which cost more, 2 notebooks or 3 pens?
**The two notebooks cost 1 cent ($0.01) more.**

**6.** What was the total that Carlos spent?
$4.75

**5.** How much change would he get from a $10 bill?
$5.25

---

## Mental Math: Special Products

**Science** Alligators, caimans, gharials, and crocodiles are all called crocodilians. There are 26 species of crocodilians.

**1.** There are 3 species of caimans. Use mental math to find the total number of caimans if there are 25 of each species sunning themselves. — **75 caimans**

**2.** Many species of crocodilians are endangered. Today there may be only about 120 gharials in the wild. If there were 8 times that many today, how many gharials would there be all together? — **960 gharials**

**3.** Crocodilians may lay as few as 12 eggs. How many crocodilians laid eggs if the total number of eggs is 84? — **7 crocodilians**

**4.** How many minutes are there in 3 hours? — **180 minutes**

**5.** How many seconds are in 9 minutes? — **540 seconds**

**6.** How many weeks are there in 5 years? (There are 52 weeks in 1 year.) — **260 weeks**

**7.** How many hours are there in 7 days? — **168 hours**

**8.** How many minutes are there in 7 days? — **10,080 minutes**

**9.** How many days are in 5 years? (There are 365 days in a year. Ignore leap year.) — **1,825 days**

---

## Multiplying 3 Factors

**Fine Art** An artist is making collages. She has the listed materials with which to work.

The artist wants to make a pattern and duplicate the pattern 5 times for each piece of artwork.

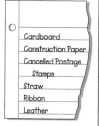

Cardboard
Construction Paper
Cancelled Postage
Stamps
Straw
Ribbon
Leather

**1.** If the artist uses 3 cancelled postage stamps in each pattern and makes 4 copies of her artwork, how many postage stamps will she need? Explain.

$3 \times (5 \times 4) = 60$ cancelled

postage stamps

**2.** Suppose the artist wants to use 2 strips of leather in each pattern and wants to make 2 copies of her artwork. How many strips of leather will she need? Explain.
$(2 \times 2) \times 5 = 20$ strips of leather

**3.** If the artist has 20 pieces of straw will she have enough to use 1 piece on each pattern and make 4 copies of her artwork? Explain.
Yes; $1 \times (5 \times 4) = 20$ pieces of straw

**4.** There are 31 floors in the Starr building. There are 3 people in each office and 7 offices on each floor. How many people work in the building? Explain.
$(31 \times 3) \times 7$; 651 people

**5.** There are 5 windows on each of the 4 sides of the building. If this is true for each of the 31 floors, how many windows are there in all?
$(5 \times 4) \times 31 = 620$ windows

---

**GPS** PROBLEM 6, STUDENT PAGE 233

ocarina $9.20

rainsticks $8.75

Joy has $50. She ordered 5 rainsticks. What is her change?

— **Understand** —

**1.** What do you know?
**Joy has $50. Joy ordered 5 rainsticks at $8.75 each.**

**2.** What do you need to find out? **Find the total cost of the 5 rainsticks. Find how much change Joy gets from her $50.**

— **Plan** —

**3.** How will you begin?
**Multiply to find the cost of the instruments.**

**4.** What's the next step?
**Subtract the total cost from $50 to find the change.**

— **Solve** —

**5.** How much change did Joy receive? $5 \times \$8.75 = \$43.75$;
$\$50.00 - \$43.75 = \$6.25$; Joy will get $6.25 in change.

— **Look Back** —

**6.** How can you check if your answer makes sense?
**Estimate: There are 5 rainsticks at about $9 each;**
$\$9 \times 5 = \$45$; $\$50 - \$45 = \$5$; the answer is reasonable.

SOLVE ANOTHER PROBLEM

Bill has $75. He ordered 8 ocarinas. What is his change? — $1.40

**GPS** PROBLEM 4, STUDENT PAGE 236

If your pattern
has 4 squares,
how many pieces
will it have in all?

| Number of squares | Number of pieces |
|---|---|
| 1 | 4 |
| 2 | 9 |
| 3 | 14 |
| 4 | |

### — Understand —
1. If the pattern has 2 squares, how
many pieces will it have in all?   **9**

2. What do you need to find out?
**how many pieces are in a pattern with 4 squares**

### — Plan —
3. Look at the table. What patterns do you see?
**As squares increase by 1, pieces increase by 5.**

4. Use the pattern to complete the table.
Fill in the table with the data you know.

### — Solve —
5. How many pieces will there be in a pattern with
4 squares?   **19 pieces**

### — Look Back —
6. What could you do to prove your answer is correct?
**Possible answer: Draw a picture.**

SOLVE ANOTHER PROBLEM

If your pattern has 7 squares, how many pieces will it have
in all?   **34**

---

## Exploring Multiplication Patterns
Find the missing factors or products.

1. a. 30 × 4 = **120**
   b. 300 × 40 = **12,000**
   c. **300** × 400 = 120,000
   d. 3,000 × **40** = 120,000

2. a. 50 × 4 = **200**
   b. 50 × **40** = 2,000
   c. **500** × 400 = 200,000
   d. 5 × **4,000** = 20,000

3. a. 9 × 30 = **270**
   b. 90 × 30 = **2,700**
   c. 900 × **30** = 27,000
   d. 90 × **3,000** = 270,000

4. a. 80 × 6 = **480**
   b. 80 × 60 = **4,800**
   c. 800 × **600** = 480,000
   d. 8,000 × **60** = 480,000

5. a. 70 × 8 = **560**
   b. 700 × 80 = **56,000**
   c. 70 × **800** = 56,000
   d. 7,000 × **8** = 56,000

6. a. 60 × 4 = **240**
   b. 90 × 40 = **2,400**
   c. **600** × 40 = 24,000
   d. 6,000 × **400** = 2,400,000

7. Describe the method you used to find the missing factors.
**Possible answer: Divide the non-zero digits of the product by
the non-zero digits of the given factor. Then use number
sense to determine the number of zeros in the missing
factor.**

8. When multiplied by a one-digit number, what multiple
of ten will always give a product with three zeros?   **1,000**

9. What is a one-digit number that will give a product
with three zeros when multiplied by 600?   **5**

10. Which one-digit numbers will give a product with
two zeros when multiplied by 500?
**1, 3, 5, 7, and 9**

---

## Estimating Products

**History** In 1873, Andrew Hallidge
introduced the cable car system
to San Francisco. At its peak just
before 1900, there were over 600
cable cars and 100 miles of track.
The great earthquake in 1906
caused extensive damage to the
cars and cable lines. Today, there
are 39 cars operating over a
10-mile network.

1. A round trip cable car ride is about 10 miles.
A cable car makes about 27 round trips
a day. Estimate how many miles the cable
car travels each day.   **About 300 miles**

2. If one cable car holds 48 people, estimate
how many people 39 cable cars will hold.   **About 2,000 people**

3. Each cable car has a brake assembly made
up of many small pieces. If each brake
assembly costs about $600, is $24,500
enough to buy brake assemblies for
39 cars?   **Yes;
40 × $600 = $24,000**

4. Each cable car is hand built by one skilled
craftsperson. It takes about 18 months
of work to build a cable car. About how
many months of work would it take to build
39 cars?   **About 800 months**

5. Mr. Benson works an average of 42 hours a week. If he
works for 48 weeks, about how many hours does he work?

**About 2,000 hours**

6. Suppose Mr. Benson works an average of 48 hours a week,
about how many more hours would he work in 48 weeks?
**About 500 hours more**

---

## Multiplying by Multiples of 10

**Recreation** Many people enjoy vacations that involve a
sport. One popular sport vacation is a bicycle tour. Bicycle
Adventures offers tours throughout the United States. You
can take a tour based on your interests and your cycling
ability.

1. There are 20 teams of bicyclists with 8 people on
each team. How many bicyclists are there?   **160**

2. a. The bicyclists travel 40 miles a day. On a 12-day
tour, how many miles will they bike?   **480 miles**

   b. The bicyclists complete 22 miles of the tour
   before lunch. How many more miles must they
   bike that day?   **18 miles**

3. The bicyclists drink water along the ride. They drink
20 cases of water. Each case contains 12 one-liter
bottles. How many liters of water do they drink?   **240 liters**

4. A van follows the bicyclists with luggage and safety
equipment. The gas tank holds 20 gallons of gasoline.
It can travel 15 miles on each gallon of gas. How
many miles can the van travel on one tank of gas?   **300 miles**

5. The bicycle tour costs $60 a day for each person.
How much will it cost a family of four each day?   **$240**

6. The average price for dinner at a local restaurant is $15. The
restaurant serves about 40 dinners a night. About how
much does the restaurant earn from dinners each day?   **$600**

7. An auditorium has 30 rows with 15 seats in each row.
Are there enough seats for 500 people? Explain.
**No, 50 more seats are needed.**

8. Alec wants to buy 30 pencils. The pencils cost $0.12
each. Alec has $3.00. Does he have enough money to
buy the pencils?
**No, he would need $3.60.**

Name _____

## Exploring Multiplying with 2-Digit Factors

Complete the multiplication.

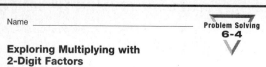

1.
$$\begin{array}{r} 32 \\ \times\ 67 \end{array}$$
$\boxed{1}\boxed{4}\ \leftarrow\ 7 \times 2$
$\boxed{2}\boxed{1}\boxed{0}\ \leftarrow\ 7 \times 30$
$\boxed{1}\boxed{2}\boxed{0}\ \leftarrow\ \boxed{6}\boxed{0} \times \boxed{2}$
$\boxed{1}\boxed{8}\boxed{0}\boxed{0}\ \leftarrow\ \boxed{6}\boxed{0} \times \boxed{3}\boxed{0}$
$\boxed{2},\boxed{1}\boxed{4}\boxed{4}$

2.
$$\begin{array}{r} 67 \\ \times\ 32 \end{array}$$
$\boxed{1}\boxed{4}\ \leftarrow\ \boxed{2} \times \boxed{7}$
$\boxed{1}\boxed{2}\boxed{0}\ \leftarrow\ \boxed{2} \times \boxed{6}\boxed{0}$
$\boxed{2}\boxed{1}\boxed{0}\ \leftarrow\ \boxed{3}\boxed{0} \times \boxed{7}$
$\boxed{1}\boxed{8}\boxed{0}\boxed{0}$
$\boxed{2},\boxed{1}\boxed{4}\boxed{4}\ \leftarrow\ \boxed{3}\boxed{0} \times \boxed{6}\boxed{0}$

3. Compare **1** and **2**. Explain how they are alike and how they differ?

**Possible answers: They have the same products; the factors are in a different order; the second and third partial products are switched.**

4. Will 23 × 76 give the same product as 32 × 67? Explain.

**No; the value of the numbers has changed.**

5. Will 47 × 52 give the same product as 57 × 42? Draw place-value blocks to show your answer.

**No; the value of the numbers has changed.**

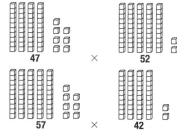

47 × 52

57 × 42

---

Name _____

## Multiplying with 2-Digit Factors

1. The Mississippi Queen was built in 1976. How many years ago was it built?

**Present year minus 1976**

2. The riverboat travels 55 miles a day up the river. How many miles will it travel in 43 days?

**2,365 miles**

3. The average weight of a suitcase brought on board the riverboat is 27 pounds. How much will 35 suitcases weigh?

**945 pounds**

4. The riverboat has 2 crew members for every 10 passengers. If there are 100 passengers, how many crew members are there?

**20**

5. There are 208 cabins on the riverboat and 78 of them have balconies. How many cabins do not have balconies?

**130 cabins**

6. There are 4 passengers in line at the breakfast buffet. Earl is ahead of Kate. Edward is behind Kate. Earl is behind Tricia. Who is first in line?

**Tricia**

7. Alan says if he reads 11 pages of his book every day for 21 days, he will finish it. How many pages are in his book?

**231 pages**

8. **Choose a Strategy** A spaceship lands in the desert. Creatures exit the spaceship. Some of the creatures have 2 large eyes. Some have 1 very large eye in the middle of their forehead. There are 19 creatures with 29 eyes. How many creatures have 2 eyes? How many creatures have 1 eye?

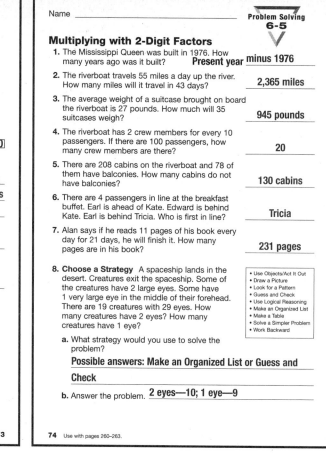

- Use Objects/Act It Out
- Draw a Picture
- Look for a Pattern
- Guess and Check
- Use Logical Reasoning
- Make an Organized List
- Make a Table
- Solve a Simpler Problem
- Work Backward

a. What strategy would you use to solve the problem?

**Possible answers: Make an Organized List or Guess and Check**

b. Answer the problem. **2 eyes—10; 1 eye—9**

---

Name _____

## Estimating Greater Products

**Science** The speed a planet travels around the Sun is measured in kilometers per second. The table shows the speed and the number of Earth days it takes a planet to revolve around the Sun.

| Planet | Speed around Sun (km/s) | Time to revolve around Sun |
|---|---|---|
| Mercury | 48 | 90 Earth days |
| Venus | 35 | 225 Earth days |
| Earth | 30 | 365 Earth days |
| Mars | 24 | 687 Earth days |

1. About how many kilometers will Venus travel in 185 seconds?

**8,000 km**

2. About how many kilometers will Mercury travel in 14 minutes?

**30,000 km**

3. About how many kilometers will Mars travel

in one minute? **1,200 km**

in one hour? **72,000 km**

in one Earth day? **1,728,000 km**

4. About how many times will Mercury revolve around the Sun in one Earth year? **4–5 times**

5. About how much farther does Mercury travel in 195 seconds than Venus?

**about 2,000 km**

6. The Jackson family spends $85 per week on food. About how much will they spend on food in one year?

**$4,500 a year**

7. A school district has 38 school buses. Each bus seats 48 students. There are 2,300 students enrolled. Estimate to find if the district will have to purchase additional buses. Explain. **Yes, 38 buses can transport only about 2,000 students. Six additional buses would be needed to transport all 2,300 students enrolled.**

---

Name _____

## Choosing a Calculation Method

**Sports** Suppose you are planning a long-distance biking trip of 1,733 miles. To find out how far you will travel, you make some comparisons with familiar lengths.

| Length | | Number in a Mile |
|---|---|---|
| Football Field | 120 yards | 15 |
| Tennis Court | 78 feet | 68 |
| Basketball Court | 28 meters | 57 |

1. How many football field lengths will you travel?

**25,995 lengths**

2. How many tennis court lengths will you travel?

**117,844 lengths**

3. How many more tennis court lengths than basketball court lengths will you travel? Explain.

**19,063 more tennis-court lengths; 117,844 − 98,781 = 19,063**

5. The biking club reached Taos, New Mexico on September 12, 1998, after traveling 6 months. About when did they begin their trip?

**March 12, 1998**

6. The desert across North Africa grows about 6 miles per year. How many miles smaller was the desert 25 years ago? 50 years ago?

**150 miles; 300 miles**

7. The temperature in Lyn's town in the winter may be as low as 12° F. In the summer it may reach 95 degrees F. What is the range of temperature?

**83°F**

8. Lilah worked on a painting 3 hours a day for 2 weeks. How many hours did it take her to complete it?

**42 hours**

**180**

## Decision Making

You and a friend go to the local Play-A-Thon. The theater group is putting on 5 plays. You can use the table below to determine how long you must wait to see each show.

You and your friend want to see 2 plays together. You can stay for an hour.

| Play | People in Line | Room Capacity | Length of play (minutes) | Reviewer's Scores |
|---|---|---|---|---|
| Time Travel | 37 | 20 | 15 | good |
| President | 68 | 30 | 20 | excellent |
| Campfire | 63 | 35 | 15 | excellent |
| Big Laugh | 49 | 25 | 30 | good |
| Cowpokes | 72 | 40 | 10 | fair |

1. How long would have to wait in line to see *President* if there is a 10-minute wait before the next show? **50 minutes**

2. Suppose the next run of each play will be starting in 5 minutes. Which plays would you be able to see without waiting any longer than 30 minutes?
*Time Travel, Campfire and Cowpokes*

3. Would you wait in line longer than 30 minutes to see any of the plays? Why?
**Possible answer: I might wait longer for *President* or**
*Campfire* **because of their high ratings.**

4. Can you see both of the plays that were rated excellent?
**Possible answer: No, the two plays lasted 35 minutes and**
**you would have to wait at least 40 minutes to see *President*.**

5. Which plays would you choose to see? Explain.
**Look for choices based on time and ratings.**

---

## Multiplying Money

**History** Life in 1900 was different from the way it is today. There were only 45 states. Women were not yet allowed to vote. Most people traveled by wagon. And prices were much lower. The chart shows the price of some grocery items.

| Item | Price in 1900 | Price Today |
|---|---|---|
| oranges (1 dozen) | $0.10 | $2.04 |
| sugar (1 lb) | $0.15 | $0.48 |
| turkey (1 lb) | $0.10 | $1.59 |
| beef (1 lb) | $0.10 | $2.49 |
| bread (1 loaf) | $0.05 | $2.49 |

Compare prices for the shopping list below.

| | a. Price in 1900 | b. Price Today |
|---|---|---|
| 1. 4 dozen oranges | $0.40 | $8.16 |
| 2. 20 lb of sugar | $3.00 | $9.60 |
| 3. 22 lb of turkey | $2.20 | $34.98 |
| 4. 12 lb of beef | $1.20 | $29.88 |
| 5. 3 loaves of bread | $0.15 | $7.47 |

5. The chorus needs red T-shirts for its 24 members. They can buy 2 shirts for $7.92. How much will the T-shirts cost in all? **$95.04**

6. There are 28 students in the Science Club. Each student needs a notebook, which costs $2.59. How much will the notebooks cost in all? **$72.52**

7. An avocado costs $1.19. How much would a crate of 40 avocados cost? **$47.60**

8. One pen costs $1.09. A packet of 8 pens cost $7.79. Which is the better buy? Explain
**The packet of 8 pens; $7.79 < $8.72.**

---

**GPS** PROBLEM 3, STUDENT PAGE 279

You want to find about how long it will take to earn enough money to buy a skateboard. You earn $3.50 for mowing a lawn. You can mow 12 lawns a month.

 a. Should you underestimate or overestimate? Why?
 b. Estimate how much you might earn in a month.

— **Understand** —

1. How much do you earn for mowing one lawn? **$3.50**

2. How many lawns can you mow in a month? **12 lawns**

3. What do you need to find out?
**How long it will take to earn money for a skateboard**

— **Plan** —

4. Consider reasons why you should overestimate or underestimate.
**Possible answer: Underestimate so you don't count on more**
**than you might actually earn.**

— **Solve** —

5. Should you overestimate or underestimate? Why?
**Underestimate; Check for reasonable answers.**

6. Estimate how much you might earn in a month. **$35.00**

— **Look Back** —

7. How can you check your answer? **12 × $3.50 = $42.00.**
**$35.00 < $42.00.**

SOLVE ANOTHER PROBLEM

You purchase 5 new stamps each month for your collection. There are 37 stamps you want to add to it. About how many months will it take you to buy all the stamps? Did you overestimate or underestimate?
**8 months; overestimate**

---

**GPS** PROBLEM 2, STUDENT PAGE 281

Max lines up his baseball cards with the same number of cards in each row. The card in the middle of the array has 8 cards to its left, 8 to its right, 8 above, and 8 below.

 a. How many cards are in each row?   b. How many are there in all?

— **Understand** —

1. What do you need to find out?
**How many cards are in each row; how many there are in all**

— **Plan** —

2. Think of a picture that will help. What will it show?
**17 rows of 17 cards in each row**

— **Solve** —

3. Draw a picture.

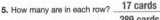

4. How many cards are above, below, to the left, and to the right of the middle card?
**8 cards × 4 directions = 32 cards**

5. How many are in each row? **17 cards**

6. How many are there in all? **289 cards**

— **Look Back** —

7. How can you check your answer?
**Possible answer: Work backward.**

SOLVE ANOTHER PROBLEM

There are 56 members in a marching band. What are two ways they could line up in rows with the same number of members in each row? **Possible answers: 1 row of 56; 2 rows of 28;**
**4 rows of 14; 7 rows of 8; 14 rows of 4; 28 rows of 2; 56 rows of 1**

## Worksheet 7-1

Name _____

Problem Solving
**7-1**

### Exploring Division Patterns

Find each quotient mentally. Then write the basic fact you used to find the quotient.

1. 240 ÷ 3 = **80**          Basic Fact: **24 ÷ 3 = 8**
2. 80 ÷ 4 = **20**           Basic Fact: **8 ÷ 4 = 2**
3. 3,200 ÷ 4 = **800**       Basic Fact: **32 ÷ 4 = 8**
4. 250 ÷ 5 = **50**          Basic Fact: **25 ÷ 5 = 5**
5. 3,300 ÷ 3 = **1,100**     Basic Fact: **33 ÷ 3 = 11**
6. 160 ÷ 4 = **40**          Basic Fact: **16 ÷ 4 = 4**
7. 1,500 ÷ 3 = **500**       Basic Fact: **15 ÷ 3 = 5**
8. 6,600 ÷ 11 = **600**      Basic Fact: **66 ÷ 11 = 6**

Use basic facts to solve these word problems.

9. A natural food store orders 1,800 pounds of whole wheat flour. It will come in 3 equal deliveries. How big will each delivery be?

   Basic Fact: **18 ÷ 3 = 6**          Answer: **600 pounds**

10. A killer whale can eat 8,000 pounds of food in 4 days. How many pounds of food is that each day?

    Basic Fact: **8 ÷ 4 = 2**          Answer: **2,000 pounds**

11. A forest has 7,200 trees. If there are 9 types of trees in the forest, how many trees of each type are there?

    Basic Fact: **72 ÷ 9 = 8**          Answer: **800 trees**

12. Frank has 280 stamps in his collection. If he puts 7 stamps on each page of his collector book, how many pages will his book need?

    Basic Fact: **28 ÷ 7 = 4**          Answer: **40 pages**

Use with pages 292–293. **81**

## Worksheet 7-2

Name _____

Problem Solving
**7-2**

### Estimating Quotients

**Recreation** Sometimes, before people play marbles, they divide the total evenly between them. Estimate how many marbles each player would get if there were:

1. 164 marbles and 3 players.          **50–60** marbles
2. 354 marbles and 4 players.          **80–90** marbles
3. 309 marbles and 7 players.          **40–50** marbles
4. 276 marbles and 5 players.          **50–60** marbles
5. 251 marbles and 8 players.          **30–40** marbles

A recipe for Scrumptious Squash Soup calls for 7 pounds of squash. Estimate the answers to the following questions.

6. Mr. Winters has 129 pounds of squash. How many times could he make Scrumptious Squash Soup this winter?

   **10–20**

7. Mrs. Summers has 234 pounds of squash. How many times could she make Scrumptious Squash Soup this winter?

   **30–40**

8. The Food Market has 465 pounds of squash. How many times could they make Scrumptious Squash Soup this winter?

   **60–70**

Jason wants to arrange 172 books on shelves.

9. About how many books will be on each shelf if Jason uses 3 shelves?

   **50–60**

10. Jason wants to use 8 shelves. How many books will be on each shelf?

    **20–30**

**82** Use with pages 294–295.

## Worksheet 7-3

Name _____

Problem Solving
**7-3**

### Exploring Division With Remainders

You bought 13 apples at the fruit market today. What will you do with them? Your recipe book is full of ideas.

1. The recipe for a dozen apple bran muffins calls for 3 apples. How many dozens of muffins could you bake? How many apples would you have left over?

   a. How many groups of 3 apples are in 13 apples? **4**

   b. How many apples are left over? **1**

2. The recipe for a pint of applesauce calls for 6 apples.

   a. How many pints of applesauce could you make? **2**

   b. How many apples would you have left over? **1**

3. The recipe for a pan of apple crisp calls for 8 apples.

   a. How many pans of apple crisp could you make? **1**

   b. How many apples would you have left over? **5**

   c. Explain how you found the number of pans of apple crisp.

   **Possible answer: Make groups of 8 apples until there are less than 8 left.**

4. You want to make 4 batches of apple bread pudding. Explain how you would divide the apples equally among the 4 batches.

   **Possible answer: Make groups of 4 apples until there are less than 4 left. Each batch will have 3 apples with 1 apple left over.**

5. Which recipe or recipes would you make? Why?

   **Possible answer: Apple bran muffins because there would be 4 dozen muffins and only 1 apple left over**

Use with pages 296–297. **83**

## Worksheet 7-4

Name _____

Problem Solving
**7-4**

### Exploring Division

There are 52 cards to be distributed equally among players in a game. Draw pictures of place-value blocks to solve each problem.

1. a. If there are 3 players, how many cards will each player get? **17**

   b. How many cards will be left over after they are all dealt? **1**

2. a. If there are 5 players, how many cards will each player get? **10**

   b. How many cards will be left over after they are all dealt? **2**

3. a. If there are 4 players, how many cards will each player get? **13**

   b. How many cards will be left over after they are all dealt? **0**

4. Explain how you regrouped to solve **3**.

   **Possible answer: To divide 5 tens into 4 groups, put 1 ten in each group, then regroup 1 ten to 10 ones. Put an equal number of ones in each group.**

**84** Use with pages 300–301.

**182**

## Dividing 2-Digit Dividends

1. An American toad can eat 48 flies in 3 minutes. How many flies can it eat in 1 minute?    **16 flies**

2. There are 50 states in the United States.
   a. If you divide them into 4 groups, how many states will be in each group?    **12 states**
   b. How many will be left over?    **2**

3. A poster with large type can fit about 9 words per line. If you have a message that is 87 words long, how many lines will your poster have?
   **10 lines**

4. Keesha's book has 73 pages. If she reads 4 pages a day, how many days will it take her to finish the book? Explain.
   **19 days; 73 ÷ 4 = 18 R1**

5. Patrick has 47 cans of soup. He can fit 8 cans in one box. How many boxes will he need? Explain.
   **6 boxes; 47 ÷ 8 = 5 R7**

6. **Choose a Strategy** A gardener has a garden space that is 12 feet by 12 feet. He wants to plant flowers and vegetables. He will use one row of flowers to divide the garden into 2 equal parts. How many ways can he do this?

   a. What strategy would you use to solve the problem?
   **Possible answer: Draw a Picture.**

   b. Answer the problem.
   **Possible answer: 4 ways**

   - Use Objects/Act It Out
   - Draw a Picture
   - Look for a Pattern
   - Guess and Check
   - Use Logical Reasoning
   - Make an Organized List
   - Make a Table
   - Solve a Simpler Problem
   - Work Backward

---

## Finding 3-Digit Quotients

**Geography** The Northeast part of the United States is often considered to be one of the most beautiful places to see the leaves change colors. The New England States and New York are easy to visit using different means of transportation.

| | Transportation | Time |
|---|---|---|
| Boston, MA to New York, NY | car | 4 hours |
| | airplane | 1 hour |
| New York, NY to Burlington, VT | train | 9 hours |
| | airplane | 2 hours |
| Burlington, VT to Portland, ME | airplane | 2 hours |
| | car | 4 hours |

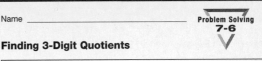

1. How fast would you need to fly to travel from New York to Burlington in 2 hours?
   **287 km per hour**

2. How fast would you need to fly to travel from Boston to New York to Burlington in 3 hours?
   **304 km per hour**

3. How fast would you need to fly to travel from Portland to Burlington in 2 hours?    **190 km per hour**

4. A factory packs 8 reams of paper in one carton. How many cartons will they need to pack 976 reams of paper?    **122**

5. How many reams of paper can be packed in 450 cartons?    **3,600**

6. If 450 cartons are packed in 3 hours, how many cartons are packed per hour?    **150 cartons**

7. 8 paper workers work 896 hours in one month. On average, how many hours does each work?    **112 hrs**

---

## 2- or 3-Digit Quotients

**Geography** North-south interstate highways have one or two-digit odd numbers. Many end with the digit 5. I-55 runs 944 miles from Chicago, Illinois to La Place, Louisiana. I-65 runs 888 miles from Gary, Indiana to Mobile, Alabama.

1. You want to travel I-55 in 4 days. How many miles should you travel each day?    **236 miles**

2. You decide to take 8 days to travel I-55. How many miles should you travel each day?    **118 miles**

3. You want to travel I-65 in 3 days. How many miles should you travel each day?    **296 miles**

4. Perry had 492 baseball cards. He planned to put them in 4 albums. How many cards should be put in each album?
   **123 cards**

5. Joan rode her bicycle a total distance of 84 miles this week. She spent 7 hours riding her bicycle. What was her average speed?
   **12 mph**

6. Li drove a distance of 378 miles. The trip took her 9 hours. What was her average speed?
   **42 mph**

7. Alex had 889 marbles which he packaged into 7 bags. How many marbles were in each bag?
   **127 marbles**

8. In a factory, 740 boxes are stacked 4 boxes high. How many stacks are there?
   **185 stacks**

---

## Zeros in the Quotient
Write the answer to each question on the line.

1. Five medium-sized strawberries have about 1,000 seeds. About how many seeds does each strawberry contain?
   **About 200 seeds**

2. Three small jars of homemade jam cost $3.27. How much does one jar cost?
   **$1.09**

3. Kevin picked 3 large baskets of strawberries. He picked 315 strawberries in all. How many strawberries were in each basket?
   **105 strawberries**

4. Aisha picked 7 strawberries from each plant in one row. In all, she picked 763 berries. How many plants are in the row?
   **109 plants**

5. Mary-Beth has 215 cranberries. She wants to make 2 loaves of cranberry bread with the same number of cranberries in each loaf.

   a. How many cranberries will be in each loaf?
   **107 cranberries**

   b. How many will be left over?    **1 cranberry**

6. **Choose a strategy** Miguel planted 4 different kinds of plants in his vegetable garden. The garden contains a total of 72 plants. Of the plants, 15 are tomato and 12 are squash. The remaining plants are either lettuce or cucumbers. The number of lettuce plants is twice the number of cucumber plants. How many lettuce plants are in Miguel's garden?

   - Use Objects/Act It Out
   - Draw a Picture
   - Look for a Pattern
   - Guess and Check
   - Use Logical Reasoning
   - Make an Organized List
   - Make a Table
   - Solve a Simpler Problem
   - Work Backward

   a. What strategy would you use to solve the problem?
   **Possible answer: Draw a picture.**

   b. Answer the problem.    **30 lettuce plants**

**GPS** PROBLEM 6, STUDENT PAGE 317

A gumbo recipe that serves 30 people calls for 45 ounces of canned tomatoes, 12 celery stalks, 3 green peppers, and 6 cups of okra, among other ingredients. Suppose you want to make enough for only 10 people.
  a. How much of each ingredient will you need?
  b. What strategy did you use to solve the problem?

**— Understand —**
1. How many people does the original recipe serve? __30__
2. How many people do you need to serve? __10__

**— Plan —**
3. Are you going to use less or more of each ingredient? __Less__
4. What part of the original ingredients will you need to serve 10 people? $\frac{1}{3}$

**— Solve —**
5. Divide each ingredient by 3. __15 ounces of tomatoes, 4 celery stalks, 1 green pepper, 2 cups of okra__

6. What strategy did you use to solve the problem?
__Possible answer: Make an Organized List__

**— Look Back —**
7. How can you check your answer? __Possible answer: Multiply the amount of each ingredient by 3. Result should be amount.__

SOLVE ANOTHER PROBLEM

Rosa's fruit salad recipe serves 16 people. It calls for 8 pounds of grapes, 40 ounces of peaches, 4 pounds of melon, 12 oranges, and 32 strawberries. Suppose you wanted to make fruit salad for only 8 people. How much of each ingredient would you need?
**4 pounds of grapes, 20 ounces of peaches, 2 pounds of melon, 6 oranges, 16 strawberries**

Use with pages 316–317. **89**

---

### Exploring Division with Money
Evan and three friends are sharing the cost of a pizza. The cost of the pizza is $6.80. To share the cost equally, how much should each person pay?

1. In the space below, draw a picture to show dollar bills and dimes totaling $6.80.

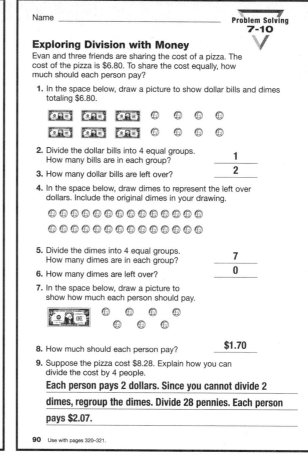

2. Divide the dollar bills into 4 equal groups. How many bills are in each group? __1__
3. How many dollar bills are left over? __2__

4. In the space below, draw dimes to represent the left over dollars. Include the original dimes in your drawing.

5. Divide the dimes into 4 equal groups. How many dimes are in each group? __7__
6. How many dimes are left over? __0__

7. In the space below, draw a picture to show how much each person should pay.

8. How much should each person pay? __$1.70__

9. Suppose the pizza cost $8.28. Explain how you can divide the cost by 4 people.
**Each person pays 2 dollars. Since you cannot divide 2 dimes, regroup the dimes. Divide 28 pennies. Each person pays $2.07.**

**90** Use with pages 320–321.

---

### Dividing Money Amounts

**Careers** Tricia is a clerk at a costume jewelry store. She sells jewelry.

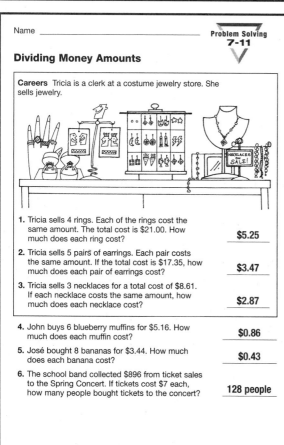

1. Tricia sells 4 rings. Each of the rings cost the same amount. The total cost is $21.00. How much does each ring cost? __$5.25__

2. Tricia sells 5 pairs of earrings. Each pair costs the same amount. If the total cost is $17.35, how much does each pair of earrings cost? __$3.47__

3. Tricia sells 3 necklaces for a total cost of $8.61. If each necklace costs the same amount, how much does each necklace cost? __$2.87__

4. John buys 6 blueberry muffins for $5.16. How much does each muffin cost? __$0.86__

5. José bought 8 bananas for $3.44. How much does each banana cost? __$0.43__

6. The school band collected $896 from ticket sales to the Spring Concert. If tickets cost $7 each, how many people bought tickets to the concert? __128 people__

Use with pages 322–323. **91**

---

### Exploring Mean
Find the typical length of four classmates' feet.

Measure the length of four of your classmates' feet and cut a strip of paper the length of each foot.

Tape the four strips together to form one long strip.

Now fold the long strip in half twice.

Open the long strip. Cut along the folds to get four equal lengths.

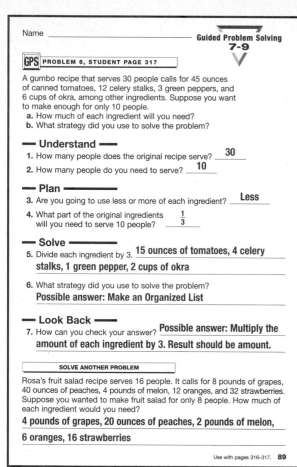

1. How long is one of these typical lengths of your classmates' feet?
**Answers will vary.**

2. Using paper strips, how could you find the typical length of eight of your classmates' feet?
**Measure 8 classmates' feet. Tape the 8 paper strips together. Fold the long strip in half 4 times. Cut along the folds. Measure each new strip.**

3. What steps would you take to find the mean of 5, 8, 9, and 6? Explain.
**Find 5 + 8 + 9 + 6 and divide the sum by 4.**

4. The mean of this set of numbers—4, 5, 6, 3, 2—is 4. What two numbers can you add to the set of numbers so the mean will still be 4?
**Any two numbers with a sum of 8: 1 and 7, 2 and 6, 3 and 5, or 4 and 4**

5. The average of 4 numbers is 30. Three of the numbers are: 20, 25, and 40. Find the fourth number. __35__

6. The average of 5 numbers is 15. If three of the numbers are 16, 17, and 18, what do you know about the other two numbers?
**Their sum must be 24.**

**92** Use with pages 326–327.

---

**184**

## Exploring Divisibility

**1.** What is an **even** number? What is an **odd** number?

**a.** Even: A number that ends with the digits 0, 2, 4, 6, or 8

**b.** Odd: A number that ends with the digits 1, 3, 5, 7, or 9

**2.** When is a number **divisible** by another number?

When it is divided and there is no remainder

**3.** Is 130 divisible by 2, 5, or 10? Write Yes or No. What rule can you use to figure out if a number is divisible by 2, 5, or 10?

**a.** by 2?  Yes  Rule: Even numbers are divisible by 2.

**b.** by 5?  Yes  Rule: Numbers that end in 5 or 0 are divisible by 5.

**c.** by 10?  Yes  Rule: Numbers that end in 0 are divisible by 10.

**4.** Is 216 divisible by 3, 6, or 9? Write Yes or No. What rule can you use to figure out if a number is divisible by 3, 6, or 9?

**a.** by 3?  Yes  Rule: Numbers that have digits with a sum divisible by 3 are divisible by 3.

**b.** by 6?  Yes  Rule: Numbers that are divisible by both 2 and 3 are divisible by 6.

**c.** by 9?  Yes  Rule: Numbers that have digits with a sum divisible by 9 are divisible by 9.

**5.** Write a number that is divisible by 3, 6 and 9.
Possible answers: 18, 36, 54, 72, 90, 108

**7.** Without dividing, can you tell if you can share $5.19 equally among 3 people? Explain. Yes, 5 + 1 + 9 = 15. 15 is divisible by 3, so $5.19 is divisible by 3.

---

**GPS** PROBLEM 4, STUDENT PAGE 333

Wendy mixed 24 ounces of tomato sauce with some olive oil. She spread 3 ounces of the mixture on each of 6 pizzas. How much of the mixture did she have left over?

### — Understand —

**1.** How much sauce with oil does she have? ___ 24 oz

**2.** What do you know?
Wendy used 3 oz of mixture on each of 6 pizzas.

**3.** What are you asked to find?
How much mixture is left over

### — Plan —

**4.** What do you need to do first?
Find out how much mixture was used.

### — Solve —

**5.** What is the amount of mixture used on each pizza? ___ 3 oz

**6.** How much mixture was used on all 6 pizzas? ___ 18 oz

**7.** How much mixture is left? ___ 24 − 18 = 6; 6 oz

### — Look Back —

**8.** How could you check your answer?
Work backward. Add 6 oz + 18 oz to find 24 oz.

SOLVE ANOTHER PROBLEM

Fernando made a fruit punch. He divided the punch into three 8-ounce glasses and had 5 ounces left over. How much punch did he start with?  ___ 29 oz

---

## Exploring Solids

Complete the table.

| | Solid | Number of Flat Faces | Number of Edges | Number of Vertices |
|---|---|---|---|---|
| **1.** | sphere | 0 | 0 | 0 |
| **2.** | cube | 6 | 12 | 8 |
| **3.** | square pyramid | 5 | 8 | 5 |

Most objects that we see around us are made up of combinations of these solids and cones and cylinders. The figure below is made up of several solids that have been joined together. Write the name of the solid used for each part of the figure.

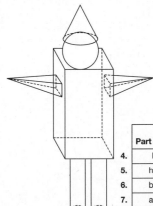

| | Part of Figure | Name of Solid |
|---|---|---|
| **4.** | hat | Cone |
| **5.** | head | Sphere |
| **6.** | body | Rectangular prism |
| **7.** | arms | Pyramids |
| **8.** | legs | Cylinders |

---

## Exploring Polygons

**1.** On the right is a picture of a soccer ball. Although the object is a sphere, it has several polygon shapes on its surface. Use a colored pencil or highlighter to outline different polygons. Name the polygons that you find.
Pentagons, hexagons

**2.** How are all the black shapes on the soccer ball similar?
Possible answer: They are all the same sized pentagons.

**3.** How are all the black shapes on the soccer ball different from the white shapes?
Possible answer: The black shapes have 5 sides and the white shapes have six sides.

**4.** If you cut a pentagon in half, what different figures would you make?
2 quadrilaterals

**5.** Draw a line across the pentagon to show how one cut could make two completely different shapes. Name the shapes.
Triangle and quadrilateral
Possible answer:

**6.** What is the name of the figure that is 36 inches around and that has equal sides, each 6 inches long?
Hexagon

**7.** If you were to cut the figure in **6** in two, what figures could you make?
Possible answers: 2 quadrilaterals or 2 pentagons

## Exploring Triangles

Look at the polygons below. What is the smallest number of triangles it will take to cover each figure? Draw the triangles. Use a ruler if you want. The first one is started for you. Then label each triangle I for isosceles, E for equilateral, or S for scalene.

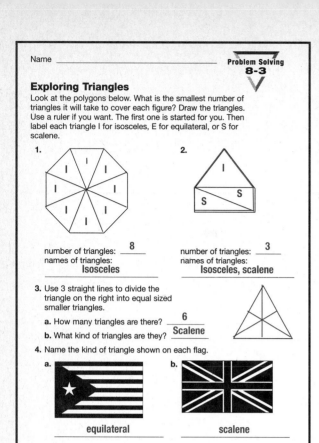

1.

2.

number of triangles: __8__
names of triangles:
_____Isosceles_____

number of triangles: __3__
names of triangles:
____Isosceles, scalene____

3. Use 3 straight lines to divide the triangle on the right into equal sized smaller triangles.

a. How many triangles are there? __6__

b. What kind of triangles are they? __Scalene__

4. Name the kind of triangle shown on each flag.

a.

b.

_____equilateral_____   _____scalene_____

## Triangles and Angles

**Fine Arts** Cubism is a type of painting or drawing where geometrical shapes and patterns are used. Pablo Picasso was a famous cubist painter. To the right is a rough sample of a cubist drawing.

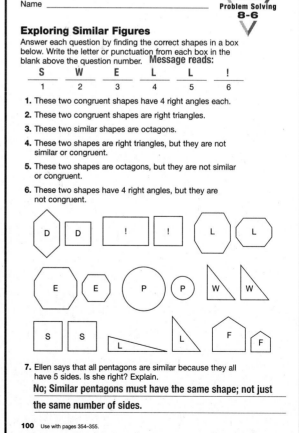

1. How many right triangles are in the drawing above? __2__

2. How many acute triangles are in the drawing? __2__

3. How many obtuse triangles are there? __1__

Name the shaded angle between each clock's hands as right, acute, or obtuse.

4.

5.

6.

**Right**   **Acute**   **Obtuse**

7. Make a drawing using right triangles, obtuse triangles and acute triangles.
**Check students' drawings.**

## Exploring Congruent Figures and Motions

Study the figures. Then decide what happens when they are flipped, turned, or slid.

# I S H O X P B A

1. What do you see if you flip the capital letter I?
**You see the same letter I.**

2. Will the capital letter B appear the same if it is flipped? __No__

3. Name 3 other capital letters that you can flip and the letter appears the same.
**Possible answers: H, O, X**

4. What motions could these two figures show?

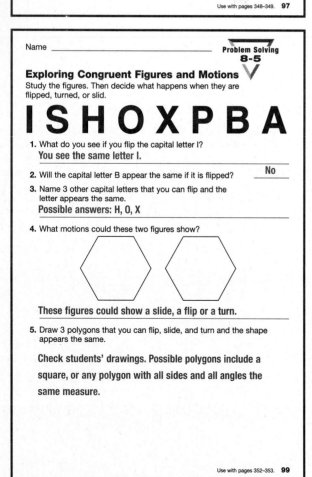

**These figures could show a slide, a flip or a turn.**

5. Draw 3 polygons that you can flip, slide, and turn and the shape appears the same.

**Check students' drawings. Possible polygons include a square, or any polygon with all sides and all angles the same measure.**

## Exploring Similar Figures

Answer each question by finding the correct shapes in a box below. Write the letter or punctuation from each box in the blank above the question number. **Message reads:**

| S | W | E | L | L | ! |
|---|---|---|---|---|---|
| 1 | 2 | 3 | 4 | 5 | 6 |

1. These two congruent shapes have 4 right angles each.

2. These two congruent shapes are right triangles.

3. These two similar shapes are octagons.

4. These two shapes are right triangles, but they are not similar or congruent.

5. These two shapes are octagons, but they are not similar or congruent.

6. These two shapes have 4 right angles, but they are not congruent.

D   D   !   !   L   L

E   E   P   P   W   W

S   S   L   L   F   F

7. Ellen says that all pentagons are similar because they all have 5 sides. Is she right? Explain.
**No; Similar pentagons must have the same shape; not just the same number of sides.**

## Lines and Line Segments

**Geography** A street map helps people find their way around a town or city. It provides a bird's-eye view so that the relationships of the street and the patterns they make become easier to remember. Use the street map below to answer the questions.

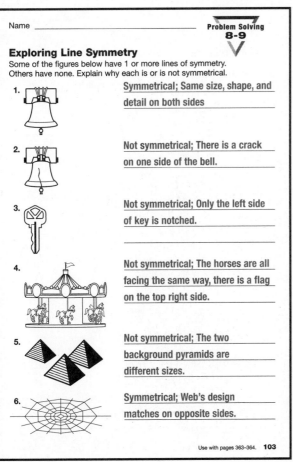

**1.** Which streets are parallel to Oak Street?

West, Lee, Elm, East

**2.** Which street is parallel to Apple Avenue?    Cherry

**3.** Elm Street is perpendicular to which streets?    Broad, Main, High

**4.** Which building marks the point where Broad Street and West Street intersect?

Library

Write if the electrical wires for each pair of poles appear to be parallel or perpendicular.

**5.**

Parallel

**6.**

Perpendicular

Use with pages 358–359.   **101**

---

## Quadrilaterals

**Fine Arts** Quadrilaterals have often been used by artists who design signs that rely on a simple symbol, rather than on words, to communicate. (These signs are called "icons.") Below are some icons. Write which quadrilateral is used. Then explain where you might find each sign.

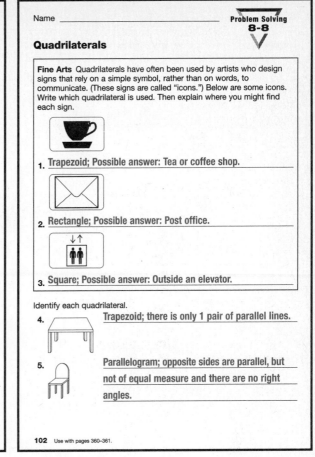

**1.** Trapezoid; Possible answer: Tea or coffee shop.

**2.** Rectangle; Possible answer: Post office.

**3.** Square; Possible answer: Outside an elevator.

Identify each quadrilateral.

**4.** Trapezoid; there is only 1 pair of parallel lines.

**5.** Parallelogram; opposite sides are parallel, but not of equal measure and there are no right angles.

**102**   Use with pages 360–361.

---

## Exploring Line Symmetry

Some of the figures below have 1 or more lines of symmetry. Others have none. Explain why each is or is not symmetrical.

**1.** Symmetrical; Same size, shape, and detail on both sides

**2.** Not symmetrical; There is a crack on one side of the bell.

**3.** Not symmetrical; Only the left side of key is notched.

**4.** Not symmetrical; The horses are all facing the same way, there is a flag on the top right side.

**5.** Not symmetrical; The two background pyramids are different sizes.

**6.** Symmetrical; Web's design matches on opposite sides.

Use with pages 363–364.   **103**

---

**GPS** **PROBLEM 3, STUDENT PAGE 365**

Mark's birthday is before Alex's but after Beth's. Ellen's birthday is before Beth's but after Orlando's. Whose birthday is first?

**— Understand —**

**1.** What do you need to find out? ___ whose birthday is first

**— Plan —**

**2.** Choose five other objects to stand for the five people. What object will represent each person?

Answers will vary.

**— Solve —**

**3.** Look at the first clue. What is the order of Mark's, Alex's, and Beth's birthdays?    Beth, Mark, Alex

**4.** Look at the second clue. Where should you put Ellen?

before Beth, after Orlando

**5.** What is the correct order?    Orlando, Ellen, Beth, Mark, Alex

**6.** Whose birthday is first?    Orlando's is first.

**— Look Back —**

**7.** How can you check your answer?

Reread each clue to be sure answers fit.

**SOLVE ANOTHER PROBLEM**

Tom finished the race before James but after Sue. Mary finished after James but before Henry finished. Who finished first?    Sue

**104**   Use with pages 364–365.

**Problem Solving**
**8-11**

## Exploring Perimeter

1. One side of a square measures 3 cm. How can you use this information to find the perimeter of the square?
   **Possible answer: Multiply 3 cm by 4.**

2. Write a rule to find the perimeter of a square, using addition.
   **Possible answer: Add length of side to itself 3 times.**

3. What rule can you write for finding the perimeter of a square using multiplication?
   **Multiply length of side by 4.**

4. Each side of a square A is 2 units. What is the perimeter?
   **8 units**

5. Multiply each side of the square by 2 to get the measurements for square B.
   a. Draw and label square B.

   4 units
   4 units [B] 4 units
   4 units

   b. What is the perimeter of square B? **16 units**

6. Multiply each side of square B by 2 to get the measurements for square C.
   a. Draw and label square C.

   8 units
   8 units [C] 8 units
   8 units

   b. What is the perimeter of square C? **32 units**

7. Does the perimeter double each time you double the sides of the square? **Yes**

8. How can you use the perimeter of square C to find the perimeter of a square with a side that measures 16 inches?
   **Multiply 32 units by 2.**

---

**Problem Solving**
**8-12**

## Exploring Areas of Rectangles

1. A rectangle has an area of 36 square inches. Write the dimensions of at least 3 different rectangles with this area.
   **Possible answers: 1 in., 36 in.; 2 in., 18 in.; 3 in., 12 in.;**
   **4 in., 9 in.; 6 in., 6 in.**

2. A rectangle has an area of exactly 100 square meters. What are all the possible dimensions for this rectangle?
   **1, 100; 2, 50; 4, 25; 5, 20; 10, 10**

3. A rectangle has an area of 48 square feet. Its width is 4 feet. How long is it?
   **12 feet**

4. Find a rectangle whose area is greater than its perimeter. What are its dimensions?
   **Possible answers: 4 in., 6 in.; 8 in., 12 in.**

5. Find a rectangle whose perimeter is larger than its area. What are its dimensions?
   **Possible answers: 1 in., 12 in.; 2 in., 6 in.**

6. A rectangle has a length of 6 cm. What is its width if its perimeter and area are the same number?
   **3 cm**

7. A square has an area of 36 square inches. What is the perimeter?
   **24 in.**

---

**Problem Solving**
**8-13**

## Exploring Volume

1. List the dimensions of 3 solids that have a volume of 24 cubic cm.
   **Possible answers: 1 cm, 1 cm, 24 cm; 2 cm, 2 cm, 6 cm;**
   **1 cm, 3 cm, 8 cm; 1 cm, 4 cm, 6 cm; 3 cm, 2 cm, 4 cm**

2. A rectangular prism has a volume of 36 cubic inches. Its length is 2 inches, its depth 9 inches. How wide is it? Explain how you found your answer.
   **2 inches wide; Possible answer: Find a third factor that when**
   **multiplied by 2 and 9 gives a product of 36.**

3. What is the volume of this cube? Explain how you know.
   5 cm

   **125 cubic cm; Possible answer: The length, width, and height**
   **of a cube are all the same measure.**

4. Explain how you can divide this solid into two prisms to find the total volume. Then find the total volume of the solid.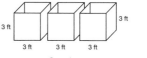

   **Possible answer: 8 units × 4 units × 3 units = 96 cubic**
   **units; 3 units × 6 units × 2 units = 36 cubic units; 96 cubic**
   **units + 36 cubic units = 132 cubic units**

5. This solid is made up of 2 prisms. Find the volume of the solid.
   **144 cubic cm**
   2 cm  2 cm
   4 cm
   8 cm
   4 cm  4 cm

---

**Problem Solving**
**8-14**

## Decision Making

Your gardening club is planning to build compost bins. You have 10 metal posts and a 35 ft roll of fencing that is 3 feet tall. Group A in the club wants to build three separate bins each 3 ft by 3 ft by 3 ft. Group B wants to build one 9-foot long structure, divided into 3 sections.

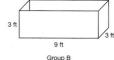
Group A                    Group B

1. The fencing is used for the sides of the bins—not the tops and bottoms. How can you find the amount of fencing Group A will need? | **Find the perimeter.**
2. a. How much fencing will Group A need for each bin? | **12 ft**
   b. For all 3 bins? | **36 ft**
3. a. What is the perimeter of Group B's design? | **24 ft**
   b. They will need two 3-ft dividers. How much fencing will this use? | **6 ft**
   c. How much total fencing will Group B need? | **30 ft**
4. A post needs to hold the bins together at every corner.
   a. How many posts will Group A need to build 3 separate bins? | **12**
   b. How many posts will Group B need? | **8**
5. Do both designs hold the same amount of compost? Explain.
   **Yes; Each of Group A's bins holds 27 cubic feet and each of**
   **Group B's sections holds 27 cubic feet.**
6. Which design do you think is the best choice? Explain your reasons.
   **Group B's design; Because it holds the same amount as**
   **Group A's design, but it uses the materials available**

## Exploring Fractions

1.
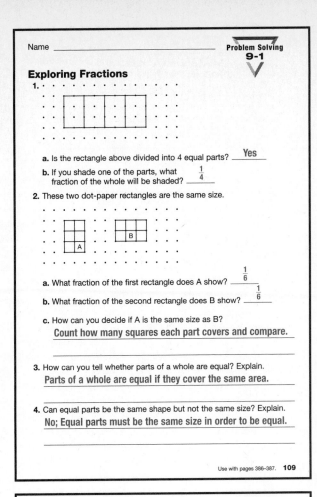

a. Is the rectangle above divided into 4 equal parts? ___Yes___

b. If you shade one of the parts, what fraction of the whole will be shaded? ___$\frac{1}{4}$___

2. These two dot-paper rectangles are the same size.

a. What fraction of the first rectangle does A show? ___$\frac{1}{6}$___

b. What fraction of the second rectangle does B show? ___$\frac{1}{6}$___

c. How can you decide if A is the same size as B?
**Count how many squares each part covers and compare.**

3. How can you tell whether parts of a whole are equal? Explain.
**Parts of a whole are equal if they cover the same area.**

4. Can equal parts be the same shape but not the same size? Explain.
**No; Equal parts must be the same size in order to be equal.**

---

## Naming and Writing Fractions

**Careers** Ms. Sparks is a baker. She owns her own bakery where she bakes all kinds of breads and pastries.

1. Ms. Sparks baked a vanilla sheet cake and cut it into 8 pieces. She sold 5 pieces of the cake in one day. What fraction of the cake was not sold?   $\frac{3}{8}$

2. Ms. Sparks made 10 raisin bagels at the beginning of the day. When she closed the bakery that day, there was 1 raisin bagel left. What fraction of the raisin bagels did she sell?   $\frac{9}{10}$

3. Ms. Sparks baked 12 oatmeal cookies. However, 5 of the cookies were burnt and had to be thrown out. What fraction of the oatmeal cookies were not burnt?   $\frac{7}{12}$

4. Ms. Sparks baked 16 loaves of bread. She saved 3 loaves for her family and sold the rest. What fraction of the loaves did she sell?   $\frac{13}{16}$

5. Together, Monday, Tuesday, and Wednesday form what fraction of the days in a week?   $\frac{3}{7}$

6. Mona gave a bouquet of flowers to her Mother. There were 2 roses, 5 carnations, and 4 daisies in the bouquet. What fraction of the flowers in the bouquet were roses?   $\frac{2}{11}$

7. Tony did yard work for 3 hours on Saturday afternoon. He spent 1 hour raking leaves and 2 hours trimming shrubs. What fraction of time he worked did he spend raking leaves?   $\frac{1}{3}$

8. John has softball practice on Tuesday, Wednesday, Friday and Saturday. What fraction of the week does John have softball practice?   $\frac{4}{7}$

---

## Estimating Fractional Amounts

**Technology** Computers have different amounts of storage space for various things. This storage space is called "memory" and is measured in "megabyte" or "meg" units. The computer in Andy's classroom has 80 megs of memory space. About 10 megs of memory space is taken up by a word-processing program. System software, which helps the computer run, takes up about 20 megs of memory space. There is about 10 megs of unused memory space in the computer.

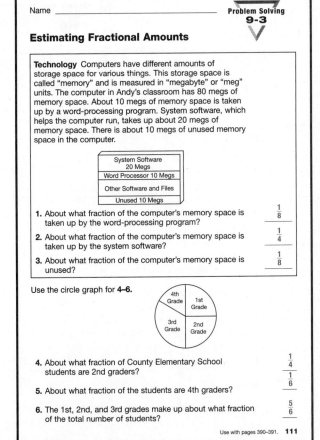

1. About what fraction of the computer's memory space is taken up by the word-processing program?   $\frac{1}{8}$

2. About what fraction of the computer's memory space is taken up by the system software?   $\frac{1}{4}$

3. About what fraction of the computer's memory space is unused?   $\frac{1}{8}$

Use the circle graph for **4–6.**

4. About what fraction of County Elementary School students are 2nd graders?   $\frac{1}{4}$

5. About what fraction of the students are 4th graders?   $\frac{1}{6}$

6. The 1st, 2nd, and 3rd grades make up about what fraction of the total number of students?   $\frac{5}{6}$

---

## Exploring Mixed Numbers

1.
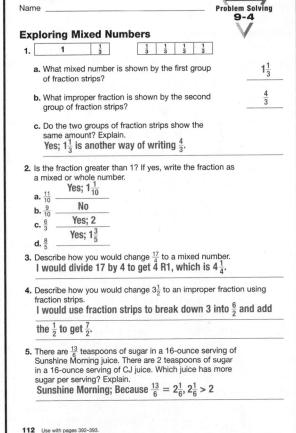

a. What mixed number is shown by the first group of fraction strips?   $1\frac{1}{3}$

b. What improper fraction is shown by the second group of fraction strips?   $\frac{4}{3}$

c. Do the two groups of fraction strips show the same amount? Explain.
**Yes; $1\frac{1}{3}$ is another way of writing $\frac{4}{3}$.**

2. Is the fraction greater than 1? If yes, write the fraction as a mixed or whole number.
a. $\frac{11}{10}$   **Yes; $1\frac{1}{10}$**
b. $\frac{9}{10}$   **No**
c. $\frac{6}{3}$   **Yes; 2**
d. $\frac{8}{5}$   **Yes; $1\frac{3}{5}$**

3. Describe how you would change $\frac{17}{4}$ to a mixed number.
**I would divide 17 by 4 to get 4 R1, which is $4\frac{1}{4}$.**

4. Describe how you would change $3\frac{1}{2}$ to an improper fraction using fraction strips.
**I would use fraction strips to break down 3 into $\frac{6}{2}$ and add the $\frac{1}{2}$ to get $\frac{7}{2}$.**

5. There are $\frac{13}{6}$ teaspoons of sugar in a 16-ounce serving of Sunshine Morning juice. There are 2 teaspoons of sugar in a 16-ounce serving of CJ juice. Which juice has more sugar per serving? Explain.
**Sunshine Morning; Because $\frac{13}{6} = 2\frac{1}{6}$, $2\frac{1}{6} > 2$**

## Decision Making

Take some lessons! The Aquatic Center offers several choices.

| Lessons | Days | Times | Prices |
|---|---|---|---|
| Swimming | M–F | 1:00, 2:00, 3:00, 4:00, 5:00 | $25 per week |
| | Saturday | 10:00, 11:00, 12:00 | $7 per lesson |
| Diving | M–F | 4:00 | $50 per week |
| | Saturday | 12:00 | $12.50 per lesson |
| Water Aerobics | M–F | 3:00, 6:00 | $3 per session |
| | Saturday | 9:00, 2:00, 3:00 | $3.50 per session |

All activities are for one hour. The per week prices are for 5 lessons.

1. Which activities fit in with your schedule?
   **Answers will vary.**

2. What is the difference in cost between a swimming lesson on a Thursday and on a Saturday?   **$2.00**

3. What is the difference in cost between a diving lesson on a Monday and on a Saturday?   **$2.50**

4. Write a fraction to show the cost of one swimming lesson during a week of lessons.   $\frac{5}{25}$ **or** $\frac{1}{5}$

5. What fraction of the total number of water aerobics M–F lessons are the classes at 3:00?   $\frac{5}{10}$ **or** $\frac{1}{2}$

6. If you had a 2-week vacation from school and $100 to spend on lessons, what could you take?
   **Possible answer: 2 weeks of swimming lessons and 1 week of diving lessons**

7. Describe how you made your decision.
   **Answers will vary. Look for consideration of schedules, prices, and interest in the activity.**

---

## Exploring Equivalent Fractions

1. a. Write three fractions that name the same amount as 2.
   **Possible answers:** $\frac{2}{1}, \frac{4}{2}, \frac{6}{3}$

   b. What pattern do you see in the denominators and numerators of the fractions?
   **The numerator is 2 times the denominator.**

2. a. List three fractions that name the same amount as $\frac{1}{4}$.
   **Possible answers:** $\frac{2}{8}, \frac{3}{12}, \frac{4}{16}$

   b. What pattern do you see in the denominators and numerators of the fractions that you have listed?
   **The denominator divided by 4 equals the numerator.**

3. How many $\frac{1}{5}$ fraction strips would you need to make a length that is $\frac{4}{5}$?
   **4**

4. How many $\frac{1}{3}$ fraction strips would you need to show $\frac{6}{9}$?   **2**

5. Suppose you were working with $\frac{1}{8}$ fraction strips and with $\frac{1}{4}$ fraction strips. Describe two ways you could show the fraction $\frac{3}{4}$.
   **Possible answers: Use six $\frac{1}{8}$-strips; three $\frac{1}{4}$-strips; or two $\frac{1}{4}$-strips and two $\frac{1}{8}$-strips.**

6. Suppose you were working with $\frac{1}{10}$ strips and with $\frac{1}{5}$ strips. Describe two ways that you could show the fraction $\frac{3}{5}$.
   **Possible answers: Use six $\frac{1}{10}$-strips; three $\frac{1}{5}$-strips; or two $\frac{1}{5}$-strips and two $\frac{1}{10}$-strips.**

---

## Naming and Writing Equivalent Fractions

You can use drawings to name and write equivalent fractions.

Find an equivalent fraction for $\frac{1}{2}$.

Here is a rectangle divided into 2 equal parts with $\frac{1}{2}$ shaded.

Divide the rectangle into different equal parts.

You can divide the rectangle into 4 equal parts with $\frac{2}{4}$ shaded.
$\frac{2}{4}$ is equivalent to $\frac{1}{2}$.

Find equivalent fractions. Use drawings to help.

1. $\frac{1}{3}$

   a. Draw a rectangle. Divide it into thirds and shade $\frac{1}{3}$.

   b. Draw three more lines in your rectangle to divide it into sixths.

   c. Write an equivalent fraction for $\frac{1}{3}$. _____ $\frac{2}{6}$

2. $\frac{3}{4} =$ **Possible answer:** $\frac{6}{8}$   3. $\frac{3}{6} =$ **Possible answer:** $\frac{1}{2}$

4. $\frac{2}{8} =$ **Possible answer:** $\frac{1}{4}$   5. $\frac{2}{3} =$ **Possible answer:** $\frac{4}{6}$

---

## Simplest Form Fractions

How do you know if a fraction is in its simplest form? Follow the steps in this flowchart to find out.

**Example**
Is $\frac{8}{32}$ in its simplest form?

Start

The numerator and the denominator can be divided by 2, so follow the Yes arrow.

$\frac{8 \div 2}{32 \div 2} = \frac{4}{16}$

Go back to the first box.

The numerator and the denominator can be divided by 4, so follow the Yes arrow.

$\frac{4 \div 4}{16 \div 4} = \frac{1}{4}$

Go back to the first box.

One is the only number that will divide both 1 and 4, so follow the No arrow.

$\frac{1}{4}$ is the simplest form fraction for $\frac{8}{32}$.

[Flowchart: Start → Can the numerator and the denominator be divided by the same number other than 1? — YES → Divide the numerator and denominator by the same number (loops back) — NO → The fraction is in simplest form → Stop]

Is each fraction in simplest form? If it is, write *yes*. If not, write it in simplest form. Follow the steps in the flowchart.

1. $\frac{10}{12}$   $\frac{5}{6}$      2. $\frac{18}{24}$   $\frac{3}{4}$      3. $\frac{4}{5}$   **Yes**

4. $\frac{9}{15}$   $\frac{3}{5}$      5. $\frac{7}{12}$   **Yes**      6. $\frac{5}{30}$   $\frac{1}{6}$

7. $\frac{6}{36}$   $\frac{1}{6}$      8. $\frac{20}{50}$   $\frac{2}{5}$      9. $\frac{12}{48}$   $\frac{1}{4}$

10. $\frac{5}{13}$   **Yes**      11. $\frac{18}{21}$   $\frac{6}{7}$      12. $\frac{19}{20}$   **Yes**

## Comparing and Ordering Fractions

You can compare fractions using drawings.

Which is greater, $\frac{5}{8}$ or $\frac{1}{3}$?

Draw two rectangles of equal size.

Divide the first rectangle into 8 equal parts.
Divide the second into 3 equal parts.

Shade $\frac{5}{8}$ of the first rectangle and $\frac{1}{3}$ of the second rectangle.

Compare the shaded areas. Are they the same size? If so, the fractions are equivalent. If not, the rectangle with the greater amount of shading is the greater fraction.

$\underline{\frac{5}{8}}$ is greater than $\underline{\frac{1}{3}}$.

Are the fractions equivalent? If so, write *yes*. If not, circle the greater fraction. Use drawings to help.

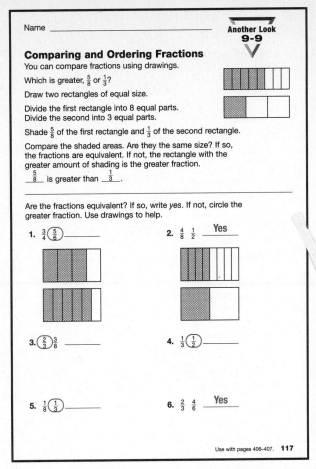

1. $\frac{3}{4}$ $\boxed{\frac{5}{6}}$ _____

2. $\frac{4}{8}$ $\frac{1}{2}$  **Yes**

3. $\boxed{\frac{2}{3}}$ $\frac{3}{8}$

4. $\frac{1}{3}$ $\boxed{\frac{1}{2}}$

5. $\frac{1}{8}$ $\boxed{\frac{1}{3}}$ _____

6. $\frac{2}{3}$ $\frac{4}{6}$  **Yes**

---

## Exploring a Fraction of a Set

Solve.

1. A group of 8 people spent a total of 64 hours planning, shopping, and decorating for a dance. Each person put in the same amount of time.

   a. What fractional part of the time did 3 people work? ___ $\frac{3}{8}$

   b. How many hours was that? __ **24 hours**

2. Miriam used 12 of the 48 exercise machines at the gym. Her friend Sam used $\frac{1}{6}$ of the machines at the gym. ___ $\frac{12}{48}$ or $\frac{1}{4}$

   a. What fractional part of the machines did Miriam use?

   b. Who used more machines? Explain.
   **Miriam; Possible answer; $\frac{1}{6}$ of 48 is 8; 12 is more than 8.**

3. Gabriella and Maxine ran for president of their class. Gabriella received $\frac{7}{10}$ of the vote. Maxine received the rest of the votes. If there are 30 students in the class, how many votes did each person receive? Explain your reasoning.
   **Gabriella received 21 votes, Maxine received 9 votes;**
   **Possible answer: $\frac{7}{10}$ of 30 is 21, $\frac{3}{10}$ of 30 is 9**

4. Aron has been into $\frac{2}{9}$ of the stores in the mall. There are 81 stores in the mall. How many stores has Aron not visited? Explain your reasoning.
   **63; possible answer: $\frac{1}{9}$ of 81 is 9, so $\frac{2}{9}$ is 18. 81 − 18 = 63**

5. Ryan said hello to $\frac{1}{5}$ of the people at the party. He said hello to 10 people. How many people were at the party? Explain your reasoning.
   **50; possible answer: $\frac{1}{5}$ of the group is 10, so $\frac{5}{5}$ = 50.**

---

## Exploring Units of Length

Replace the false measurements below with more reasonable units of length. Replace with inches, feet, or yards. Follow the example.

Example: The table is 36 yards long. __36 inches__

1. The dictionary is about 4 yards thick. __4 inches__

2. The doorway is about 1 inch wide. __1 yard__

3. A child is 2 inches tall. __2 feet__

4. The soccer field is about 120 inches long. __120 yards__

5. The butterfly has a wingspan of 3 feet. __3 inches__

6. The kitchen is about 15 yards wide. __15 feet__

7. The flagpole is 18 inches tall. __18 feet__

8. A compact disc is about 5 yards wide. __5 inches__

9. The hamster is 4 feet long. __4 inches__

10. The length of the car is 10 yards. __10 feet__

11. The tallest giraffe ever recorded was almost 20 ft tall. Is this more or less than 250 in.? How much more or less?  **Less, 10 in.**

12. The largest animal on the earth is the blue whale. The longest ever recorded was about 110 ft long. Is this more or less than 36 yd? How much more or less?  **More, 2 ft**

13. Would you choose inch, foot, or yard to measure these?

    a. length of a football field? __Yard__

    b. length of a skateboard? __Inch or foot__

    c. width of this page? __Inch__

    d. average cat? __Foot or inch__

---

## Measuring Fractional Parts of an Inch

This is an enlarged view of the scale on a ruler. Notice that it is divided into 8 sections. The longest lines are inch marks and are labeled with whole numbers. The next longest lines mark $\frac{1}{2}$ inches. The next longest mark $\frac{1}{4}$ inches. The shortest lines on this ruler mark $\frac{1}{8}$ inches.

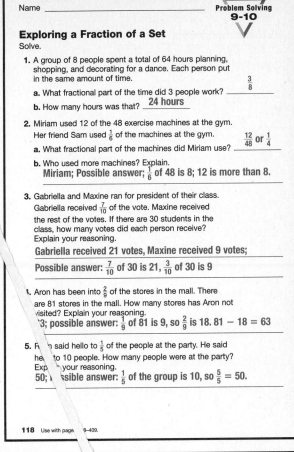

The mark at A shows a length of $3\frac{3}{8}$ in.

The mark at B shows a length of $3\frac{1}{2}$ in.

The mark at C shows a length of $3\frac{3}{4}$ in.

The following drawings show a partial view of arrows being measured with rulers. Give the length of each arrow to the nearest:

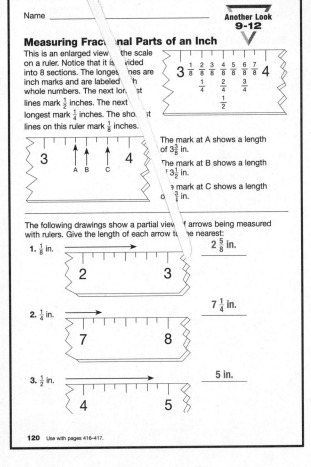

1. $\frac{1}{8}$ in.  _____  **$2\frac{5}{8}$ in.**

2. $\frac{1}{4}$ in.  _____  **$7\frac{1}{4}$ in.**

3. $\frac{1}{2}$ in.  _____  **5 in.**

## Exploring Feet, Yards, and Miles

The high school cross country team is participating in a track meet. The map shows the seven sections of the course, each measured in yards.

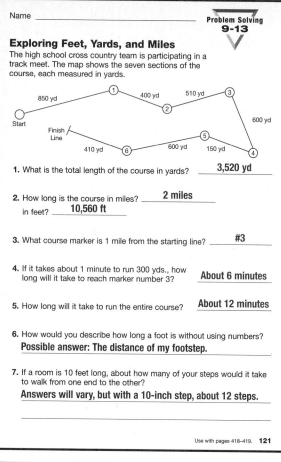

**1.** What is the total length of the course in yards? **3,520 yd**

**2.** How long is the course in miles? **2 miles**
in feet? **10,560 ft**

**3.** What course marker is 1 mile from the starting line? **#3**

**4.** If it takes about 1 minute to run 300 yds., how long will it take to reach marker number 3? **About 6 minutes**

**5.** How long will it take to run the entire course? **About 12 minutes**

**6.** How would you describe how long a foot is without using numbers?
**Possible answer: The distance of my footstep.**

**7.** If a room is 10 feet long, about how many of your steps would it take to walk from one end to the other?
**Answers will vary, but with a 10-inch step, about 12 steps.**

---

**GPS** PROBLEM 4, STUDENT PAGE 421

A group of 50 climbers took part in this year's mountain cleanup. For 29 climbers this was their second year helping. 10 had never helped before. How many of the 50 climbers had helped before last year?

### — Understand —

**1.** What do you know?
**50 climbers participated this year, 29 climbers participated the year before, 10 climbers never participated before this year.**

**2.** What do you need to find out? **The number of climbers who participated before last year**

### — Plan —

**3.** Describe how you can solve the problem. **Use Logical Reasoning.**

**4.** Of the 50 climbers, how many helped last year? **29**

**5.** How many climbers had participated in a cleanup before? Write the number sentence. **50 − 10 = 40**

### — Solve —

**6.** How many of the 50 climbers had helped before last year? Write the number sentence. **11; 40 − 29 = 11**

### — Look Back —

**7.** How can you check your answer?
**Possible answer: Work Backward**

SOLVE ANOTHER PROBLEM

A crew of 28 people picked up trash in a local park. 18 people picked up trash along the hiking trails. 15 people picked up trash in the picnic areas. How many people helped in both areas?
**5 people**

---

## Exploring Adding Fractions with Like Denominators

**1.** How many $\frac{1}{12}$ fraction strips does it take to make $\frac{12}{12}$? **12**

**2.** How many $\frac{1}{7}$ fraction strips would you need to show the sum of $\frac{2}{7}$ and $\frac{3}{7}$? **5**

**3.** Write 4 addition problems that have 2 fractions with a sum of $\frac{8}{9}$. **Possible answers:**
$\frac{1}{9} + \frac{7}{9}$  $\frac{2}{9} + \frac{6}{9}$
$\frac{3}{9} + \frac{5}{9}$  $\frac{4}{9} + \frac{4}{9}$

**4.** What fraction strips would you use to find the sum of $\frac{3}{8}$ and $\frac{4}{8}$? Explain.
**7 $\frac{1}{8}$-fraction strips; To show the sum 3 + 4**

Use fraction strips or draw pictures to solve each problem.

**5.** Bob ate $\frac{1}{4}$ of his sandwich at 10:15. He ate $\frac{1}{4}$ more at 11:30. How much of his sandwich did Bob eat? **$\frac{2}{4}$ or $\frac{1}{2}$**

**6.** Laverne walked $\frac{1}{8}$ of a mile. Then she ran $\frac{3}{8}$ of a mile before stopping to catch her breath. How far did Laverne go before stopping? **$\frac{4}{8}$ or $\frac{1}{2}$ mi**

**7.** Kim did $\frac{1}{3}$ of her homework after school. She did $\frac{2}{3}$ of it after dinner. How much of her homework did Kim complete? **$\frac{3}{3}$ or all**

**8.** James spent $\frac{1}{5}$ of his lunch money on a drink and $\frac{3}{5}$ of it on a sandwich. What fractional part of his lunch money did James spend on these 2 things? **$\frac{4}{5}$**

**9.** Shelley read $\frac{1}{6}$ of her magazine before lunch and $\frac{3}{6}$ after lunch. How much of her magazine did she read? **$\frac{4}{6}$ or $\frac{2}{3}$**

---

## Exploring Adding Fractions with Unlike Denominators

**1.** $\frac{1}{3} + \frac{1}{6}$
**a.** Which fraction would you rename to solve the problem? **$\frac{1}{3}$**
**b.** Rename the fraction. **$\frac{2}{6}$**
**c.** Use the renamed fraction to solve the problem. **$\frac{2}{6} + \frac{1}{6} = \frac{3}{6}$**
**d.** Simplify the sum, if possible. **$\frac{3}{6} = \frac{1}{2}$**

**2.** $\frac{1}{2} + \frac{1}{4}$
**a.** Which fraction would you rename to solve the problem? **$\frac{1}{2}$**
**b.** Rename the fraction. **$\frac{2}{4}$**
**c.** Use the renamed fraction to solve the problem. **$\frac{2}{4} + \frac{1}{4} = \frac{3}{4}$**
**d.** Simplify the sum, if possible. _____

**3.** $\frac{1}{3} + \frac{1}{4}$
**a.** Explain why you cannot rename just one fraction to solve this problem.
**Possible answer: 3 doesn't divide evenly into 4 and 4 doesn't divide evenly into 3.**
**b.** Rename both fractions as 12ths. **$\frac{4}{12}, \frac{3}{12}$**
**c.** Find the sum and simplify. **$\frac{7}{12}$**

**4.** $\frac{1}{3} + \frac{1}{2}$
**a.** What denominator could you use to rename these as equivalent fractions? **6**
**b.** Rename the fractions. **$\frac{2}{6}, \frac{3}{6}$**
**c.** Find the sum and simplify. **$\frac{5}{6}$**

## Adding Fractions

**Geography** New York City is made up of five boroughs (or parts). Some boroughs are large in size and some are small.

This table shows about how much of New York City's 319 square miles is contributed by each of its boroughs.

| Manhattan | $\frac{1}{15}$ |
|---|---|
| The Bronx | $\frac{1}{8}$ |
| Queens | $\frac{1}{3}$ |
| Brooklyn | $\frac{1}{4}$ |
| Staten Island | $\frac{1}{6}$ |

1. What fraction of New York City is Manhattan and Queens?  $\frac{6}{15} = \frac{2}{5}$

2. What fraction of New York City is Brooklyn and the Bronx?  $\frac{3}{8}$

3. What fraction of New York City is Staten Island and Queens?  $\frac{3}{6} = \frac{1}{2}$

4. What should the sum of all 5 fractions be?  1

Here are the ingredients for a batch of Zack's All-Natural Granola bars:

$\frac{1}{2}$ cup raisins          $\frac{2}{3}$ cup chocolate chips

$\frac{3}{4}$ cup of oats          $\frac{1}{4}$ cup coconut

$\frac{1}{3}$ cup peanuts          $\frac{1}{8}$ cup maple syrup

5. How many cups of peanuts and chocolate chips are used?  $1$

6. How many cups of oats and maple syrup are used?  $\frac{7}{8}$

7. You asked your classmates to name their favorite writer. $\frac{2}{3}$ of the class chose Jack Prelutsky. $\frac{1}{6}$ of the class chose Shel Silverstein. The rest chose other writers. What fraction of your class chose either Prelutsky or Silverstein?  $\frac{5}{6}$

---

## Decision Making

Your class wants to paint a mural on the wall of the school gymnasium. The wall is large, about 800 square feet. One gallon of paint will cover about 100 square feet.

After getting permission from the school board, the class collected paint from people in the neighborhood on two different days last week. Here is what they got:

| Color | Amount Collected on Monday | Amount Collected on Friday |
|---|---|---|
| White | 1 gallon | 1 gallon |
| Black | $\frac{1}{2}$ gallon | $\frac{1}{2}$ gallon |
| Blue | $\frac{1}{6}$ gallon | $\frac{1}{3}$ gallon |
| Red | $\frac{1}{4}$ gallon | $\frac{1}{2}$ gallon |
| Green | $\frac{1}{8}$ gallon | $\frac{1}{8}$ gallon |
| Purple | 3 gallons | 1 gallon |
| Brown | $\frac{1}{3}$ gallon | $\frac{1}{6}$ gallon |

1. How much paint of each color was collected?
**2 gallons of white, 1 gallon of black, $\frac{1}{2}$ gallon of blue, $\frac{3}{4}$ gallon of red, $\frac{1}{4}$ gallon of green, 4 gallons of purple, and $\frac{1}{2}$ gallon of brown**

2. Do you have enough paint after 2 collection days to start your mural? Explain.
**Possible answer: Yes, there are over 8 gallons of paint.**

3. Some students want the mural to show people playing basketball. Another group of students wants to paint a pattern in the team's colors, which are purple and white. Which mural would you choose? Explain your reasoning.
**Answers will vary.**

---

## Exploring Subtracting Fractions

1. $\frac{1}{2} - \frac{1}{6}$

a. Which fraction would you rename to solve the problem?  $\frac{1}{2}$

b. Rename the fraction.  $\frac{3}{6}$

c. Solve the problem.  $\frac{2}{6}$

d. Simplify, if possible.  $\frac{1}{3}$

2. $\frac{3}{10} - \frac{1}{5}$

a. Which fraction would you rename to solve the problem?  $\frac{1}{5}$

b. Rename the fraction.  $\frac{2}{10}$

c. Solve the problem.  $\frac{1}{10}$

d. Simplify, if possible.  _____

3. $\frac{2}{3} - \frac{1}{2}$

a. Explain why you cannot rename just one fraction to solve this problem.
**Possible answer: 3 cannot divide 2 evenly and 2 cannot divide 3 evenly.**

b. Rename both fractions as 6ths.  $\frac{4}{6}, \frac{3}{6}$

c. Find the difference and simplify.  $\frac{1}{6}$

4. $\frac{1}{3} - \frac{1}{4}$

a. What denominator could you use to rename these as equivalent fractions?  12

b. Rename both fractions.  $\frac{4}{12}, \frac{3}{12}$

c. Find the difference and simplify.  $\frac{1}{12}$

---

## Subtracting Fractions

A certain city gets its electricity from several different sources:

| Source of power | Fraction of total energy |
|---|---|
| Wind power | $\frac{1}{10}$ |
| Nuclear power | $\frac{1}{2}$ |
| Solar power | $\frac{1}{5}$ |
| Hydroelectric power | $\frac{1}{5}$ |

1. What is the greatest source of electricity in this city?
**Nuclear power**

2. How much of the city's electricity comes from hydroelectric power and wind power?  $\frac{3}{10}$

3. How much more of the city's electricity comes from nuclear power than from wind power?  $\frac{4}{10}$ or $\frac{2}{5}$

4. Compare the amount of electricity coming from nuclear power to the total amount coming from all the other sources.
**They are equal. Nuclear power gives the city $\frac{1}{2}$ of its electricity; the other sources also give $\frac{1}{2}\left(\frac{1}{10} + \frac{1}{5} + \frac{1}{5}\right)$.**

5. **Choose a strategy** $\frac{1}{2}$ of a city park is being planted with trees. Another $\frac{1}{4}$ of the park is being used for a baseball field. Another $\frac{1}{8}$ of the park is being used for a wading pool. How much of the park is still unplanned?

| Strategy box |
|---|
| • Use Objects/Act It Out |
| • Draw a Picture |
| • Look for a Pattern |
| • Guess and Check |
| • Use Logical Reasoning |
| • Make an Organized List |
| • Make a Table |
| • Solve a Simpler Problem |
| • Work Backward |

a. What strategy would you use to solve the problem?
**Possible answer: Draw a Picture.**

b. Answer the problem.  $\frac{1}{8}$ **of the park**

Name _____

## Guided Problem Solving
### 10-7

**GPS** PROBLEM 7, STUDENT PAGE 453

How much longer is the wingspan of the Western pipistrelle bat than the wingspan of hog-nosed bat?

| Smallest Bats |
| --- |
| World record: Hog-nosed bat<br>Location: Thailand<br>Wingspan: $\frac{13}{24}$ ft |
| U.S. record: Western pipistrelle<br>Wingspan: $\frac{2}{3}$ ft |

### — Understand —

1. What do you know?
   **Wingspan of hog-nosed bat is $\frac{13}{24}$ ft; wingspan of pipistrelle is $\frac{2}{3}$ ft**

2. What do you need to find out? **How much longer is the wingspan of the Western pipistrelle bat than that of the hog-nosed bat?**

### — Plan —

3. What operation should you use? **subtraction**

4. What words in the problem tell you this operation is needed?
   **how much longer**

### — Solve —

5. Rename $\frac{2}{3}$ so the fractions have like denominators.   $\frac{2}{3} = \frac{16}{24}$

6. Solve the problem.   $\frac{1}{8}$ ft

### — Look Back —

7. How can you check your answer? **Possible answer: The sum of $\frac{1}{8}$ and $\frac{13}{24}$ should be $\frac{2}{3}$.**

SOLVE ANOTHER PROBLEM

Seth has two pieces of wire. One piece is $\frac{1}{10}$ ft long and the other piece is $\frac{3}{5}$ ft long. What is the total length of the two pieces of wire?   $\frac{7}{10}$ ft

Use with pages 452–453.  **129**

---

Name _____

## Problem Solving
### 10-8

### Exploring Weight

1. You have learned that a slice of bread weighs about 1 oz. Look around the classroom. Name one object that weighs about as much as a slice of bread. What is your item?
   **Answers will vary.**

2. How many oz are in 1 lb? **16 oz**

3. How many slices of bread would weigh 1 lb? **16**

Use the weight of a loaf of bread to estimate the weight of each object below. Write whether each object weighs *less than*, *greater than*, or *about the same as* a loaf of bread.

**Estimates will vary. Possible answers are shown.**

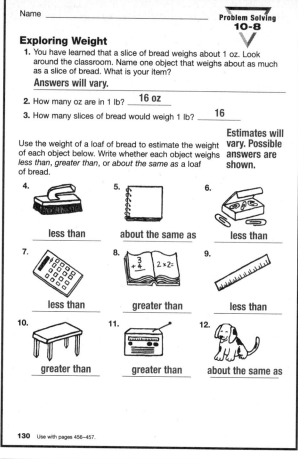

4. **less than**   5. **about the same as**   6. **less than**

7. **less than**   8. **greater than**   9. **less than**

10. **greater than**   11. **greater than**   12. **about the same as**

**130**  Use with pages 456–457.

---

Name _____

## Problem Solving
### 10-9

### Exploring Capacity

List two things you might measure with each unit of capacity. **Possible answers:**

1. teaspoon   **Pepper, medicine**
2. tablespoon   **Honey, baking soda**
3. cup   **Juice, raisins**
4. pint   **Cottage cheese, yogurt**
5. quart   **Water, milk**
6. gallon   **Soup, stew**

7. Joan says she served 50 gallons of fruit punch at a party.

   a. If there were 50 people at the party, could this be true? Explain.
   **Possible answer: No, that would mean that each person drank 1 gallon of punch.**

   b. Suppose there were 25 people at the party. Complete the following sentence with a reasonable unit of measure.
   Joan served 50 **cups** of fruit punch.

   c. How many people do you think could have been at the party for Joan to serve 50 gallons of fruit punch? How much did each person drink on average?
   **Possible answer: If each person drank 1 quart of punch, there could be 200 people at the party. If each person drank 1 pint, there would have to be 400 people at the party.**

Use with pages 458–459.  **131**

---

Name _____

## Problem Solving
### 10-10

### Changing Units: Length, Weight and Capacity

**Health** The table shows serving sizes of some foods that are rich in calcium.

| Item | Serving Size |
| --- | --- |
| Sardines, with bones | 3 oz |
| Yogurt | 1 c |
| Oysters | $\frac{3}{4}$ c |
| Cottage cheese | $\frac{1}{2}$ c |
| Swiss cheese | 1 oz |

Use the table to help solve the problems.

1. Stacy bought a pound of sardines.
   a. How many servings is that? **5 servings**
   b. How many ounces would be left over? **1 oz**

2. This week, Jerome ate a pint of cottage cheese. How many servings is that? **4 servings**

3. How many servings of yogurt are in a quart? **4 servings**

4. Suppose you purchased 1 lb of Swiss cheese. If you ate 2 servings of Swiss cheese per day, how long would it last? **8 days**

5. a. How many cups of oysters should Karla buy to make 24 servings? **18 c**
   b. How many quarts is that? **$4\frac{1}{2}$ qt**

Solve.

6. Quincy ran 45 yds. How many feet is that? **135 ft**

7. Roger's table is 3 ft long. How many inches is that? **36 in.**

**132**  Use with pages 460–461.

---

**194**

## Top Left Panel

Name _____

**Guided Problem Solving
10-11**

**GPS** PROBLEM 1, STUDENT PAGE 463

A school required three adult leaders for every 24 students. If 168 students signed up for a field trip to the Alamo, how many adults were needed?

| Students | 24 | 48 | 72 | 96 | 120 | 144 | 168 | 192 |
|---|---|---|---|---|---|---|---|---|
| Adult leaders | 3 | 6 | 9 | 12 | 15 | 18 | 21 | 24 |

**— Understand —**

1. What do you know? **3 adults for every 24 students;**
**168 students going on the trip**

2. What do you need to find out? **how many adults are needed**

**— Plan —**

3. How are the numbers in the top row of the table changing?
**They increase by 24.**

**— Solve —**

4. Describe the pattern in the table.
**Students increase by groups of 24; adults increase by 3.**

5. Complete the table.

6. How many adults are needed for the trip? **21 adult leaders**

**— Look Back —**

7. How could you use a picture to solve the problem?
**Possible answer: Draw 1 adult leader for every 8 students.**

SOLVE ANOTHER PROBLEM

In Karen's photo album, there are 4 photographs per page. If there are 24 pages in the album, how many photographs does Karen have? **96 photographs**

Use with pages 462–463. **133**

## Top Right Panel

Name _____

**Problem Solving
10-12**

**Exploring Algebra: Using a Balance Scale Model**

1. These two equations mean the same thing. Explain how you know.

$n + n = 12$        $12 = n + n$

**It doesn't matter which side of the equal sign a value is on.**

2. If you start with a balanced scale and subtract the same amount of weight from each side, what happens to the scale?
**The scale stays balanced because the weight on each side would still be the same.**

3. If you start with a balanced scale and add 4 counters to the right side and 2 counters to the left side, what happens to the scale?
**The scale would tip lower on the right side since it has more weight. The scale would not balance.**

4. Suppose you start with a balanced scale that has an unknown weight on one side and 2 one-pound weights on the other side. What is the unknown weight? How do you know?
**Since 2 pounds balance the unknown weight, the unknown weight is 2 pounds.**

5. Suppose you start with a balanced scale that has an unknown weight and 3 one-pound weights on one side. On the other side are 5 one-pound weights. What could you do to the scale to show the unknown weight?
**Remove 3 one-pound weights from each side of the scale to show that the unknown weight is 2 pounds.**

**134** Use with pages 464–465.

## Bottom Left Panel

Name _____

**Problem Solving
11-1**

**Reading and Writing Decimals**

**Careers** Ms. Alonzo is a professional gardener. She runs a nursery in the country.

1. Look at the picture of the garden plot above.

a. Write the decimal showing the number of pumpkins compared to the total number of plants in the garden plot. **0.3**

b. Write the decimal for broccoli compared to the total. **0.7**

2. Ms. Alonzo has a garden plot of 100 rose bushes. Forty-one of the bushes are yellow rose bushes. Fifty-nine of the bushes are red rose bushes.

a. Write the decimal showing red rose bushes compared to the total number of bushes in the garden plot. **.59**

b. Write the decimal for yellow rose bushes compared to the total number of bushes in the garden plot. **.41**

3. Four out of the ten orange trees in Ms. Alonzo's nursery died due to a long frost. Write the decimal for the number of orange trees that survived the frost, compared to the original number of trees. **0.6**

4. Complete the number line. Write the missing decimals.

0    0.1    0.2    0.3    **0.4**    0.5    0.6    0.7    **0.8**    0.9    1

5. Write the decimal for the number of shaded figures below compared to the total number of figures. **0.5**

Use with pages 476–477. **135**

## Bottom Right Panel

Name _____

**Problem Solving
11-2**

**Exploring Decimal Place-Value Relationships**

1.

0.4                    0.40

a. Shade the tenths grid to show 4 tenths. Write the decimal amount below the grid.

b. Shade the hundredths grid to show 40 hundredths. Write the decimal amount below the grid.

c. Is 4 tenths the same as 40 hundredths? Explain.
**Yes; 4 of 10 shaded sections of a tenths grid equals 40 of 100 sections of a hundredths grid.**

2. Is 11.43 greater or less than eleven and five tenths? Explain how you know.
**Less than; 43 hundredths is less than 50 hundredths.**

3. Write the word names for 13.20 in tenths and hundredths.
**Thirteen and two tenths, thirteen and twenty hundredths**

4. John said that since 7 is less than 70, 2.7 is less than 2.70. Is he right? Explain.
**No; 2.7 = 2.70, because seven tenths is the same as seventy hundredths.**

5. Write $\frac{1}{10}$ in two ways, once with two decimal places and once with one decimal place.
**0.10** , **0.1**

**136** Use with pages 478–479.

**195**

**Guided Problem Solving**
**11-3**

**GPS** PROBLEM 3, STUDENT PAGE 481

Suppose you have the same number of pennies and dimes. The coins total $1.21. How many of each coin do you have?

— **Understand** —

1. What do you know? The total amount—$1.21; there is an equal number of dimes and pennies.

2. What do you need to find out? The number of dimes and number of pennies

— **Plan** —

3. Will you make an organized list or use objects to solve the problem? Students may choose either strategy.

— **Solve** —

4. Use your strategy to solve the problem.

   a. If you decided to make an organized list, write the list on another sheet of paper. If you decided to use objects, draw a picture of the objects you used. Answers will vary.

   b. How many of each coin do you have? 11 dimes, 11 pennies

— **Look Back** —

5. Use a different strategy to check your answer. Is your answer reasonable? Explain.

   Answers will vary. Students may use the strategy that they didn't choose above to show that their answer is reasonable.

```
SOLVE ANOTHER PROBLEM
```

Renee has 1 dollar, 6 quarters, and 5 nickels. Does she have enough to buy a book that costs $2.95? Explain.

No, Renee only has $2.75.

---

**Problem Solving**
**11-4**

## Comparing and Ordering Decimals

**Physical Education** Nadia's gym class practiced their distance running. They decided to see how far they could run in 20 minutes. Here are the results:

| Student | Distance in 20 Minutes |
|---|---|
| Karen | 1.67 miles |
| Neil | 1.98 miles |
| Patricia | 1.7 miles |
| Antonio | 1.76 miles |
| Nadia | 1.90 miles |

1. Who ran the longest distance in 20 minutes? **Neil**

2. Who ran the shortest distance in 20 minutes? **Karen**

3. Who ran farther, Patricia or Antonio? **Antonio**

4. Order the distances the students ran from shortest to longest.
   **1.67 mi, 1.7 mi, 1.76 mi, 1.90 mi, 1.98 mi**

5. In the high school women's gymnastics meet, five students competed on the balance beam. Bonnie got a score of 9.89, Fiona got 8.98, Alison got 9.8, Cindy got 9.08, and Mia got 9.19.

   a. Who got the highest score on the balance beam? **Bonnie**

   b. Who got the lowest score? **Fiona**

   c. Order of the scores of the balance beam competition from 1st place to 5th place.
   **9.89, 9.8, 9.19, 9.08, 8.98**

---

**Problem Solving**
**11-5**

## Rounding Decimals

**Careers** Mr. Kowalski is a cartographer. A cartographer is a person who makes maps. Most maps have a key telling the distances between different places on the map. Sometimes the distances are given to the nearest mile. The cartographer rounds to the nearest mile to make the map convenient and easy to use.

1. Mr. Kowalski is drafting a map of Livingston County in New York State. The exact distance between the villages of Avon and Geneseo is 11.31 miles. What is the distance between the two villages rounded to the nearest mile? **11 miles**

2. The distance between the villages of Dansville and Livonia is 29.88 miles. What is the distance rounded to the nearest mile? **30 miles**

3. Mr. Kowalski wrote that the distance between Lakeville and Mount Morris is 17 miles, rounded to the nearest mile. Write the greatest and least possible distances between the two villages, in decimals to hundredths.
   **Greatest distance—17.49 miles, least distance—16.50 miles**

4. Circle the two decimals in each set that round to the same whole number. Write the whole number.

   a. (2.52) 2.49 (2.60) _____ 3

   b. (0.61) 1.51 (1.06) _____ 1

   c. (3.45) (3.02) 3.53 _____ 3

5. John has $1.50, Alice has $1.75, and Akheem has $1.45.

   a. Who has an amount that rounds to $2.00? **John and Alice**

   b. Who has an amount that rounds to $1.00? **Akheem**

---

**Problem Solving**
**11-6**

## Exploring Fractions as Decimals

1.

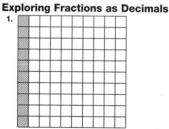

   a. What fractional amount do the shaded squares show? $\frac{10}{100}$

   b. What decimal amount do the shaded squares show? **0.10**

2. How would you find a decimal amount for $\frac{3}{5}$? Explain the process step by step.
   **Possible answer: Multiply both the numerator and the denominator by 2 to get $\frac{6}{10}$. $\frac{6}{10} = 0.6$, so $\frac{3}{5} = 0.6$.**

3. Which is greater, $\frac{6}{25}$ or 0.25? Explain.
   **0.25; $\frac{6}{25} = \frac{24}{100} = 0.24$, 0.24 < 0.25.**

4. What fraction of a dollar is 70 pennies? Write the fraction. Then write the amount using a decimal point.
   **$\frac{70}{100}$ or $\frac{7}{10}$; $0.70**

5. Explain how knowing that $\frac{1}{4} = 0.25$ can help you find the decimal for $\frac{3}{4}$. What is the decimal?
   **$\frac{3}{4}$ is three times as much as $\frac{1}{4}$. $3 \times 0.25 = 0.75$.**

## Estimating Sums and Differences

**Recreation** Do your sneakers weigh more than you think?
Use the table to solve the problems.

| Shoe | Weight of 1 shoe |
|---|---|
| Brand A | 19.5 oz |
| Brand B | 11.1 oz |
| Brand C | 15.8 oz |

**1.** Estimate how much a pair of Brand B sneakers weighs.
**About 22 oz**

**2.** Estimate how much a pair of Brand A sneakers weighs.
**About 40 oz**

**3.** Estimate the difference in weight between a pair of
Brand A and a pair of Brand C sneakers.
**About 8 oz**

Use the table to solve **4–7.**

| Ring | Bracelet | Necklace |
|---|---|---|
| $1.55 | $2.06 | $4.34 |

**4.** Estimate the cost of a bracelet and a ring. **About $4**

**5.** Venise bought a bracelet with a $5 bill. About how
much money does she have left? **About $3**

**6.** Alanna has $10. Can she buy a ring, a bracelet, and a
necklace? Explain.
**Yes; $2 + $2 + $4 = $8**

**7.** Becky has $5. Can she buy a ring and a necklace?
Explain.
**No; $2 + $4 = $6**

---

## Exploring Adding and Subtracting Decimals

**1.** Shade the grid to show
0.09 + 0.42. What is
the sum? **0.51**

**2.** Shade the grid to show
0.56 − 0.2. What is
the difference? **0.36**

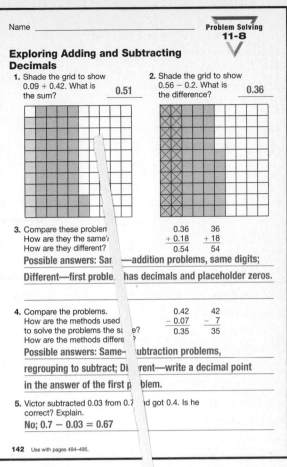

**3.** Compare these problems.
How are they the same?
How are they different?

| 0.36 | 36 |
|---|---|
| + 0.18 | + 18 |
| 0.54 | 54 |

**Possible answers: Same—addition problems, same digits;**

**Different—first problem has decimals and placeholder zeros.**

**4.** Compare the problems.
How are the methods used
to solve the problems the same?
How are the methods different?

| 0.42 | 42 |
|---|---|
| − 0.07 | − 7 |
| 0.35 | 35 |

**Possible answers: Same—subtraction problems,**

**regrouping to subtract; Different—write a decimal point**

**in the answer of the first problem.**

**5.** Victor subtracted 0.03 from 0.7 and got 0.4. Is he
correct? Explain.
**No; 0.7 − 0.03 = 0.67**

---

## Adding and Subtracting Decimals

Gerry and Liz went shopping for bargains. They priced
t-shirts with logos at three different stores. Here's what
they found.

| Store | Price |
|---|---|
| Shirts Ahoy! | $24.99 |
| Bargain Basement | $19.99 |
| Your Store | $21.49 |

Use the table for **1–3.**

**1.** How much more was the most expensive
shirt than the least expensive shirt? **$5.00**

**2.** How much would 2 shirts from the Bargain
Basement cost? **$39.98**

**3.** Estimate the difference in price between a
shirt from Your Store and one from Shirts
Ahoy! **About $4.00**

**4.** Adam has $10. He bought a paint brush for
$1.99 and a tube of paint for $2.25. How
much money does he have left? **$5.76**

**5.** Tyron ran 0.86 of a mile. Mariah ran 0.57 of
a mile. How much further did Tyron run? **0.29 mile**

**6. Choose a Strategy.** Mikhail wants to make punch for
everyone in his class. There are 25 students. If each
student gets 1 cup of punch, how many quarts of punch
will he need? Will there be any punch left over?

**a.** What strategy would you use to solve the
problem?
**Possible answer: Use Objects/**
**Act It Out**

• Use Objects/Act It Out
• Draw a Picture
• Look for a Pattern
• Guess and Check
• Use Logical Reasoning
• Make an Organized List
• Make a Table
• Solve a Simpler Problem
• Work Backward

**b.** Answer the problem.
**7 quarts with 3 cups left over**

---

## Exploring Centimeters, Decimeters, and Meters

Complete the table.

| | Centimeters | Decimeters | Meters |
|---|---|---|---|
| **1.** | 100 cm | 10 dm | 1 m |
| **2.** | 200 cm | 20 dm | 2 m |
| **3.** | 300 cm | 30 dm | 3 m |
| **4.** | 400 cm | 40 dm | 4 m |
| **5.** | 500 cm | 50 dm | 5 m |
| **6.** | 600 cm | 60 dm | 6 m |
| **7.** | 700 cm | 70 dm | 7 m |
| **8.** | 800 cm | 80 dm | 8 m |
| **9.** | 900 cm | 90 dm | 9 m |
| **10.** | 1,000 cm | 100 dm | 10 m |

**11.** What pattern do you see in the centimeter column?
**It increases by 100.**

**12.** What pattern do you see in the decimeter column?
**It increases by 10.**

**13.** What pattern do you see in the meter column?
**It increases by 1.**

**14.** What pattern do you see in each row? **Possible answers:**
**The number of centimeters divided by 10 equals the number**
**of decimeters, the number of decimeters divided by 10**
**equals the number of meters; as you move to the right,**
**each number has 1 less zero than the previous number.**

## Meters and Kilometers

**Geography** The table shows the highest mountain on each continent.

| Continent | Highest Point on Each Continent | Mountain Height |
|---|---|---|
| Africa | Kilimanjaro | 5,895 m |
| Asia | Everest | 8,854 m |
| Antarctica | Vinson Massif | 4,897 m |
| S. America | Aconcagua | 6,960 m |
| Europe | Blanc | 4,810 m |
| Australia | Kosciusko | 2,231 m |

1. Which continent has the highest mountain?   **Asia**

2. How much higher is Kilimanjaro than Vinson Massif?   **998 m**

3. About how high is Aconcagua in kilometers?   **About 7 km**

4. About how many kilometers higher is Blanc than Kosciusko?   **About 3 km**

5. The swim team has to swim the following laps at practice today: 400 m, 600 m, 200 m, 800 m, with a rest between each set of laps. How many kilometers will they swim in all?   **2 km**

6. Mary stayed in the pool from 11:00 A.M. to 3:30 P.M. How many hours did she stay in the pool?   **4.5 hr or $4\frac{1}{2}$ hr**

7. On the first day of practice, Rick could only swim 225 meters without stopping. Now he can swim 1 kilometer. How much further can he swim now?   **775 m**

8. The boys' swimsuits cost $17 each. There are 12 boys. The coach has received $187. Have all the boys paid? Explain.
**No. If all 12 boys had paid, the coach would have $204.**

---

## Exploring Length and Decimals

A cubit is a unit of length used by many early civilizations. It is based on the length of a person's arm from the elbow to the tip of the middle finger.

1. Name one advantage of using the length of a person's arm as a unit of measurement. Name one disadvantage.
**Possible answers: Advantage: convenience; Disadvantage:**
**Not everyone's arm is the same length**

2. The length of the English cubit is 46 cm. What is the length in meters?   **0.46 m**

3. Mark used the English cubit to measure a picture that he wanted to frame. The picture was 1.5 cubits by 2 cubits. What are the picture's dimensions in centimeters? Explain how you solved the problem.
**69 cm by 92 cm; Multiplied 1.5 by 46; multiplied 2 by 46**

4. The Egyptian cubit is 53 cm. How many more meters is it than the English cubit?   **0.07 m**

5. Suppose a rug measured 2.2 English cubits by 1.4 English cubits. If you used Egyptian cubits, would the measures be greater or less? Explain your reasoning.
**Less; Fewer Egyptian cubits are needed to measure the rug**
**since Egyptian cubits are longer than English cubits.**

6. Why do you think the Egyptian cubit is larger than the English cubit?
**Egyptian arms must have been longer than English arms.**

7. Suppose an English company is building in Egypt. The planners used cubits for all the measurements. If you were in charge of the construction, what is the first question you would ask? Explain your answer.
**Possible answer: Ask if measurements are in English cubits**
**or Egyptian cubits. The difference in units would effect the**
**building plans.**

---

## Exploring Mass

Labels on packaged foods contain nutrition information. The amount of nutrients are given in grams. Use the cereal box label to answer 1–4.

1. How many grams of protein are in 5 servings?   **20 g**

2. If you eat a serving each day for 7 days, how many grams of carbohydrates will you consume?   **168 g**
How many kilograms?   **0.168 kg**

**WHEAToaties**
Serving Size ....................30 g
Nutrition Information per serving
Calories ...........................115
Protein ..............................4 g
Carbohydrates ................24 g
Fat ....................................0 g
Cholesterol .......................0 g
Ingredients: oat bran, wheat, corn, raisins, honey

3. a. A box of cereal weighs 390 g. How many servings are in one box?   **13**
   b. A family of four each has a cereal serving every day. Will 2 boxes of cereal be enough for the week? Explain.
   **No. 4 × 30 = 120 g each day; 120 g × 7 = 840 g each**
   **week; 2 boxes = 780 g; 840 g > 780 g.**

4. Sue bought 4 loaves of bread. Each loaf weighed 700 g. How many kilograms did the bread weigh all together?   **2.8 kg**

5. Write g or kg to complete the sentence. Katrina went grocery shopping; she bought one 200 __g__ bar of soap, a 5 __kg__ turkey, a 310 __g__ can of soup, and a 2 __kg__ pork roast.

6. Samuel and his father bake bread. To make 5 loaves, they need 2.5 kg of flour. They have a 1 kg bag and 250 g of flour in a container. How many more kilograms of flour do they need?   **1.25 kg**

7. A bag of popcorn is twice the size of a bag of oranges. Will the popcorn have the greater mass? Explain.
**No; Popcorn has a much smaller mass than oranges.**

8. Does a larger object always weigh more than a smaller object? Explain.
**No; Weight doesn't always depend on size.**

---

## Exploring Capacity

The basketball team has a party to celebrate a winning season. They serve lemony punch. Use the recipe to answer questions 1–5.

**Lemony Punch**
360 mL   Lemonade
1 L   Pineapple juice
1.4 L   Cranberry juice
5 L   Ginger ale
945 mL   Lemon sherbet
Place liquids in punch bowl.
Add sherbet before serving.

1. How much more pineapple juice than lemonade is used?   **640 mL**

2. How many milliliters of ginger ale is used?   **5,000 mL**

3. How many more liters of ginger ale than cranberry juice is used?   **3.6 L**

4. How many milliliters of ingredients are in the punch?   **8,705 mL**
How many liters?   **8.705 L**

5. A punch cup holds 225 mL. Is there enough punch to serve one cup of punch to 40 people? Explain.
**No; 225 × 40 = 9,000 mL > 8,705 mL**

6. Marcie has to put eyedrops in her eyes twice a day for a week. Do you think the bottle the medicine comes in is measured in liters or milliliters? Explain your reasoning.
**Milliliters; eyedrops are usually measured in small amounts**

7. Marcie puts 2 drops in each eye twice a day. If a drop is 1 mL, about how many milliliters will she use in a week? Explain how you know.
**14 mL; 2 × 7 = 14 mL drops per week**

8. At a rate of 2 milliliters a day, how long would a one-liter bottle of eyedrops last? Why do you think eyedrops are not sold in liter containers? Give two reasons.
**500 days; Possible answers: Small quantities are used;**
**an eyedropper that would reach to the bottom of a liter bottle**
**would be very hard to use.**

## Temperature

**Science** Meteorology is the study of the atmosphere, weather, and climate. A meteorologist studies atmospheric conditions and makes predictions about the weather, based on the data.

| Record Temperatures | | | | |
|---|---|---|---|---|
| | High | | Low | |
| State | °C | °F | °C | °F |
| Washington | 47.7 | 118 | −44.4 | −48 |
| North Dakota | 48.8 | 121 | −51.1 | −6. |
| California | 56.6 | 134 | −42.8 | −45 |
| Florida | 42.7 | 109 | −18.8 | −2 |
| Georgia | 44.4 | 112 | −27.2 | −17 |

1. What is the difference between the highest and lowest temperatures in degrees Fahrenheit? __194°F__ in degrees Celsius? __7.7°C__

2. What is the difference between the highest and lowest temperatures for the state of Washington
in degrees Fahrenheit? __166°F__ in degrees Celsius? __92.1__

3. Which state has the greatest difference between the high and low temperature? __North Dakota__

4. Order the states from the greatest to least difference between the high and low temperatures.
**North Dakota, California, Washington, Georgia, Florida**

5. Ramón has a fever. His body temperature is 40°C. Normal body temperature is 37°C. How many degrees will his body temperature have to drop to reach normal body temperature? __3°C__

6. A freezer cools itself down 8°F per minute until it reaches the correct temperature. If the freezer is 72°F now, how many minutes will it take before the freezer can make ice cubes? __5 minutes__

7. If it is snowing, is the temperature more likely to be 30°F or 30°C? __30°F__

---

## Decision Making

A carousel has horses on an inside ring, one or more middle rings, and an outside ring. If you want to ride one of the fastest horses, which ring should you select?

1. Think about a carousel ride. Does any horse ever pass another one? __No__

2. Does any horse go around the track more times than any other horse? __No__

3. Does any horse cover more distance than any other horse? Explain.
__Yes; Outside horses have a longer track.__

4. Think about a way to demonstrate the speed of various horses on a carousel. Explain how you would do it.
__Possible answer: Have five friends hold hands and walk__
__around in a circle, counting their steps. The person__
__farthest away from the center of the circle will take many__
__more steps than the inside person.__

5. Which horse would you choose if you wanted to go the fastest possible speed on a carousel?
__Any horse on the outside lane__

6. Explain how you decided which horse would be the fastest.
__Outside horses have a longer track, yet they complete the__
__circle in the same amount of time as the inside horses;__
__so, they must be going faster.__

---

## Exploring Division Patterns

Show place-value patterns to the millions for the following basic facts. Follow the example.

**Example:**

Basic fact: 49 ÷ 7 = 7

490 ÷ 70 = 7

4,900 ÷ 70 = 70

49,000 ÷ 70 = 700

490,000 ÷ 70 = 7,000

4,900,000 ÷ 70 = 70,000

1. Basic fact: 8 ÷ 2 = 4
80 ÷ 20 = __4__
__800__ ÷ 20 = 40
8,000 ÷ __20__ = 400
__80,000__ ÷ 20 = 4,000
800,000 ÷ 20 = __40,000__

2. Basic fact: 12 ÷ 4 = 3
120 ÷ __40__ = 3
1,200 ÷ 40 = __30__
__12,000__ ÷ 40 = 300
120,000 ÷ __40__ = 3,000
1,200,000 ÷ 40 = __30,000__

3. Basic fact: 36 ÷ 6 = 6
__360 ÷ 60 = 6__
__3,600 ÷ 60 = 60__
__36,000 ÷ 60 = 600__
__360,000 ÷ 60 = 6,000__
__3,600,000 ÷ 60 = 60,000__

4. Basic fact: 9 ÷ 3 = 3
__90 ÷ 30 = 3__
__900 ÷ 30 = 30__
__9,000 ÷ 30 = 300__
__90,000 ÷ 30 = 3,000__
__900,000 ÷ 30 = 30,000__
__9,000,000 ÷ 30 = 300,000__

5. Will has a recipe for potato salad which serves 4. It uses 24 potatoes. He is making the salad for a party and he has 240 potatoes. How many people will the salad serve?
__40 people__

---

## Estimating Quotients with 2-Digit Divisors

**Geography** Use the table to solve the problems.

| Road Mileage Between Selected U.S. Cities | |
|---|---|
| Boston to Chicago | 963 miles |
| Denver to Dallas | 781 miles |
| Indianapolis to Atlanta | 493 miles |
| Minneapolis to Cincinnati | 692 miles |
| Kansas City to Cleveland | 770 miles |

1. If Kahlil drives 65 miles per hour, about how much driving time will it take to get from Boston to Chicago?
__About 15 hours__

2. Denise left Indianapolis at 6:00 A.M. driving 60 miles per hour. About what time will she arrive in Atlanta if he stops for an hour for lunch?
__About 3:00 P.M.__

3. About how many hours of driving time would it take to get from Kansas City to Cleveland at an average rate of 55 miles per hour?
__About 14 hours__

4. About how many hours would it take to drive from Denver to Dallas, at 65 miles per hour, if you stop every 4 hours to take a 20-minute break?
__About 13 hours__

Estimate before you answer yes or no.

5. At 35 miles per hour, can you go 150 miles in 4 hours? __No__

6. At 55 miles per hour, can you go 150 miles in 2 hours? __No__

7. At 65 miles per hour, can you go 120 miles in 2 hours? __Yes__

8. At 45 miles per hour, can you go 200 miles in 4 hours? __No__

9. At 50 miles per hour, can you go 240 miles in 5 hours? __Yes__

## Dividing by Tens

**Careers** Fishermen go out on their boats very early in the morning, in order to get fish to the market by the time it opens. Use the table to solve the problems.

| Fish Market: Today's Catch | |
|---|---|
| Salmon | 586 |
| Halibut | 819 |
| Petrale Sole | 733 |
| Crabs | 986 |
| Trout | 648 |

The Fish Market has 40 regular customers who are buyers for local restaurants. Each customer buys the same amount of fish.

1. About how many salmon can each customer buy? __14__

2. About how many halibut can each customer buy? __20__

3. About how many petrale sole can each customer buy? __18__

4. 10 customers are not interested in crabs. How many crabs can each of the remaining 30 customers buy? __32__

5. 20 customers do not want trout. How many trout can each of the remaining 20 customers buy? __32__

6. Clancy the Clown has 198 balloons to give out equally to 60 children. How many balloons will each child get? __3__

7. Pricilla has to type 148 pages. She can usually type about 10 pages an hour. How many hours will it take her to finish? __About 15__

8. An auditorium can hold 348 people. There are 20 full rows of seats.

   a. How many people are in each full row? __17__

   b. How many people are in the one shorter row? __8__

## Dividing with 2-Digit Divisors

**Careers** The table shows the maximum weight allowed by the U.S. Post Office for packages sent by air to some other countries. Use the table to solve the problems.

| Country | Maximum Weight Limit |
|---|---|
| Argentina | 44 |
| Denmark | 66 |
| Ireland | 50 |
| Israel | 33 |
| Lebanon | 11 |
| Portugal | 22 |

For each situation, answer these questions:

   **a.** How many boxes will be needed?

   **b.** Will every box be full?

1. Corinne, a shipping clerk, has to send 892 pounds of computer parts to Argentina.   a. __21__  b. __No__

2. The Portuguese branch of Marvin's company needs 547 pounds of denim to complete an order.   a. __25__  b. __No__

3. A customer in Israel ordered 264 pounds of chocolate from Abe's Chocolate Factory.   a. __8__  b. __Yes__

4. Tadashi must send 426 pounds of iris bulbs to a customer in Denmark.   a. __7__  b. __No__

5. A customer in Ireland ordered 750 pounds of coffee beans from Mick's company.   a. __15__  b. __Yes__

6. Fateema is sending 40 copies of her company's 3-pound catalog to Lebanon.   a. __11__  b. __No__

7. 936 pairs of shoes will go on 26 long shelves in the back room of your shop. How many pairs will go on each shelf? __36__

8. You need to store 882 zippers in 14 drawers. How many zippers will go in each drawer? __63__

## Decision Making

There are two main routes to get from Daniel's house to his grandparents' house by car. Here are the pros and cons of each.

| Route | Pros | Cons |
|---|---|---|
| Scenic route (530 miles) | • Some ocean views and interesting towns<br>• Varied choice of restaurants for lunch<br>• Easy access to service stations | • Takes about 10 hours<br>• Towns slow you down because of stop lights and traffic<br>• Occasional stop-and-go traffic |
| Direct route (406 miles) | • No traffic jams<br>• All freeway driving<br>• Takes about $6\frac{1}{2}$ hours | • Boring drive<br>• Very few places to stop for lunch<br>• Service stations can be up to 30 miles apart |

1. How many miles longer is the scenic route? __124 miles__

2. Which route would be better if Daniel's car has some problems? Why?
   **Scenic; Easier to get to service stations**

3. Which route would be better if Daniel is in a hurry to get there? Why?
   **Direct; Shorter drive**

4. At 35 miles per gallon, about how many gallons would the direct route take? __About 12 gallons__

5. At 27 miles per gallon, about how many gallons would the scenic route take? __About 20 gallons__

6. Why might you choose the direct route?
   **Possible answer: To get there quickly**

7. Why might you choose the scenic route?
   **Possible answer: To see the ocean**

8. Make a decision. Which route would you choose? Explain.
   **Answers will vary. Check students' reasonings.**

## Exploring Likely and Unlikely

Read each statement about the numbers in the box. Suppose you put your finger on one number in the box without looking. For each statement, write impossible, unlikely, equally likely as unlikely, likely, or certain.

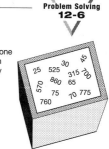

1. The number has 4 digits.
   **Impossible**

2. The number has two or three digits.
   **Certain**

3. The number has a 0 in the ones place.
   **Likely**

4. The number has an 8 in it. __Unlikely__

5. The number has a 9 in it. __Impossible__

6. The number has a 4 in it. __Unlikely__

7. The ones digit is a 0 or 5. __Certain__

8. You can count by 2s to reach the number. __Likely__

9. You can divide the number by 5. __Certain__

Suppose you choose 1 number from the hat without looking.

10. The number is evenly divided by 3.
    **Certain**

11. The number is a 2-digit number.
    **Equally likely as unlikely**

12. The number is a 3.
    **Unlikely**

13. The number is evenly divided by 10.
    **Impossible**

14. The number is greater than 8.
    **Likely**

## Exploring Fairness

Write whether each situation is fair or unfair.

**1.** Isaiah and Ismael want to play a game. They have to decide who plays first. To do so, they place one hand behind their back. On the count of three, they face their hand palm up or palm down. If both hands are palm up or palm down, Isaiah plays first. If one palm is up and the other is down, Ismael plays first. Is this fair or unfair? Explain.

**Fair; There is an equally likely chance of having palm**

**up or down.**

**2.** You want to watch a movie on TV. Your brother wants to watch a baseball game. You say to your brother, "I'll write "movie" on 3 slips of paper and "baseball" on 2 slips of paper. I'll put the papers in a hat, and without looking, I'll let you choose a paper from the hat. We'll watch whatever you choose." Is this fair or unfair? Explain

**Unfair; There is more of a chance of picking "movie".**

**3. a.** Flora and Marisol make a game to practice their division facts. They label a number cube with the numbers 3, 4, 6, 8, 9, and 12. In turn, they roll the number cube. If the number can be evenly divided by 3, Flora wins 1 point. If it can be evenly divided by 4, Marisol wins 1 point. Is this a fair or unfair game? Explain.

**Unfair; Flora has a greater chance of winning; 4 numbers**

**can be divided by 3; 3 numbers can be divided by 4.**

**b.** Suppose Flora and Marisol use the same rules but with a number cube numbered 8, 16, 18, 20, 21, and 27. Is this a fair or unfair game? Explain.

**Fair; 3 numbers are divisible by 3 and 3 are divisible**

**by 4.**

---

## Listing Possible Outcomes

tiger = frog     tiger = squirrel

**Fine Arts** An artist likes to create crazy animal pictures by combining two different animals into one.

The artist uses a tiger, gorilla, frog, squirrel, and giraffe to create the crazy animals. One animal is used in front; the other in the back.

**1.** What are the possible outcomes if the front animal is a tiger?

**tiger-gorilla, tiger-frog, tiger-squirrel, tiger-giraffe**

**2.** Is a tiger-giraffe picture different from a giraffe-tiger picture?           **Yes**

**3.** How many possible crazy animal pictures are there using the five animals?           **20**

**4.** If a camel is added to the list of animals, how many more pictures can be created?           **10**

**5.** Suppose you roll a pair of number cubes. One of them is labeled 1, 3, 5, 7, 9, 11 and the other is labeled 2, 4, 6, 8, 10, 12.

**a.** How many different sums are possible?   **11**

**b.** What is the greatest possible sum?   **23**

the least possible sum?   **3**

**c.** How many ways can you roll a sum of 13?   **6**

**d.** How many ways can you roll a sum of 9?   **4**

**e.** Which outcome is more likely, 7 or 17?   **17**

**f.** Which sums are least likely to occur?   **3, 23**

---

## Exploring Probability

**1.** The probability of rolling a 3 on a number cube is $\frac{1}{2}$. How many faces on the cube have a 3?           **3**

**2.** A sack contains 15 marbles. The probability of drawing a red marble without looking is $\frac{3}{5}$. How many red marbles are in the sack?           **9**

**3.** A spinner is divided into 6 equal parts. The probability of spinning yellow is 1. How many of the 6 parts are colored yellow?           **6**

**4.** A box contains 18 markers. The probability of picking a green marker without looking is $\frac{2}{9}$. How many green markers are in the box?           **4**

**5.** A sock drawer contains 15 pairs of socks. The probability of pulling out a pair of white socks without looking is $\frac{1}{5}$. How many pairs of white socks are in the drawer?           **3**

**6.** There are 6 teddy bears in a toy chest filled with stuffed animals. The probability of pulling out a teddy bear without looking is $\frac{3}{10}$. How many stuffed animals are in the toy chest?           **20**

**7.** Lauren has 12 coins in her pocket. The probability of her pulling out a penny is $\frac{1}{2}$. How many pennies are in her pocket?           **6**

**8.** Shawn has 2 nickels in his pocket. The probability of him pulling out a nickel is $\frac{1}{3}$. How many coins are in his pocket?           **6**

**9.** Ronnie has less than 12 nickels, dimes, and quarters in his pocket. The probability of pulling out a nickel or a quarter is $\frac{1}{4}$. The probability of pulling out a dime is $\frac{1}{2}$.

**a.** How many coins could Ronnie have in his pocket?   **4 or 8**

**b.** How many of each coin could Ronnie have?

**either 1 nickel, 1 quarter, and 2 dimes or 2 nickels,**

**2 quarters, and 4 dimes**

---

## Exploring Predictions

Andrea passed out a survey which asked people to choose their favorite color from a list of five different colors. From her results, Andrea concluded that she could make the following predictions:

$\frac{1}{2}$ of all people would choose blue as their favorite color.

$\frac{1}{12}$ of all people would choose yellow as their favorite color.

$\frac{1}{8}$ of all people would choose green as their favorite color.

$\frac{1}{4}$ of all people would choose red as their favorite color.

$\frac{1}{24}$ of all people would choose orange as their favorite color.

**1.** Evan says "I think Andrea gave the survey to 10 students." Could Evan be right? Why or why not?

**No, Evan could not be right because Andrea has predictions**

**of $\frac{1}{12}$ and $\frac{1}{24}$, so she had to survey at least 24 people.**

**2.** Suppose Andrea made her predictions from 48 completed surveys. How many people do you think chose each color as their favorite?

Red **12**     Yellow **4**     Blue **24**

Green **6**     Orange **2**

**3.** Suppose Andrea gave her original survey to 24 people. She wants to check the reasonableness of her predictions by giving the survey to either 120 people or 240 people. Which number of people would best show whether Andrea's original predictions were reasonable? Explain.

**Andrea should give her survey to 240 people because**

**the more people she surveys, the more accurate her**

**predictions will be.**

**GPS** PROBLEM 3, STUDENT PAGE 551

A 2-letter group has A, B, C, or D as its first letter, and E or F as its second letter.

**a.** Write all possible 2-letter groups.   **b.** How many possibilities are there?

## —Understand—

1. How many letters make a group? _____2_____

2. What letters can be used as the first letter? A, B, C, or D

   second? E or F

## —Plan—

3. Solve a Simpler Problem. Suppose a 2-letter group has either A or B as its first letter and E as its second letter.

   **a.** Write a 2-letter group that starts with A. ___AE___ with B. ___BE___

   **b.** How many 2-letter groups in this simpler problem

   are possible? _____2_____

## —Solve—

4. Make an organized list of arrangements with letter A as the first letter. Continue with arrangements using B, C, and D. How many arrangements are possible?

   AE, AF, BE, BF, CE, CF, DE, DF; 8 arrangements are possible.

## —Look Back—

5. Look for a pattern in your list. How can you use the pattern to check your answer?

   Possible answer: There are two 2-letter groups for each

   of the first letters. $4 \times 2 = 8$

   SOLVE ANOTHER PROBLEM

Stephen's little sister has 1 red, 1 green, 1 blue, and 1 yellow block. She randomly grabs 2 blocks. How many different combinations of blocks could she pick up? _____6_____